THE COMPLETE GUIDE TO

MAGAZINE ARTICLE WRITING

JOHN M. WILSON

Phillip ardries
Washington
August   1996

WRITER'S DIGEST BOOKS
CINCINNATI, OHIO

This hardcover edition of *The Complete Guide to Magazine Article Writing* features
a "self-jacket" that eliminates the need for a separate dust jacket. It provides sturdy
protection for your book while it saves paper, trees and energy.

97 96 95 94   5 4 3 2

Library of Congress Cataloging-in-Publication Data

Wilson, John M.
      The complete guide to magazine article writing / by John M. Wilson.
         p.   cm.
      Includes index.
      ISBN 0-89879-547-8
      1. Feature writing. 2. Journalism — Authorship. I. Title
PN4784.F37W55   1993
808'.02 — dc20
                                                        93-24157
                                                          CIP

Cover design by Impact Studio

Note: To avoid exclusion of one gender, pronouns such as "he" or "she" and "his"
or "her" will alternate from chapter to chapter.

ACKNOWLEDGMENTS

My eternal gratitude to Brenda Day, who provided invaluable research, assistance and advice in helping me put this book together.

Also, deep thanks to Pat H. Broeske, Lee Green, Carol Easton, Barbara Hopfinger, Muriel Schloss, John Merryman, Martina Wynn, Bud Lesser, Stacy Jenel Smith, Ellen Alperstein and Don Chase, among many other writers, editors and former students, for their contributions.

Special thanks to just about everyone, past and present, at The UCLA Extension Writers' Program, *Writer's Digest* and Writer's Digest Books. Extra special thanks to Irv Letofsky, Arthur C. Wimer, John Brady, Linda Venis and Bill Brohaugh, and to Beth Johnson, the production editor on this book, for making it — and me — looking infinitely better.

A nod of admiration to my agent, Alice Martell, who knows what she's doing and does it well.

Finally, my love and appreciation to close friends and family for their patience and support over the years, especially Judy, Bob-O, Darryl, Tom, all the Mariners (wives, associate members), Pooh and Buzz, Aunt Betty and Uncle Bud, and Dad and Bonnie.

I'd like to think I carry within me a small part of the patience, sense of craft, and satisfaction in work well done that I've long observed in my father; an appreciation for language and wordcraft instilled in me by my mother; and the value of emotional honesty, learned from Jon-Noel, who was surely born to write, but ran out of time much too soon.

ABOUT THE AUTHOR

John M. Wilson has sold several hundred freelance pieces to a wide range of magazines and more than a dozen major newspapers. These include *The New York Times*, *The Washington Post*, *The Los Angeles Times*, *The Chicago Tribune Magazine*, *California Magazine*, *Los Angeles Magazine*, *Entertainment Weekly*, *TV Guide*, *Western's World*, *Alaska Outdoors*, *Christopher Street* and *Writer's Digest*.

A graduate with a journalism degree from San Diego State University, he served as a staff reporter with *The Los Angeles Herald-Examiner*, a staff editor with *The Los Angeles Times*, and was the founding publisher of his own alternative community newspaper, *Easy Reader*, in Hermosa Beach, California. A longtime columnist for *Writer's Digest*, he teaches classes and workshops through The UCLA Extension Writers' Program, where he has served on the department's Guidance Committee.

for Irv Letofsky

the editor who let me find my voice

into your writing. Microscopic line editing and better word choice. Sixty-eight questions to ask yourself during revisions.

Step Thirteen
TURNING IT IN
242
Step-by-step guidelines for packaging and submitting your manuscript and accompanying materials. Making a professional presentation, from the stamps you select to the cover letter you enclose. Proper manuscript format. When and how to submit photos. International mailings. Copyediting symbols.

Step Fourteen
DEALING WITH EDITORS
255
Understanding editors, their needs and the special pressures they face. How to build relationships with editors, including submission follow-up, offering support services, working out further revisions, handling galley proofs, presenting new ideas, staying in touch. When and how to use the phone. Advice on coping with unbusinesslike and abusive editors.

Step Fifteen
TAKING CARE OF BUSINESS
268
Freelance writing as self-employment; how to approach it as a business. Understanding the publishing rights that you sell. Contracts, invoices, getting paid. Preparing for taxes. Developing additional "customers" for your articles, through syndication, self-syndication, foreign markets and books. The basics of writing book proposals. Pros and cons of using a pseudonym.

Step Sixteen
KEEPING THE FAITH
284
Understanding and tapping our deep, personal need to write; using it as a source of inspiration and motivation. Using mentors, writers and writer's organizations as resources for networking and moral support. Realities of the writing life; developing the confidence and discipline to sustain a writing career through frustration and rejection. Self-reliance.

INTRODUCTION:
WHAT'S IT ALL ABOUT?

Introductions can be awkward, but I think you should know who you're dealing with, so please bear with me for a minute or two.

At the age of nineteen, without formal journalism training, I started writing for my local newspaper. At the time, I was a dropout from a midwestern university, where I had been on the wrestling team. Brash, cocky, with nothing to lose, I walked into the headquarters of the *South Bay Daily Breeze*, a Copley newspaper then serving about 45,000 readers in southern California, and asked to see the sports editor, Dick White.

"You guys are doing a terrible job covering local wrestling," I told him.

White was a big, gruff, crew-cut guy with a loose tie and a soft lead pencil behind his ear.

"You think you can do a better job," he said, barely looking me over, "there's a typewriter over there."

I felt I was a pretty good writer, so I sat down and wrote a feature story that summed up the state of high school and college wrestling in the area. It was part commentary, part survey piece, but I didn't know those terms at the time. I didn't even know what a "feature" was. I just wrote what I knew and felt.

"This isn't bad," he said when I handed it in. "Now I'm going to show you how to write for a newspaper."

He drew an inverted pyramid in the middle of my first page (now an outdated concept except for hard news stories).

"This means you put the most important facts at the top of the story, and the least important at the bottom," he said. "When we're on deadline, we cut from the bottom to make it fit, and we don't have time to rearrange things or smooth 'em out. Now go rewrite it. Oh, yeah, and cut it in half. Trim the fat, keep the meat."

Reluctantly, I did as I was told. To my surprise, I found I could still say what I wanted to say, and give him what he wanted. In fact, at half the length, it was *better*. A lot better.

I had just completed my first nonfiction writing workshop and learned a valuable lesson: Being a "good writer" and writing *professionally* are not the same thing.

Three days later, my article appeared on the front page of the sports section. There was my byline, for all the world to see. It was an incredible boost to a teenager's pride, and I was hooked on journalism.

Learning How to Freelance

As a "stringer," I wrote two or three dozen articles for the *Daily Breeze* over the next six months, covering track and basketball along with amateur wrestling. I worked without pay, and by the time I hit the ripe old age of twenty, I was ready to move on.

I enrolled as a journalism student at San Diego State, where I discovered a professor named Arthur C. Wimer. A former Marine drill instructor and newspaper man, Wimer was close to seventy but still stood trim and ramrod straight behind his neat bow tie and wire-rimmed glasses. A terse, sometimes crusty manner concealed a warm heart and surprisingly open mind; he didn't give a whit about his students' political views if they worked hard and wrote well—not an easy adjustment for a former Marine D.I. in the fervent 1960s.

Wimer taught a class called Magazine Article Writing, which introduced students to the world of freelance writing, showing us how to work therein.

He had a strict grading procedure: To earn an A in the class, you had to sell four articles within the semester; to earn a B, you had to sell three articles; for a C, you needed two sales; one sale got you a D. Otherwise, you flunked, no exceptions.

In the fifteen or so years he taught the class with this tough criterion, Wimer failed only half a dozen students. With his practical "system" of studying and prioritizing markets and careful follow-up, he turned the remainder into published freelance writers.

Happily, I was among them. That semester, I sold articles to two small national magazines, *American County Government* and *American Bicyclist and Motorcyclist*; the popular Midwest tabloid, *Grit*; and a local newspaper, *The San Diego Independent*. Small markets, perhaps—I earned $95 from the bunch—but places to get started, and to grow.

I got my A, but Art Wimer gave me much more—a practical knowledge of what it takes to break into the freelance writing marketplace. He was a stern taskmaster, but also a wonderful motivator. He stripped away the mystery of freelancing and gave us the simple but necessary tools to succeed.

Passing On the Knowledge

For much of my adult life, I've earned a living as an independent writer, rather than under the thumb or time clock of an employer or supervisor. I've sold hundreds of freelance pieces on a wide range of subjects to a dozen major newspapers, from *The New York Times* on down, and to nearly three dozen magazines, including leading regional, national and Sunday publications. In the late 1970s, John Brady, then editor of *Writer's Digest*, asked me to write a monthly column covering freelance markets, which I filed for nearly a decade. Eventually, in the mid-1980s, I joined *The Los Angeles Times* as a part-time editor, assigned to help freelance contributors develop and polish their articles, a role that lasted several years.

When Art Wimer retired many years ago, he sent me the handouts he used in his San Diego State classes. He suggested I might continue to teach his approach in workshops of my own.

For the past decade, I have done just that, updating and expanding on his material, primarily through the UCLA Extension Writers' Program. While I'm supportive and encouraging in class, I also play the role of a tough, "no-nonsense" editor, stripping away the illusions about freelance writing and marketing.

Over the years, I've found that's what most adult students want and need: no more coddling, no more vague or unrealistic theory, no more false pats on the back; instead, practical, professional feedback to help them see their weaknesses, improve specific skills, find their writing voice, and move ahead in the nonfiction marketplace.

Not every one of my students succeeds, but many do. Some make their first sales in class; throughout this book, you'll find examples of their published work, along with that of others, illustrating a wide range of writing approaches, elements and techniques.

As you move through the sixteen steps in *The Complete Guide to Magazine Article Writing*, you may find the format unusual. I've organized and laid it out much the way I do a ten-week class, following what I feel is the natural, step-by-step progression of a developing article, with craft and marketing closely related. That means you'll encounter various techniques gradually, at different points over time, rather than having to digest them in one overwhelming mass.

In trying to create a comprehensive "workshop on a shelf," I've plumbed nearly thirty years as a nonfiction writer, editor and writing instructor, including advice gleaned from the more than 500 editors and publishers I interviewed during the past fifteen years for *Writer's Digest*. Throughout this book, I'll also point you to guidebooks written by others that I think are especially valuable.

I will never guarantee anyone success in the field of nonfiction writing. But I can show beginning writers how it's done, and give more experienced writers a nuts-and-bolts "refresher" course, with the emphasis on craft, technique and professionalism.

Nonfiction writing is much more than just marketing know-how and acquired skills, with rewards that far exceed the paychecks you'll earn. Nonfiction writing is a state of mind, a way of life, an extra set of eyes and ears. It's a key that can open many doors, a passport to travel far and wide, an introduction to fascinating people, a guide to wonderful adventures, an excuse to ask any question you want, a reason to be curious and to learn, a way to reach out to readers and to the world.

If you want to learn how to do it—or how to do it better and more profitably—please join me as we take our first steps together.

John M. Wilson

What Kind of Writer Am I?

Several years ago, Barbara Hopfinger was a student in one of my writing classes. A mother and public school teacher, she burned with passion about issues such as racism, inequitable medical care and deteriorating public education.

Barbara yearned to become an investigative reporter, exposing social injustice. But after a few weeks, she was frustrated and floundering with half-baked ideas and aborted writing projects. Research, extensive interviewing and other facets of in-depth reporting took special skills and lots of time, and she soon realized she had neither.

Because she was a natural storyteller, with a rich sense of humanity and humor, I suggested she write something in the first person on a subject from her life experience, close to her heart.

She came to the next class with a 1,200-word recollection of a crafty but endearing youngster named Ernie, whom she'd met on a trip to Mexico, and what he had meant to her. She put the article through several revisions, then sold it to *Trailer Life.*

She followed that sale with one to *Woman's World,* a humor piece about changing the color of her lipstick after many years — and how it failed to transform her life, as she'd hoped. Then came "My Son, The Rock Musician," for *The Jewish Journal of Greater Los Angeles,* in which she confronted conflicting feelings about the career choice of her nonacademic son. These early rewards came after many months of hard work, and didn't pay an awful lot, but they gave Barbara the start she needed.

She found success by finding out what kind of writer she was — and what kind she was not.

Let's put that another way, as Barbara has since written longer pieces that required more research and reporting: She found her initial success with shorter, first-person pieces because she realized what kind of writing was right for her *at the time.*

BORN TO WRITE

You're probably a born writer, or you wouldn't be reading this book. You enjoy writing. You aspire to do more of it, more visibly and profitably. It's likely that over the years, many people — friends, relatives, teachers — have commented on what a talented writer you are. Or perhaps you just know it, deep within yourself.

You're lucky; you've been blessed with the gift of writing talent. But: *There's a big difference between a gifted writer and a professional writer.*

I once read a perceptive piece in *The Writer* espousing the theory that "talent" was the most dangerous and destructive concept a writer could embrace. It was directed at writers who are so convinced of their innate "talent," they think that all they must do is jot down their brilliant thoughts, and the work is done; that the world is waiting for their precious prose, exactly as it pours from their exceptional minds.

In truth, it is often the "gifted" writer, so convinced of her own artistic specialness, who has the most difficulty shaping and honing her creative material into publishable form.

That's particularly true in the nonfiction field, where a wide range of skills, techniques and specific journalistic elements are as important as a creative impulse and the natural instinct to "write well."

In the beginning, the most important thing is to *write*, and write a lot to find and develop your natural writing voice and rhythms. To develop as a *professional*, however, you need to understand the difference between "writing" and "reporting." The difference between "news" and a "feature." The difference between a "survey" and a "service" article, a "lead" and a "kicker," a "billboard" and a "bullet," a "deck" and a "sidebar." And on and on.

For many assignments, you must know how to locate sources, do research, substantiate statements, differentiate between libel and fair comment. You may have to handle challenging interviews, a craft all its own. And when the piece is finally done, you might be asked to do a fast rewrite, find a completely different slant, do more research and interviewing, trim away long blocks of text, or all these and more.

Such requirements should be neither discouraging nor intimidating to an aspiring nonfiction writer. They are simply the nuts and bolts of nonfiction writing, skills to be practiced if one wants to develop from "gifted writer" to published pro.

CRAFT AND MARKETS: INSEPARABLE

We'll explore virtually all of those basic — and some not-so-basic — elements and techniques, step by logical step, in the course of this book.

Most books on nonfiction writing start with the craft of writing, then move on to marketing. As I mentioned in the introduction, I've designed this book differently, following the steps one often takes in putting an article together, with craft and marketing constantly bumping into each other or trading places. The sixteen steps, or chapters, go something like this:

1. Figuring out what kind of nonfiction writer you are, and which types of assignments to go after right now, to increase opportunity, productivity and confidence.

2. Finding ideas for articles; the crucial difference between a good idea and a marketable angle. Understanding different article types, and what each requires.

3. Knowing the marketplace in general and studying individual markets in particular, page by page; learning to spot the fertile freelance market, and opportunities within.

4. Pitching your ideas by writing effective query letters, with many samples of successful queries.

5. An organized "system" for prioritizing your markets and querying in volume; finding many slants from one basic idea to maximize research efficiency and sales opportunity.

6. Writing effective leads, or openings, for your queries and articles.

7. Writing the "billboard paragraph," and how it can affect article focus and structure.

8. Exploring a range of other nonfiction tools and techniques, such as anecdotes, quotes, kickers and bullets.

9. Tips on research and other approaches for putting detail and substance into your work.

10. The craft of interviewing, from preparation to the interview itself, with tips on framing effective questions.

11. The elements and techniques of strong nonfiction writing, including structure, style, tone, pacing and voice.

12. Rewriting—your opportunity to improve and polish your work; how to develop your "inner editor," protecting your unique voice while making your work more marketable.

13. Guidelines for packaging and submitting the manuscript, along with accompanying materials.

14. Building relationships with responsive, supportive editors, and coping with those who aren't so terrific.

15. Taking care of business, such as rights, contracts, taxes; syndication, self-syndication; book proposals; etc.

16. Realities of the writing life; developing the confidence and discipline to sustain a writing career.

That's more or less the order in which marketable ideas are hatched, refined, targeted, assigned, researched, written and sold — and the progression in which most freelance writers develop as professionals.

The craft and the marketing of nonfiction writing don't exist separately; they are interdependent, something that's often ignored in the academic world. You don't just "write an article"; which type of article you write, what you put in it, and how you write it depend to a great extent on the specific market you've targeted.

That's why, as you go through the steps in this book, we'll discuss craft and markets in a "connected" way, just as they are connected in the real world of professional writing.

KNOW THYSELF!

As with any field, professional growth takes discipline, commitment and time — and a healthy dose of humility. When you start as a freelance writer, or find yourself professionally bogged down, it can be as important to understand your limitations as it is to believe in your talent and potential.

Before you ever send off a proposal letter or begin a manuscript, you need a sense of what kind of article you intend to write — and if you have what it takes to execute that particular piece. Have what it takes not only in terms of experience and skill, but in time and resources to do the research, interviewing, organizing and actual writing. You must not only understand the wide range of article types — profile, service, roundup, investigative, op-ed, et al. — but also the specific market you intend to write for, and what it requires of its contributors. (We'll discuss article types in detail in Step Two.)

You must know not only what you want from writing, but what you are willing and able to give to it.

Some questions to ask yourself:

• What are my goals as a freelance writer, and how hard am I willing to work to reach them?

• Am I willing to clear a regular part of my life every day or every week and devote it to the craft and business of writing?

• How many hours a week can I give up? Sixty? Forty? Twenty? Five?

• How much progress can I realistically expect to make in the time I'm willing to commit? Not just progress in monetary terms, but in developing skills and finding my natural voice as a writer?

CONTRACT VS. "SPEC"

Until you're established as a nonfiction writer, you will probably have to write on "spec."

"Spec" is short for speculation, the opposite of working under contract.

When an editor says, "I'd be happy to look at your article on spec," she means that she finds your idea interesting, but because you lack much in the way of credits or have yet to establish a relationship with the publication, she cannot give you a firm contract, guaranteeing you a kill fee (or partial payment) should she decide not to use the article for some reason.

If you decide to write on spec, it's with the understanding that the editor looks forward to reading the piece when it's completed, but with no strings attached.

Some of the high-paying magazines only work on a contract basis, guaranteeing a kill fee (generally 20 to 50 percent of the contract fee). They are also considerably more selective about who gets those contracts, giving assignments only to established writers or those who intrigue them with knockout ideas and proposals.

Many established writers are against kill fees in concept, feeling that a writer should be paid in full if his work is written under contract but not used, but most publications still hold to the practice of partial or token payment in such cases. If you receive a kill fee for a rejected piece of work, you retain complete ownership of the material and the right to sell it anywhere else you please.

Some veteran nonfiction writers claim they would never write on spec, but it's the way most get started; some even write for free in the beginning, accumulating experience and clips.

- Am I determined to become a full-time freelance writer, or am I willing to pursue it part-time, at least in the beginning?
- How much of my income do I expect to make from freelancing this year, and in the years ahead? Will I be happy selling only a dozen articles a year? Half a dozen? One or two?
- Am I continually trying to break into big, prestige markets when I'm essentially a novice? Am I trying too much, too soon?
- Conversely, am I working below my potential? Do I feel professionally *stuck*? Afraid to take risks?
- What kind of writer am I? What kinds of articles do I like to read?

When I close my eyes, what published work do I see with my byline attached? What type of article is it? What specific market is it in?

• Do I have the personality to write probing investigative pieces, doing weeks and months of backgrounding and research and confronting interviewees with tough questions? Or am I better suited to lighter or more personal features, at least for now?

• Do I really know the marketplace? Am I acquainted with the thousands of freelance writing markets that exist in the United States alone? Am I willing to do the kind of market study that will expand my options and opportunities?

• Am I willing to try my hand at a wide range of article genres, to discover what feels right for me?

• Am I prepared to deal with the business that goes along with being a self-employed writer?

• Am I motivated primarily by dreams of big money and fame, or by the satisfaction of the writing process and work well done, which will have to sustain me through hard times and painful frustration?

• Do I have the discipline to sit down alone every day and write, without a boss to motivate me or give me orders? Should I consider collaborating?

• Do I have the courage to put my work into the mail? The backbone to deal with inevitable rejection? The guts to try again?

• Do I have the deep, abiding desire to master the craft of writing? Or am I just a "dabbler"—a dreamer and a dilettante—who would rather talk about it than do it?

Almost all successful writing careers come about not because of a "big break" but because of a series of small breaks, stretching over many years, and resulting from the writer's discipline and persistence.

◆ ◆ ◆

Barbara Hopfinger was no dilettante; she worked hard. But in the beginning, she bit off more than she was able to chew, and her frustration was clearly painful. It nearly caused her to quit.

Fortunately, she scaled down her immediate ambitions and was able to generate projects that fit into her busy schedule, that were closer to her skill and resource level. Her willingness to "think small" paid off big—it got her started as a professional writer.

Adjusting Your Scope

Many years ago, when *Life* magazine was resuming publication after a long hiatus, an editor contacted me on a trip to the West Coast. She was looking for correspondents, and we met for lunch.

IS TWO BETTER THAN ONE?

For many writers, the toughest aspect of the profession is the isolation. Not just the loneliness, but the need for creative stimulation and a partner to help maintain discipline and productivity.

For some, the answer is collaboration.

You'll find potential collaborators everywhere. They might be a writing friend with similar interests, whose strengths complement your weaknesses, and vice versa; someone you meet in a writing class or at work, especially if you have a writing job. Writer's groups and organizations are also places where collaborators often first make contact.

Working with a nonwriter is a more difficult challenge; the responsibility for writing and organizing your project will fall primarily on your shoulders. For that kind of partnership to work, you must be especially confident in your professional skills. You should also verify your prospective partner's credentials in her field of specialty—psychology, health, education, women's issues, dieting, etc.—before agreeing to work with her.

Nonwriting collaborators turn up wherever your interests lead you: classrooms, seminars, media interviews, conversations with strangers. If you know of someone who has something valuable to say or a terrific story to tell, and you can find a hook and market for it, you may have found a writing partner. What matters is that you each have professional expertise to contribute to a specific project, and feel you can work together productively.

Some tips:

• Don't join with the first writer who's looking for a partner. Meet lots of writers, spend time with those who might be right for you, and get to know them—their habits, manners, personalities.

• Beware of overly strong egos. In any writing partnership, flexibility and the willingness to compromise are two of the most important qualities.

• Make sure there's mutual professional respect; it's essential that the partnership be equitable.

• Don't underestimate the importance of geographic proximity. Your partner should live close to you.

• Be sure you're both interested in similar subject matter.

• Find someone with compensating strengths and weaknesses—i.e.,

continued

if research is your forte but not writing, find a strong writer who works quickly and handles deadline pressure well.

- If you share the writing, which is likely, be sure your writing styles are compatible. The writing will ultimately have to blend. Ideally, one of you is a particularly strong editor who will handle the final polish.

- Draw up a simple contract spelling out the terms of your partnership (presumably 50/50 on all sales in all markets for all time). Exchanging letters that outline the basic terms might be enough, with each of you signing the letters and keeping copies. If you are entering a partnership with a nonwriting partner, a more detailed contract is in order.

- Most important, choose someone you feel good about in your gut, someone with whom you enjoy spending time.

"Are you a writer or a reporter?" she asked. "Do you get your primary satisfaction gathering the facts, or sitting down and writing the story?"

"The actual writing," I told her truthfully, even though I had a strong background in reporting.

"Then I don't think you'd be happy working for us," she said. "We need people who are willing to do the digging, then let us rewrite the raw material they turn in."

It was the first time I'd ever thought about the difference between writers and reporters. At the time, I was making my mark as a reporter, but I was gradually becoming more skilled and expressive as a writer; I knew that the writing process "turned me on" more than laborious research. But as a writer, I still had a long way to go before I cracked a prestige market like *Life* (as a matter of fact, I still haven't!).

Conversely, there are some excellent reporters who have the persistence and thoroughness of first-rate detectives, but who are lousy writers, and never get much better. They love the chase, the discovery. Having to put it all together is a necessity, and polishing a nuisance; it feels tedious and anticlimactic to them. Often, they need a lot of editing, but because of their tenacity and reporting skills, they're invaluable as journalists, a special breed that wins most of the prizes.

Good writers who are not at least fair reporters, however, are not much use to most newspapers and magazines. Even a soft celebrity feature, or an inoffensive business profile engineered by a public relations person, requires some minimal ability at backgrounding, researching, interviewing and fact-checking.

What does all this mean to you?

The less your training and skill as a reporter, the better your writing must be.

Humor writers, for instance, needn't be good reporters, in the sense of doing exhaustive research. Erma Bombeck or Dave Barry, for example, write humorously from life experience and seemingly off the top of their heads. But humor writing also requires an almost flawless sense of style, voice, economy and craft. (More on humor writing in Step Eleven.)

The point I'm getting at is this: *The less experience you have as a reporter and professional writer, the more you need to seek out assignments within your scope, assignments that allow you to get started and to grow as a writer.*

"AS TIME GOES BY"

Once, while teaching a one-day workshop, I encountered a student who had made a sale to *Reader's Digest*. *RD* had reprinted her piece worldwide in its international editions, and the student had earned many thousands of dollars from it. I'd been trying for years, without success, to break into *RD*. Why, I wondered, did this woman need to take my workshop on free-lance writing basics after reaching such an enviable level?

"Because they took my personal experience story and completely rewrote it," she said. "I thought that first sale made me a 'pro'—I made a lot of money from it! But I haven't sold a thing in the years since. I've been wasting time submitting material to other big markets, and only getting rejections."

Ironically, this woman's quick and enviable success with *Reader's Digest* was also something of a setback. With a staff of nearly 100 editors, this venerable and widely read magazine can afford to put raw drafts through heavy revisions, particularly the many dramatic first-person pieces it pub-lishes. That's what happened to my "lucky" student. It earned her a fat check, but also fooled her into thinking she had jumped easily into the big time, and would remain there, making sale after sale.

She handed me a two-page query letter that had met repeated rejections; she said she had trimmed and revised it as much as was humanly possible. I looked it over; the woman clearly had a natural talent for language and storytelling, but just as clearly lacked the ability to tighten and polish her work. Within minutes, I trimmed her query nearly in half, deleting entire paragraphs and dozens of individual words; when I read it back to her, she seemed amazed how clear, focused and compelling her writing had suddenly become. There was nothing magical in what I did; I simply read her piece with a fresh eye and performed some basic editing, skills that come only with experience.

She was in the same position as many aspiring nonfiction writers: She'd

AFRAID OF SUCCESS?

As much as we want to be successful writers, many of us fear that success even more. There's one voice inside telling us we can do it, driving us to work hard, fueling our dream. There's another voice telling us we aren't good enough, can't deliver, better give up.

In some, that negative voice is louder. *Fear of success* wins out over confidence and determination.

Why would some of us, who are so ambitious, be *afraid of success* — the one thing we want so badly? Because deep inside, unconsciously, we feel that should we be successful, it will be just a fluke. That if we get a break, by some ridiculous stroke of fate, we won't be able to deliver. Oh, maybe we'll get lucky and deliver once, but we'll never measure up. We're certain that we can't live up to the new standard of performance that first taste of accomplishment suggests.

To make sure we never have to face that challenge, we unconsciously sabotage our opportunities.

Some of the symptoms:

• We're constantly late — to classes, to interviews, to appointments, to meet deadlines.

• We're slovenly in our appearance, telling ourselves it reflects our individualism and casual style.

• We constantly misplace things and can't seem to get organized.

• Our personal life is so challenging and trying at the moment, we just don't have the time or energy to get our professional life "together."

• We take frequent shortcuts in our work — doing a half-baked job of researching, fact-checking, proofreading, et al.

• We convince ourselves that rewriting and polishing our work will destroy its originality, spontaneity and artistic vision.

• We're cheap in buying materials; we use frugality to justify the shoddy presentation of our work.

• We remind ourselves that we're writers, not salespersons, and refuse to market our work adequately.

• We're confrontational with editors when there's no good reason for it.

• We act arrogant, make unreasonable demands, and generally behave in a manner that makes people *not* want to work with us. Or, conversely, we're passive or obsequious to a discomfiting degree.

continued

- We can't generate enough ideas.
- We have so many ideas, we can't choose one.
- We pick grandiose ideas that we won't have time to research, write, or otherwise follow to completion.
- We're offered an assignment and find perfectly logical reasons why we can't accept it or turn it in.
- We rarely study markets carefully, continually submitting inappropriate ideas and manuscripts.
- We try only for markets beyond our reach in terms of our experience and skill, because smaller markets where we might break in are "beneath us."
- We write regularly for smaller markets but don't attempt to move up to more demanding markets because we're comfortable where we are, and we "know our limits."
- We look for and dwell on contradictory advice from writers and writing teachers so we won't have to make up our own minds, rely on ourselves, and get down to work.

And so on.

How do we overcome our fear of success?

Listen to the other voice, the supportive one. Nurture it. Trust it. Believe in it.

spent years trying to break into the big markets, getting constant rejection but no useful feedback about what she was doing wrong.

THERE'S NO SHAME IN BEING REALISTIC

Some successful writers, in *Writer's Digest* and elsewhere, recommend that writers shoot straightaway for the biggest, highest-paying markets. If you're really a writer, they say, and you believe in yourself, why not take on the greatest challenge?

I respect every one of these well-meaning mentors, and the success they've had personally; but never, as they've exhorted writers to skip the smaller markets, have I seen any mention of the markets they first sold their articles to, the smaller publications that gave them their starts before they moved on to those prestigious credits they list in their biographical sketches. Perhaps they're embarrassed to admit they wrote their first articles for small newspapers or magazines that paid a nickel or dime a word.

Advising a beginning writer to aim immediately for prestige markets is like telling a teenager with a new driver's license to head straight for the Indy 500. By targeting more accessible markets, and writing the kinds of articles you're ready to write, you will develop confidence and skills as a writer, the same way a professional in any field develops. For some, it takes a relatively short time to achieve steady sales in markets that pay respectably or that offer prestige. For others, it may take many years. But few jump right into the big time and stay there.

Be objective about your experience and your skill level.

Swallow your pride, and admit that you have a few things to learn. Be realistic about the time and commitment you have to give to writing in general, and an assignment in particular, should you land one.

It's possible you're ready right now for top markets. If so, that's great. Go for it!

But if you're not quite at that stage, admit it. Be willing to start on a lower rung of the ladder, one that you can firmly grasp, and climb your way up. If necessary, enroll in classes, join a writer's group, or volunteer your writing services to a worthy organization — anything to gain experience and develop professionally. Just remember:

The more you write, the faster your climb up the ladder will be.

The less you write, the longer it will take.

Should I Specialize?

When I started freelancing, I wrote on a wide variety of subjects. I was a "generalist." I didn't know that's what I was. I only knew I was desperate to write and be published, and pitched ideas on anything I figured would make a good article.

Although I was not a churchgoer, I wrote a piece for *Christian Life* about a wrestling coach who used his religious beliefs in his daily work. On a surfing trip to Mexico, I spent a day in jail and turned it into an article for *Surfer* advising readers how to stay out of Mexican hoosegows. For a Canadian film magazine called *Take One*, I wrote a humor piece about losing a movie review contest. I profiled a legendary female saddlemaker for *Grit*, examined an experimental halfway house for criminals for *American County Government*, and interviewed a European bike racing champion for *American Bicyclist and Motorcyclist*.

By generalizing, I had gotten a start and was accumulating some respectable clips. But I was not making a living and, still in my early twenties, took a job as a page with CBS in Hollywood, working TV shows ranging from "All in the Family" to "The Price Is Right."

I quit a year later and wrote about my backstage experiences for "Calendar," the arts and entertainment section of *The Los Angeles Times*, cracking my first major market.

That's when I discovered specializing. I knew a lot about television and film. They were among my primary interests, filling my head with endless ideas. Because of my interest in them, I had something special to say about them, which is the key to breaking into new markets. And there were plenty of publications using media-related articles.

Over the next couple of years, I pitched and sold celebrity or media angles to *Tennis Illustrated*, *Los Angeles Magazine* and *West*, a prestigious Sunday magazine then published in *The Los Angeles Times*; that paid $500, my first significant money. I sold original articles and spin-offs to small publications whose names I can't remember.

Still, the payoffs were sporadic. After a year or two of living at the poverty level, I took a job as a public relations writer. But I continued to grind out query letters to several publications, concentrating on show business angles, with a goal to be a full-time freelancer by age thirty.

Finally, after rejecting a dozen of my ideas, an editor named Guy Flatley at *The New York Times* assigned me a film production piece. A *TV Guide* editor happened to see it and asked if I wanted to profile celebrities for his magazine. I began contributing entertainment pieces to Sunday magazines in major newspapers across the country. A roundup piece on screenwriting for *Writer's Digest* led to a regular *WD* column on freelance writing. *The New York Times*, *The Los Angeles Times* and *TV Guide* kept calling with assignments.

Shortly after turning thirty, I quit my job to freelance full time, working at home, a situation that lasted many years. It didn't happen accidentally, easily or quickly, but it happened. Specializing did it.

Does that mean you should specialize?

There's no easy answer. To repeat: *You must assess what you want from writing, and what you are able and willing to give to it.*

Many of my students are employed full time, are parents, or both. They do not have eight or ten or twelve hours a day to write and market their work.

I suggest they at least consider specializing.

"If you are an avid gardener," I say, "you may want to write about gardening. If begonias are your passion, write about begonias. If you are a parent, consider articles on parenting. If you fix leaky pipes, think about ideas related to plumbing."

Here's why:

- When you specialize, ideas tend to generate themselves.
- Because you are an expert in a given area, you stand out; you have a trademark. Editors tend to remember you, trust you, be more receptive to your pitches.
- Much of your knowledge is already in your head or your files. You have a jump start on background and research.
- In recent years, general interest magazines have been in decline, while the specialty market has grown.
- Relationships with editors built on a specialty can be used as a springboard to more diverse assignments.
- Specializing leads not only to editor-generated assignments, but to columns and books, because you become known as an authority in one or more fields.

The downside: Specializing can limit your pool of ideas and your range of assignments; working the same subject matter too much can lead to boredom and writer burnout.

If you specialize, of course, you can always branch out later, and vice versa. For some, specializing is a boon. For others, it's too confining.

Gregory Von Dare, the writer-producer-host of a daily radio show on cars, enrolled in one of my nonfiction writing classes several years back. He wanted to learn how to write articles, and turned his knowledge of cars into several pieces for automotive magazines. He went on to edit a couple of automotive publications and write specialty books on classic cars. For Greg, specializing in car matters became his calling card.

Barbara Hopfinger, on the other hand, let her heart and mind wander, and that worked for her. One of her freelance pieces, for *The Los Angeles Times*, profiled a nurseryman named Kiyoshi Yoshida, who has devoted much of his life to planting and nurturing bamboo groves.

"I knew nothing about bamboo when I wrote the article," Barbara recalls. "Yoshida's quiet obsession with bamboo intrigued me. I set about to read everything I could about the plant. I learned from writing this article that an individual's passion makes a great subject for an article."

Barbara also learned that a writer's curiosity and willingness to explore can lead to rewarding assignments, just as well as specializing can.

A lot of it has to do with what kind of person you are, what kind of writer you are. And only you know that—or have the capability to find out.

GLOSSARY OF TERMS

Angle. Also *slant, hook* or *peg.* The special facet of a larger topic that you choose to focus on that sets your article apart and makes it useful to an editor. As in: "That's too broad a subject. What's your angle?"

Billboard paragraph. A paragraph that comes high in an article, summing up the general angle or theme of the piece. Also known by various other terms, such as guidepost, signpost, theme, nut, essence graph, etc.

Bullets. Brief bits of information, related to one subject, and listed and set apart from the body of the text by a graphic symbol.

Byline. The writer's name on her article, usually under the headline.

Biocredit. Biographical information about the writer that accompanies some articles, often at the end.

Clips. Samples of your published work (usually two or three, cleanly photocopied) that may accompany your query as evidence of your experience, writing ability or expertise in a certain area of reporting.

Company publication. Published by a company to serve its employees, clients, customers, etc.

Copy. Actual lines of writing, as in, "Please proofread your copy carefully."

Copyeditor. The editor whose job it is to proofread and clean up ("copyedit") your manuscript, which is performed at the "copy desk."

Copywriting. The creation of advertising copy.

Copyright. The registration of your personal work with the Library of Congress for protection of your work.

Credits. Although this can mean a complete list of your published articles or books, it more often refers to a few of the better markets where your work has appeared, part of a statement of your credentials in a query letter.

Deck. Body of type below the headline that amplifies the head and gives the reader a summary or teaser of what the story is about.

Evergreen. An almost timeless article that an editor can hold for many months or even longer and use when needed with little or no updating.

Feature. Generally used to differentiate writing style from straight news reporting, or from shorter pieces. "Feature length" generally refers

continued

to articles of roughly 1,200-1,500 words or more, with "short features" being less.

Filler. Mini-item, usually of fewer than 100 words, used by editors to fill in a small hole on a page.

First person. Material for an article written in the first person is drawn from one's own experiences or feelings. Also called a *personal experience piece.*

Front-of-the-book, back-of-the-book. Magazine sections or departments of shorter items or articles found at the beginning and the end of magazines.

General interest. As in "general interest magazine," a publication that defies categorization. It appeals to a broad readership, with a wide range of subject matter.

Graph. Short for "paragraph." As in: "Cut the graph about the pink elephants."

Handouts. Free publicity material, such as photographs, given to you for use with your article.

Head. Short for headline. Also called *hed.*

How-to. An article providing authoritative advice on how to perform a particular task or general activity, such as how to bake perfect cookies, write a billboard graph, survive a snowstorm while backpacking, etc.

In-house. Staff-written, as in: "That's an article we'd handle in-house." Not to be confused with in-house (corporate) publications, a magazine category.

Kicker. The final element, often the last sentence, in your article that pulls it together, offers a concluding touch or statement, and gives the reader a satisfying finish.

Kill fee. An amount guaranteed a writer (frequently by written contract) if her assigned material is not used by a publication. This is customarily 25 to 50 percent of the full payment and sometimes paid as an "advance."

Lead. Beginning of an article, usually the first sentence, designed to get the piece started and grab the reader's attention. Also spelled "lede."

Lead time. The period of time that a final manuscript must be submitted prior to publication date (e.g., "At *Writer's Digest*, we work on a three-month lead time").

continued

List article. An article that unifies several related bits of information or advice, often in the how-to, self-help or service vein, such as "Ten Ways to Save Money at Tax Time" or "Ten Great Bible Bedtime Stories."

Masthead. Listing of publication's staff and their titles, usually found at the front of the book. Also called a *staff box.*

ms. Abbreviation for "manuscript." Plural: mss.

On acceptance, on publication. A publication's policy governing when you will be paid for written work. "On acceptance" means when the article is accepted (and after accounting has been notified). "On publication" means when your article actually appears in print.

Op-ed. Opinion-editorial, as in op-ed page or op-ed piece.

Over the transom. Unsolicited manuscripts. Folklore has it that they were once tossed "over the transom" of an editor's closed door.

Page rate. Payment based on number of pages of material actually printed, e.g., "We pay $50 a page." More common is payment by word or total word length.

Pull quote. Pithy quotation "pulled" from an article and graphically highlighted in larger typeface to help "sell" the article to readers, much like a headline or deck.

Query. Letter proposing your idea to an editor, used in lieu of a completed manuscript, to "sell" your idea.

Rights. The publishing rights you sell when your article is purchased.

Roundup. Article that "rounds up" a wide range of information or opinion on a single subject, often polling experts in a given field. Also known as a *survey piece.*

SASE. Self-addressed, stamped envelope, which accompanies your query or submission.

Self-help. As in a "self-help" piece, providing authoritative advice on how to change or improve human behavior, psyche, emotions, relationships, health, etc. A "how-to" for the mind, emotions and body.

Service piece. An article, often aimed at the consumer, providing readers with information to help them make a better choice. Example: "Pittsburgh's Ten Best Pizza Parlors."

Short. A brief item, often only a couple hundred words long. Often found on a special page or in a special section of "shorts."

Sidebar. Succinct accompanying article, often only a few hundred

continued

words, set off graphically (usually boxed) from a much longer article on related subject matter. Frequently used to highlight a block of material that is pertinent but slows or weighs down the main piece.

Spec. Short for speculation, as in "writing on spec." Meaning an editor will look at a manuscript based on your idea, but without any guarantees of purchase (no firm assignment or contract).

Spin-off. A new article fashioned from leftover research material or published material rewritten in a different way (rights permitting).

Stringer. Correspondent or nonstaff writer for a newspaper or magazine.

Subhead. Short headlines inside the article, usually a word or two, that help break up the copy and act as section dividers.

Tearsheet. Original sample of your published work, "torn" from a publication. Prior to photocopying, tearsheets were customary, but have largely been replaced by photocopied clips, which are cleaner and cheaper.

Terms. Stipulated payment, length, deadline, rights to be purchased, etc. when assignment is made. As in "terms of the contract."

Think piece. Essay or analytical article, usually longer on thought than facts, but often combining the two.

Trade journal. Publication aimed at members of a particular profession, generally carrying articles directly related to that field, especially job skills.

Well. Main editorial section of a magazine, usually toward the middle, where the longer features appear.

Every published article begins with the idea, and the writer's ability to find the marketable angle within that idea.

That's up next—Step Two.

Getting Started

I don't know about you, but I'm the kind of writer who has more ideas than he knows what to do with.

Ideas for articles, books and scripts flutter around in my head like a swarm of butterflies (sometimes, unfortunately, they feel more like *bats*). I wake up with ideas. They hit me while I'm driving, eating, reading the newspaper, watching television, exercising, conversing with friends, making love. I make lists of ideas, fill notebooks with them, keep endless idea files. A fraction ends up getting written, and earns me a living.

Ideas, and plenty of them, are the lifeblood of a professional writing career. To mix metaphors, they are the vital seeds without which there is no cash crop.

Once, in the first article-writing workshop I taught, a young man raised his hand and said a bit pitifully, "I can't come up with enough ideas."

That surprised me — really surprised me. I assumed all writers were like me: overactive imagination, head constantly bombarded and muddled with "neat things" to write, if only there were enough time.

I asked the class if anyone else had trouble finding ideas. Up went several hands.

I was forced to think hard about how and where a nonfiction writer discovers marketable ideas. In brief, this is what I concluded:

1. Ideas are everywhere, all around us.
2. If something makes you say to yourself, "Mmmm, I'd like to know more about that," arouses strong feelings in you or presents a problem, it's at least the beginning of an idea.
3. Markets help define ideas. Put another way, specific markets turn nebulous ideas into viable, workable ideas. Without a keen understanding of markets, we're blind to good ideas.
4. As with markets, an awareness of the wide range of article types, how they differ, and what's required of them, further sharpens our

perception of ideas.

5. Ideas are only as good as the *angle* we find within them, the special slant that gives marketable focus to a general topic.

VOLUME OR SELECTIVITY?

There are basically two schools of thought about selectivity when you're starting out as a freelancer. One—the "beggars can't be choosers" view—says you should grab any assignment you can, gaining as much experience and as many credits as quickly as possible. The other says that since freelancing is your "second job," not your primary source of income, you have the luxury to be more picky, to follow your heart.

The danger in being choosy when you're getting started is in being unproductive. It's easy to use "selectiveness" as an excuse for not getting down to work. On the other hand, heartfelt work is invariably *better* work, if the craft is there.

A former student of mine, Brenda Day, had never sold an article when she enrolled in one of my UCLA Extension classes. She was a skilled writer—she'd spent four years as a journalism student at the University of Southern California—but when it came to coming up with her own ideas as a freelancer, she seemed lost.

During that class, she sold an article to *The Los Angeles Times*—her first freelance sale—and followed it with an article for *Los Angeles* magazine. Both were related to mystery and crime-solving, a passion of hers. She has turned out dozens of self-generated pieces since, many related to nonmainstream music, another field she follows with enthusiasm. Her advice? "Choose ideas and write articles," says Brenda, who freelances part time, "that you feel only *you* can write."

Ellen Alperstein, a full-time freelancer whose work calendar always seems full, offers a different perspective. "If you write to soothe your soul, and that makes you happy, be as picky as you want," she says. "If you write to eat, do what it takes to pay the bills."

Turning down assignments because the subject matter doesn't quicken your pulse may be a subconscious excuse for not taking chances as a writer, Ellen warns. And when you restrict yourself too much, she adds, you'll never know what fascinating story you might have stumbled across.

"Curiosity," she says, "can really be rewarding."

But only, she adds sagely, if you do something to satisfy it—by turning it into an assignment.

THE PROFESSIONAL APPROACH

From now on, you are a professional writer.

Never mind how few sales you may have. A professional *attitude* will often get you into the marketplace while you work to acquire experience, credits and clips.

That mind-set is as important to you at home as it is in the outside world. Here and now, vow to leave amateur outlooks behind, and to think and behave like a pro. That means, among other things, spending a little money (keep those receipts for tax deductions).

Some actions to take immediately:

• Create a workplace that is yours, and yours alone. Ideally, it will be outside your home. Short of that luxury, it can be a separate room in your home. But even if it is only a desk in a corner, it should be strictly for work, nothing else. And it must be your personal choice; it must feel right to *you*.

• Furnish it with a big desk, a good chair and a file cabinet, preferably with several drawers. You are a writer with big plans, big ideas, big self-confidence.

• Stock your home *work* library with appropriate resource books, such as a top-quality dictionary, thesaurus, world atlas, almanac and so on. Suggestion: Put them prominently on your holiday wish list.

• Buy a business wall calendar for jotting down assignments, deadlines, interviews, et al. Begin filling it in with regular tasks, even if it's only query letters you "assign" to yourself. Then observe those hours as rigorously as if you were at the office—because you *are* at the office.

• Buy file folders. Not a dozen—a *hundred*. You're a working writer, with loads of ideas. When you get one, slug a file folder with a key word or working title, then fill it with notes, names of possible sources, related clippings and so on. You'll be surprised how quickly a file folder fills up with preliminary research.

• Create a post-office-in-a-drawer. You can get a scale for a few dollars at most office supply stores. Purchase a variety of stamps ranging in value up to a dollar, and pick up a free postal-rate card while you're at it. If possible, select stamps that reflect your personality or taste, not just the standard stamp. Buy plenty of mailing envelopes in a variety of sizes, and get businesslike mailing labels.

Why a post office at home? It will encourage you to complete queries

continued

and manuscripts and get them into the mail without proscrastination.

• Purchase a ream of stationery with a clean, professional-looking letterhead and corresponding envelopes. If you can afford it, have it personally designed on quality stock. Keep it simple and straightforward. Don't embellish or overadvertise.

Like it or not, most editors feel gimmicky insignias such as typewriters, quill pens and cameras are a tipoff that the writer is an amateur. The same goes for the term "Freelance Writer" after a name; it means nothing, because anyone can use it, regardless of training, skill or experience. Leave it off. Let your work speak for itself.

In addition, order note-sized stationery with your name at the top. If you're working hard, you'll use it a lot.

• You may want to have business cards printed. This is when a notation such as "Freelance Writer" or "Photo-Journalist" is more appropriate. If you're uncomfortable about publicizing your address, get a postal box. (Personally, I've never used business cards, but many professional writers do.)

• Get an answering machine or voice mail. It is not an editor's responsibility to continually call a writer with an assignment or question as a deadline nears. If he can't reach you, he'll quickly stop trying—and call someone else.

• If you don't work on a PC, get some training and start. Mac, IBM, IBM clone, it doesn't matter; what matters is that you get up to speed as a productive nonfiction writer.

Be sure to use a surge protector to protect against sudden power surges that can destroy PC circuitry. Even better, buy a UPS (uninterrupted power source) standby unit, which combines surge protector with backup battery to allow you time to save the file you're working on and shut down your computer properly in case of electrical problems. Contrary to popular belief, standard surge protectors vary in quality and capability, and they do not guarantee against *every* power surge.

• Just as you'll need lots of file folders, you'll need plenty of diskettes. Ideally, you'll have a PC with both A and B drives to supplement your hard drive, not only to provide an extra backup copy in case of a faulty diskette, but because some publishers prefer to work with 3½-inch diskettes rather than 5¼-inch. Costwise, however, this ideal may be out of the financial reach of many writers.

continued

> • Please, no dot matrix printers, unless they approximate letter quality, such as Hewlett-Packard's excellent Laser Jet series, at this writing the top of the line (check out the market, because it constantly changes). What's wrong with low-quality dot matrix? Generally, the printing looks cheap, and it's hard on the eyes; editors don't like copy that's hard on the eyes.
>
> • Consider a fax machine, if you don't already have one. Not necessary (yet), but certainly handy.
>
> You now have your own home office.
>
> *You are now your own boss.*
>
> Be the toughest boss you've ever had. If necessary, during your self-prescribed working hours, post your door with a warning to visitors that they are not welcome, and cut incoming personal calls short, or turn on your answering machine and return calls later.
>
> Convince your friends and family that writing is your new, part-time job—because it is.
>
> *You're a professional!*

THE CURIOSITY FACTOR

When I was starting out and grabbing just about any byline I could, even I turned down assignments that didn't spark my interest at least in some small way. And I think that's the single most important motivating factor in choosing an idea: *curiosity.*

"Don't write what you know," Art Spikol has advised in his *Writer's Digest* column, "write what you'd *like* to know. Follow your natural curiosity, which usually rears its inquisitive head for one of two reasons: one, because you *have* to find out and, two, because you *want* to find out."

I'm looking at a copy of *Fly Fisherman*, which has in it an article by a Colorado writer named Chester Anderson called "Drifting Mayflies." It examines the habits of this insect in relation to using homemade imitation mayflies as trout bait.

In the midst of the second paragraph is this sentence: "I wondered, why do mayflies drift?"

That's all. Just the curiosity of an avid fly fisherman.

If drifting mayflies are of interest to me, the writer must have figured, surely they will interest others who fish with fly rods. Simple curiosity turned into an informative article.

Write about those things that arouse your curiosity and motivate you to find out more.

Look Around!

From the time we get up in the morning to the time we go to bed—even while we sleep (or try to)—potential articles swirl around us. They are *everywhere*.

Ripped off by a carpet cleaning scam? Might be a cautionary how-to piece for a women's magazine, or a consumer-oriented exposé for your local newspaper.

Trouble getting your child to eat his breakfast? Maybe it's a self-help article for a parenting journal.

Inspired by a neighbor who's overcome a disability and gone on to a special accomplishment? Could be a profile for your local newspaper, or even a national magazine.

Getting ready to move, and worried that it might disrupt your child's schooling? Another how-to or self-help article in the making.

Studying yoga with an elderly instructor who's unusually flexible? Could it be the focus of an interview for a health or seniors' magazine?

Traveling to a favorite weekend getaway spot? Why not pitch it to a newspaper travel section?

Bothered by faulty car alarms, including your own, that go off at all hours, interrupting your sleep? I was, so I turned my problem into a 1,100-word, first-person humor piece that helped me vent my feelings. It required a few hours' work—and earned me $300.

Those are just a few examples of potential article ideas, which can be found in what we read, watch, eat, feel, dream, enjoy, hate, think and talk about. If you have a problem, chances are many others have the same problem, and want advice on how to solve it. If you have deep feelings about something, many others surely do, too. If you've had a particularly rewarding experience, it's probably worth sharing.

If you're fascinated by a particular fact or set of facts, others are bound to be interested.

What's New?

The more things change, the more things there are to write about.

Editors look for writers who plow fresh ground. They covet those writers. They *depend* on those writers. They give those writers assignment after assignment.

Here are some catchwords that often indicate whether a subject area is ripe for exploitation: *unique, unusual, new, first, trend-setting, change, one-of-a-kind, different, timely, groundbreaking, pacesetting, making waves.*

When a movie called *Bebe's Kids* was in production, I sold an item on the film to *Entertainment Weekly*. The hook: It was the first animated feature with black characters from black filmmakers. Note that word *first*.

I was planning a short trip to San Felipe, Mexico, and wanted a travel assignment. Several years had passed since *The Los Angeles Times* had run a piece on the coastal resort town. In that time, the first luxury hotels and condos had gone up, and an international airport was in the works. I got my assignment with this peg: *San Felipe is changing fast. See it now, before the last vestiges of a sleepy fishing village are gone.* Note the words *changing* and *now*.

For *Alaska Outdoors*, I profiled the National Outdoor Leadership School not long after it set up new regional headquarters outside Anchorage — the first environmentally conscious organization to do so. Note the words *new* and *first*.

Look around. What's happening in your world to shake things up? What's new on the horizon? What's making an impact? What's drawing your attention, and the attention of others? What's not being covered that should be? What's being reported in one publication that can be covered differently in another?

If you don't write about it, someone else will.

How Ideas Become Marketable

At this point, you're undoubtedly jotting ideas down right and left. It's time to break the bad news.

"Ideas" aren't worth a dime.

To be *viable* ideas, they must have four things: (1) an *angle*, (2) *timeliness* (in most cases), (3) an *identifiable article type*, and (4) an *appropriate market*.

Henceforth, let's stop thinking of ideas and think only of angles, because angles are what you sell.

Take my car alarm problem, for example. That's all it was, a nagging problem. Until I . . .

• Figured it would make a good piece for *The Los Angeles Times*. Not just *The Los Angeles Times*, but the View section. And not just the View section, but a regular column in View called "First Person," which purchased freelance material. I had my target market.

• Because the "First Person" column obviously used first-person material, I had my *article type*. But I honed this further when I decided to take a humorous approach. My article type became a *humorous personal experience piece*.

• I needed a slant. Car alarms is not a slant. It's a broad subject. Erratic car alarms is still just a vague topic, too broad for an editor to envision as an article. *How I learned to live without a car alarm and reclaim my sanity.* That's an angle. And in Los Angeles, a car-crazy city plagued at the time by erratic car alarms, it was a particularly marketable angle.

By finding my market, knowing my article type, coming up with my own special angle — and a timely one — I was able to turn a nebulous idea into a salable one.

TOPIC VS. ANGLE

Jack Hart, a veteran editor and writing coach at *The Oregonian*, once told me, "Right after writers pitch me a story, I often say to them, 'OK, that's your topic. Now what's your *angle?*' "

Hart learned long ago, first as a reporter and later as an editor, the difference between a broad topic and a workable angle.

Finding the angle or hook for your story is one of the most crucial aspects of the nonfiction trade.

Let's take as an example the "idea" of gardens in England. That's a big subject — a book, not an article. We must find a slant that's manageable as an article of a couple thousand words, a slant with enough focus to catch and keep the interest of editors and readers.

Let's microscope our topic and see what happens:

Topic: "England's gardens."

Still a topic: "England's summer gardens."

Still a topic: "England's colorful summer gardens."

Still a topic: "Photographing England's colorful summer gardens."

Still a topic, but getting some focus: "Photographing England's colorful coastal summer gardens."

Angle: "How to find and photograph England's most colorful coastal gardens this summer," now a potential how-to piece, seasonally timed, for a travel section or a photography magazine.

Finding that peg for your material enables an editor to envision:

• What kind of article you plan to write, its scope, and what it will be about.

• How it differs from other takes being pitched or published on the same subject.

• Whether it fits into current editorial needs.

• Where it might fit into the actual publication, even how it might be laid out, illustrated, promoted.

• How it might serve the reader.

A sharp angle will do all those. A more general topic will only get rejected.

Give an Editor a Reason

How different or well-defined an angle do you need? Generally speaking, *the more widely covered a subject, the sharper or fresher the angle must be.*

Let's take the topic of AIDS. Obviously, it's a subject that will be with us for years, probably decades. At this point, we can't even begin to know its far-reaching medical, economic, social and political ramifications.

Yet AIDS has also been covered *in extremis*, in countless feature articles. That means that outside of news developments, such as research breakthroughs and changing statistics, you must come up with a new take on it to interest an editor.

In 1992, Donna St. George, a reporter for Knight-Ridder Newspapers, faced that dilemma. She wanted to write about the spread of the disease to the general population, beyond high-risk groups, but that was already "old news." She needed a timely, dramatic peg. So St. George wrote about an isolated farm town of 16,000 people in the Florida Everglades in which more than 1,000 were HIV-infected, most of them black. Residents of the tiny community of Belle Glade were literally dying by the hundreds. It was a story that found a sharp focus for the subject of AIDS while simultaneously broadening the scope of the story, and did so with emotional impact. St. George narrowed her focus further to one particular family, and even more sharply to that family's matriarch. Nearly 3,000 miles from Belle Glade, in southern California, *The Orange County Register* ran the piece under the headline, "AIDStown," with this deck:

A mother's grief for her ravaged family and the tale of a devastated community foreshadow the coming heterosexual epidemic in the central cities and in pockets of poverty across the United States.

It's a classic example of finding an intriguing, manageable angle—a *focus*—within a broad topic.

The more demanding the market and the editor, the clearer and more provocative your take must be. That's especially true with subjects that are nationally or internationally prominent and stale from overexposure.

When actress-producer Jane Fonda was about to broadcast her first made-for-television movie, *The Dollmaker*, I wanted to profile her for *The Los Angeles Times*. At the time, Fonda was a preeminent public figure and multimedia star, a success with films, fitness books and tapes, TV production, health clubs, et al., one of the most influential women of her generation. That made her an intriguing subject; it also meant she was overexposed.

Like all editors, *The Los Angeles Times* arts and entertainment editor Irv Letofsky had a limited budget and limited space for freelance purchases; and he was not fond of puff pieces rolled off the publicity-driven assembly line. To get an assignment, I had to give him a *reason*.

I did some research and found that only one publication, the business magazine *Forbes*, had done a major piece on the problems and contradictions Fonda faced after evolving from outspoken leftist to head of a lucrative business empire.

I pitched that angle to Letofsky, assuring him that I would ask tough questions the entertainment press wasn't asking. My piece appeared as a Sunday Calendar cover story, which I reprinted profitably in nearly a dozen other major newspapers (I'll cover reprint rights and syndication in Step Fifteen).

Without my special take on Fonda, without giving my editor a reason to run that article, I would never have gotten the assignment.

Before pitching an idea, try to see it through the editor's eyes; ask what needs it will satisfy, and why he would choose your approach over others.

◆ ◆ ◆

Footnote: A decade earlier, I had profiled Fonda for *The New York Times* when she was making a movie called *Dick and Jane*, her first mainstream film after years of antiwar protest. The angle then was: "Can Jane Fonda's popularity and career survive her controversial political activism?" (Obviously, they did.)

Which brings us to another element of a marketable angle: *timeliness*.

IT'S ALL IN THE TIMING

There is a genre of article, the "evergreen," that defies topicality.

It is that rare piece that is useful *because* of its timelessness; editors keep evergreens on hand knowing they can schedule them now or a year from now, as needed, with little or no updating. Many historical accounts are evergreens; so are many nostalgia or cooking pieces. Virtually all of the how-to articles I've sold to *Writer's Digest* are in the same mold—their advice on writing craft doesn't age much.

Evergreens are the exception to the rule: Most angles generate assignments because they are fresh, timely, even forward-looking.

Perhaps 80 percent of the media-related articles I've written have been tied to specific dates: movie release dates, television air dates, book publica-

TESTING YOUR ANGLE

To sell to editors, you must learn to think like editors think—what they want, need, don't need. And that begins with the angle you decide to pitch to them.

In getting out their magazines or newspaper sections, editors have certain tasks. Among them are the following: determining if a feature should be a major article, department piece, short, etc. ("what's the scope?"); summing up an idea succinctly for other editors; writing headlines, decks and cover copy.

If you go through these same tasks as an exercise at your end, before you ever contact an editor, you'll be able to better sift out unfocused ideas from marketable angles.

Put your angle through this five-step test:

1. Are you trying to write everything there is to know about a subject, with a topic ("Earthquake Preparedness") more suitable for a book? Or have you carved off a sharp enough slant that you can handle it in a limited word length ("Ten Precautions Californians Can Take Right Now to Surive the Next Jolt")?

2. Can you state your angle in a concise phrase or single sentence ("How the National Football League tackled the drug problem and rescued ruined lives")?

3. Are you able to capture the essence of your article in a headline or title that suits the target publication? Let's suppose your target market was *Parents*: "Picking a Babysitter Can Be a Nightmare—Or a Dream Come True."

4. Can you follow up that title with a "deck" that sums up what your article is about? ("Finding the right person to stay with your child is one of the most important challenges you'll ever face. The decision can be nerve-wracking and traumatic. But it doesn't have to be. A child-care expert and mother of three tells why.")

Don't include a deck on the manuscript you submit; write it only as an exercise to test your angle.

5. Can you shorten both title and deck to a promotional blurb that's appropriate for the cover of your target publication? (Again, for *Parents*: "Finding a Babysitter—Without the Worry!")

Before you pitch or write an article, apply this five-step test. If you have trouble with any of these criteria, you've probably bitten off too big a subject, or you may be going off on tangents.

Rethink, refocus, and find your angle.

tion dates and the like. The outdoor and travel pieces I've filed have been planned for seasonal travel and outdoor recreation. Even human interest material can have timeliness: I once profiled a mother who radically changed her life to care for her paralyzed son; placing it in the newspaper near Mother's Day helped give it a special poignancy, and marketability.

I'm not one of those writers who obsess about timing, planning months and years ahead to take advantage of seasonal, holiday and historical pegs. Some writers do, though, and quite profitably.

Thanksgiving, Christmas, Hanukkah, Easter, Mother's Day, Father's Day, Valentine's Day, Presidents' birthdays, notable assassination or war dates, et al., offer article opportunities. Every year, or on incremental anniversaries, hundreds of publications run features slanted to these and other calendar events, including ethnic holidays such as Chinese New Year and the Mexican Day of the Dead.

Some examples of seasonal or holiday pegs, right off my corner newsstand:

"Charming South Florida Inns," a November issue of *South Florida* magazine, timed just before the winter season.

"Flatlanders Beware," a February edition of *Flying*, on the dangers of piloting planes in winter.

"Indian Summer Picnics," a September/October issue of *Virtue*, with special autumn recipes.

"Everything's Coming Up Roses," a December issue of *Entrepreneurial Woman*, profiling a woman who turned a Christmas gift-making tradition into a multimillion-dollar business producing fabric-wrapped frames.

"New Year, New Gear," a January issue of *Sea*, on new boating products.

Seasonal/holiday pieces like these are a mainstay with many magazines, and a profitable way to find angles simply by studying your calendar.

With the immigration influx and changing ethnic face of America, there are countless other special days to write about that are still foreign to many of us, yet deserve attention. It's a fertile area for generating sales.

Planning Ahead

Since all markets work with "lead times"—up to several months for monthly magazines, and longer for holiday scheduling—that means you must think ahead, plan ahead and pitch ahead for seasonal or holiday pegs. In fact, the best time to consider them is not as they approach—when it's much too late—but shortly after their last appearance on the calendar. Thinking "timing" is the kind of professional approach that editors appreciate, and that gives them one more reason to assign and schedule your story.

I once wrote a trend piece, for instance, on how television was tackling subject matter that had previously been taboo. A Calendar cover story, it was planned for the start of the new fall TV season. It was my sense of a trend that made the piece marketable. A year earlier might have been too soon, before some key made-for-television movies were in production; and a few months later too late, because the movies would have aired by then, and other reporters would have done the story.

Yet I could have done that story again two or three years later, asking the question, "By breaking down barriers in recent years, has television served the public, or merely trivialized and exploited important social issues?"

Most of the big pieces I've done have had a similar sense of timing: Hollywood's response to the AIDS crisis, the cultural boycott of South Africa, the struggle of Latinos to find an equitable place in Hollywood, the increasing trend of "beefcake" and male sensuality in mainstream movies, the emergence of African-American filmmakers in the commercial marketplace and so on. Every one of those articles was timely when it appeared, and every one could be updated today with a fresh slant.

A sense of trends, of timing, is crucial to most freelance writing careers.

From the briefest new product item to an in-depth report of global magnitude, timeliness is usually a vital ingredient, the difference between a useful idea and a stale one.

CHOOSING YOUR CATEGORY

"What type of article is it?"

That's a question I frequently put to students just after they've shared an idea or new manuscript with the class, especially if it feels ragged, rambling, unfocused. Too often, the response is a blank stare or stammer.

Before you propose or develop an article, you must be able to identify what *type* of article you have in mind. If you feel muddled about the essential purpose of the piece, so will editors.

Among the basic article types: how-to, self-help, personal experience (or first person), profile, roundup (or survey), service, historical, nostalgia, essay (including commentary or op-ed), investigative/exposé, humor and general interest. (See sidebar on article types and their functions, page 36).

These categories are arbitrary and, sometimes, the lines between them blur. For example, a *profile* of a remarkable person could also be a *personal-experience* piece, written in the first person — how the writer knew and experienced the subject. If it's first and foremost a profile, think of it as that. A profile could also be historical, investigative and written in the first person,

WHAT TYPE OF ARTICLE IS IT?

Most articles fall into the following categories and serve these general purposes (the examples/titles are strictly hypothetical):

How-To

An article that shows the reader how to better perform an activity.

Example: "Ten Tips for Growing Healthy Roses."

How It Might Serve the Reader: teach/instruct, update techniques, generate ideas, save time or money, inspire confidence, encourage, help improve (work, craft, activities, hobbies, etc.).

Self-Help

Similar to a how-to, but offering advice and guidance in the area of psychology and human behavior.

Example: "Ten Ways to Improve Your Marriage—Tonight."

How It Might Serve the Reader: help cope, feel less alone, feel better, improve life, find solutions, change.

Personal Experience

An article written in the first person recounting a firsthand experience.

Example: "Overcoming Heartbreak: How I Learned to Cope With My Child's Autism."

How It Might Serve the Reader: entertain, stir emotion, instruct in some way, help him to see himself, broaden his perspective, provide hope and inspiration, let him into another's life, help him feel less alone.

Profile

A personal or professional portrait—sometimes both—of a particular individual (or even a pet).

Example: "Joan Chen: An Actress Who Defies Asian Stereotypes."

How It Might Serve the Reader: entertain, inform, update, give insight into a person's character, reveal little-known details, inspire, touch emotions, instruct, warn.

Roundup or Survey

A "roundup" of comment, advice, quotes, etc. on a particular subject from notable sources or experts. The content can be opinions, remembrances, hard information, tips—just about anything on one

continued

theme. This format is often used to report on emerging trends.

Example: "Five Safety Experts Tell You What to Look for in a New Car."

How It Might Serve the Reader: inform, update, make him think, broaden perspective and awareness.

SERVICE

An article, often aimed at the consumer, that gives the reader a range of choices or helps him make a better selection.

Example: "Ten Places to Get a Great Pizza for Under $10"

How It Might Serve the Reader: guide/advise, help make better choices, reassure, provide ideas, avoid problems or disappointment, save time or money, make a purchase, find help or needed service, expand enjoyment, fight boredom.

ESSAY, COMMENTARY, OP-ED

A piece that expresses the opinion of the writer or explores a subject or issue in a distinctly personal way. (Note: "op-ed" stands for "opinion-editorial.")

Example: "Political Correctness Is Destroying Free Expression!"

How It Might Serve the Reader: inform, enlighten; broaden perspective; stimulate to think, change opinion or cause to become involved; help in some way, including to become a better person.

HISTORICAL

Informs about a particular time in history, focusing on people, places and events.

Example: "The Real Story of the Crack in the Liberty Bell"

How It Might Serve the Reader: educate, enlighten, give new insight, entertain, amuse, stimulate recall of old memories, correct misconceptions or misinformation, call to action.

NOSTALGIA

Historical, but looking at the past fondly, generally with a warm, positive tone.

Example: "In Our House, Sunday Was for Church and Baking Cookies"

How It Might Serve the Reader: entertain, inform, stir fond memories or emotions.

continued

INVESTIGATIVE/EXPOSÉ

In-depth reporting, heavily researched and documented, that brings to light new information on an important and/or controversial subject.

Example: "Pulling the Mask Off Cancer Cure Quackery"

How It Might Serve the Reader: inform, stir to action, generate public or official concern, right wrongs.

GENERAL INTEREST

An article of fairly broad interest that provides basic information on a given subject but does not fit into a particular category.

Example: "Wheelchair Racers: True Athletes on Wheels"

How It Might Serve the Reader: entertain, inform, educate, provide insight, broaden perspective, change opinion, caution, inspire.

HUMOR

Although a humorous tone characterizes some articles, a humor piece is one written principally and expressly to amuse, often in essay or personal-experience form.

Example: "This Christmas, I'm Hiding Until the In-Laws Leave!"

How It Might Serve The Reader: amuse, entertain, offer insight or message in lighthearted way.

Most articles fit into these caregories. If they don't, they don't — whatever works, works. But categorizing articles by type, when possible, can be a useful guide for shaping and honing your ideas into commercial nonfiction.

Suggestion: Clip articles that you find particularly well crafted and satisfying. Identify them as to type. Note their distinctive qualities and what they offer the reader. File these samples according to type, for easy reference and inspiration when you work on your own articles.

such as: "My Life with JFK: The Untold Story of Deception in the White House." An essay could certainly be historical or nostalgic. And so on. You alone must decide what kind of piece you intend to write, and focus accordingly. It's OK when categories cross over and mix with one another, as long as the piece works.

It's not OK if it means you're unclear about what you're writing.

SLANTING FOR THE MARKET

There's probably more to this "getting started" business than you expected.

Well, hang on, because we have yet to discuss finding the right angle for the *right market*.

When I sold my article on the National Outdoor Leadership School (NOLS) to *Alaska Outdoors*, I pegged my pitch to the opening of the school's Alaska headquarters and the controversy such an environmentally conscious group might generate in a state known for its individualistic citizens.

When I pitched a piece on NOLS to *Western's World*, my focus was a two-week kayaking expedition in Prince William Sound that NOLS had designed especially for professionals. Since most airline passengers travel for business reasons and businesspersons make up the bulk of *WW*'s readership, and because Alaska was on Western's destination route, the angle was a natural.

When I proposed an article on NOLS to the lifestyle section of *The Los Angeles Times*, my emphasis was a five-week summer backpacking trek in Utah aimed at helping young people build confidence and character.

I was able to sell three articles from the same general subject by coming up with three completely different slants aimed at three completely different markets. (We'll deal with reslanting for multiple markets and related issues in Step Five.)

An angle is only as good as its appropriateness for a specific market, and that market's unique readership and needs.

Take a look at some published articles and how their angles are ideally suited for their publications:

Topic: hazing on college campuses
Angle: sorority hazing, focusing on large women as special targets
Market: *Big Beautiful Woman*
Why it's on target: A unique angle on the issues of discrimination and abuse of heavy women for a magazine that speaks exactly to those problems. Keen market understanding.

Topic: cat safety
Angle: tips for protecting your feline on Halloween
Market: *Cat Fancy*
Why it's on target: It's got three things going for it—an angle that's a natural for this market, seasonally pegged to a holiday, focusing on a growing problem in urban areas.

Topic: cholesterol
Angle: how to enjoy soul food while lowering cholesterol
Market: *Upscale*
Why it's on target: *Upscale* is a magazine aimed at upwardly mobile African-Americans, many of whom enjoy soul food—but worry about the health risks. Savvy market slanting of a health topic.

Topic: business telephone communication
Angle: etiquette tips for putting customers "on hold"
Market: *Your Company* (business trade journal)
Why it's on target: Offers specific tips for a problem that everybody complains about, but which isn't written about much. Clever slanting to fill an editorial "hole."

Topic: Japanese culture
Angle: Japan's recent proliferation of Caucasian geishas
Market: *Transpacific*
Why it's on target: Taps into a trend that's offbeat and still fresh; aimed at an audience keen to read and learn about both traditional and changing Japanese culture.

Topic: Hispanic fiction writers
Angle: how they are making an impact in mainstream publishing after years of exclusion
Market: *Hispanic*
Why it's on target: Again, a timely angle aimed carefully at this particular magazine's sophisticated Hispanic readers, with an appropriate tone and viewpoint.

Topic: army "Casualty Assistance Officers"
Angle: the surprising rewards of helping grieving families
Market: *Soldier*
Why it's on target: A surprisingly upbeat twist on a grim subject for readers interested in military matters; another example of thinking of the fresh slant, the untold story.

Topic: dining in Atlanta
Angle: where to nosh on authentic, New-York-style deli
Market: *Atlanta* (city magazine)
Why it's on target: A good example of "going against the grain," thinking against stereotype, and coming up with a helpful article for Atlantans

with adventurous palates as well as East Coasters who have settled in the southern city.

Eight angles, eight markets with different readers and different needs.

Obviously, the article on cholesterol and soul food would not fit in *Cat Fancy*, *Transpacific*, or most of the other markets. But with a bit of retailoring, it probably would work in *Atlanta*, because of the city's large black population and the magazine's interest in dining.

By knowing markets, writers know how and what to pitch — and when.

◆ ◆ ◆

None of the four key elements — angle, timing, article type and market — exists alone. They complement each other to produce salable articles for welcoming publications.

Much of your success will depend on your awareness of the marketplace in general and understanding of individual markets in particular.

That's our next step.

Step Three

Markets: Getting to Know You

Warning!
All publications, names, titles and other market-related details
mentioned in this book are subject to change.

◆ ◆ ◆

When my friend Lee Green saw a TV news report about a Los Angeles Police Department "antistalking unit," designed to stop suspects from following and harming human prey, he immediately figured it would make a good magazine piece. If it intrigued him, he assumed it would interest others.

The first market he pitched was *Playboy*, which is aimed at sophisticated, upscale men. Lee had written previously for the magazine, but there were other reasons why he targeted that publication:

• The police unit was staffed primarily by male cops, which gave Lee male characters to write about.

• The victims were usually women, often ex-wives or lovers, which added an element of sexuality, however deviant.

• At the same time, Lee says, "stalking is a growing problem and phenomenon in society, the kind of thing *Playboy* covers frequently and in a serious way."

• The unit was new, the only one in the country, which meant *Playboy* hadn't written about it, and most readers wouldn't know much about it.

Even as a *Playboy* "insider," Lee's query (reproduced on page 72) was a long shot—the magazine generates most ideas in-house, according to one editor, developing perhaps two dozen nonfiction pieces yearly from the thousands of proposals that come in.

Lee's pitch paid off, however; he got the assignment.

Was it luck? Serendipity? A nice gesture from an editor he'd worked with before? Not at all.

He got the assignment because he knew the publication inside and out, and pitched an article that was right on target.

STUDYING THE MARKETPLACE

Two questions will take you a long way toward pointing an angle at the right market:

- What are they looking for?
- What haven't they done?

The best way to find that hole? Study the publication, regularly and thoroughly.

If that's not motive enough, here are some others:

- Your idea might be totally inappropriate for that publication's core readership.
- Perhaps a similar angle just ran there.
- Even if you studied the market some time ago, its editorial direction may have since changed.
- The publication may be staff-written or use limited freelance material.
- The number of pages — and assignments — might be changing.
- Freelance departments may have been added, or dropped.
- Editorial staff could have changed.
- The magazine or newspaper section might rely on certified experts to cover certain subjects.
- It may come out seasonally or irregularly.
- It may publish special issues for which you're well suited.

The average editor probably rejects 90 to 95 percent of all ideas pitched by freelance writers and sends back an even higher percentage of unsolicited manuscripts. Editors expect some proposals to be a bit off the mark and, if the writing is good, will even take note of writers who miss but come close. That's how I got started at *The New York Times*, pitching ideas that just weren't quite right at the time, until the editors came up with an assignment from their end.

But if you continually send queries on ideas that indicate you've never bothered to carefully study the market, it will wear out your welcome and mark you as an amateur. Besides, it gluts the marketplace with junk and wastes everyone's time — one reason replies take so long is that editors are backed up with literally tons of inappropriate and unprofessional submissions.

"Don't propose an idea to me until you've read my section every day for at least six months," the editor of a newspaper lifestyle section warned a group of my students. "I'm not kidding!"

Three types of letters, in particular, irritate an editor:

- Those addressed to their predecessors.
- Those addressed to them, but with their names misspelled.
- Those pitching an idea similar to one that just ran.

As a freelancer, you need to separate yourself from the herd, to distinguish yourself as a professional with something to offer. Slow down, take a broader look at the general marketplace, and peer deeper into individual markets. It makes all the difference.

Going to Market

Periodical publishing falls into two general groups: (1) consumer publications and (2) trade, technical and professional journals. From there, periodicals break down into dozens of categories, such as women's magazines, men's magazines, parenting journals, sports publications, New Age magazines and so on (see list of market categories, pages 45-46). These umbrella markets encompass virtually every field of human interest. By being aware of them, you become aware of the enormous range of possibilities for marketing your work, and you're better able to stay on top of marketing trends.

But you can't stop there. Within each of those umbrella nonfiction markets are dozens, even hundreds of individual publications. The most visible and tempting, of course, are the big national publications with which we're already familiar, those prominent markets that often pay higher rates. But because they are so big and so visible, everyone tries to write for them. They can pick and choose among the country's most skilled and experienced nonfiction writers.

That's why it's so vital, when you get started, to also pay attention to the smaller markets, the ones where you're most likely to break in. That includes not just the lesser-known consumer publications that are so hungry for freelance contributors, but the trade journals and company publications that rarely can afford to keep staff writers or top freelance writers under contract.

Don't let categories like trade journals and company publications put you off if you don't have expertise in a particular area. *Friendly Exchange*, for instance, is the company publication of Farmers Insurance Group. This

THE MARKETPLACE

Generally, periodical publishing falls into two groups: (1) consumer publications and (2) trade, technical and professional journals. Within these two giant categories are subject areas covering virtually every interest on earth (as broken down by *Writer's Market*):

Consumer

Animal

Art and Architecture

Associations

Astrology, Metaphysical and New Age

Aviation

Business and Finance

Career, College and Alumni

Child Care and Parental Guidance

Comic Books

Consumer Service and Business Opportunity

Contemporary Culture

Detective and Crime

Disabilities

Entertainment

Ethnic/Minority

Food and Drink

Games and Puzzles

General Interest

Health and Fitness

History

Hobby and Craft

Home and Garden

Humor

Inflight

Juvenile

Literary and "Little"

Men's

Military

Music

Mystery

Nature, Conservation and Ecology

Personal Computers

Photography

Politics and World Affairs

Psychology and Self-Improvement

Regional

Relationships

Religious

Retirement

Romance and Confession

Rural

Science

Science Fiction, Fantasy and Horror

Sports (which has nearly two dozen subdivisions)

Teen and Young Adult

Travel, Camping and Trailer

Women's

Trade, Technical and Professional Journals

Advertising, Marketing and PR

Art, Design and Collectibles

Auto and Truck

Aviation and Space

Beverages and Bottling

Book and Bookstore

continued

Brick, Glass and Ceramics
Building Interiors
Business Management
Church Administration and Ministry
Clothing
Coin-Operated Machines
Dental
Drugs, Health Care and Medical Products
Education and Counseling
Electronics and Communication
Energy and Utilities
Engineering and Technology
Entertainment and the Arts
Farm
Finance
Fishing
Florists, Nurseries and Landscaping
Government and Public Service
Groceries and Food Products
Hardware
Home Furnishings and Household Goods
Hospitals, Nursing and Nursing Homes
Hotels, Motels, Clubs, Resorts and Restaurants
Industrial Operations
Information Systems
Insurance
International Affairs
Jewelry
Journalism and Writing
Law
Leather Goods
Library Science
Lumber
Machinery and Metal
Maintenance and Safety
Management and Supervision
Marine and Maritime Industries
Medical
Music
Office Environment and Equipment
Paper
Pets
Photography Trade
Plumbing, Heating, Air Conditioning and Refrigeration
Printing
Real Estate
Resources and Waste Reduction
Selling and Merchandising
Sport Trade
Stone, Quarry and Mining
Toy, Novelty and Hobby
Transportation
Travel
Veterinary

Suggestion: Go through these two lists, and check those areas in which you have expertise or a special interest. Collect and study as many individual publications within those selected areas as possible, and begin to formulate ideas for them, based on your new market knowledge.

well-edited quarterly rarely deals with insurance; it's aimed at policyholders and uses wide-ranging articles of general interest to families and consumers — and it's 80 percent freelance written.

A recent winter issue of *Friendly Exchange* contains subject matter as diverse as "Unforgettable Holiday Journeys," "Burglarproof Your Home," visiting California's Mojave Desert, mountain train rides and Tennessee music. The lead article, "City Holidays Past and Present," explores holiday traditions in three "typical American communities" (San Antonio, Cleveland and St. Louis). The biocredit reads like this:

Bob Stewart is a freelance writer living in San Antonio who enjoys piñatas, luminaries, and the River Walk.

Bob Stewart, I would add, is probably a man of many interests who knows how to study a market and turn his interests into magazine and newspaper sales.

THINK "GROUPS"

Sometimes, if you look carefully at the broad marketplace, you will find many of these smaller markets in *bunches*, under subcategories, if you will.

One night at a fire department training center, during the taping of a television show I was writing, I discovered these magazines in the firefighter's lounge: *Rescue* ("Uniting Rescue and Basic Life Support"), *Response* ("Promoting Search, Rescue & Emergency Response Professionalism"), *The California Firefighter, The California Fire Service, Fire Chief, Fire Command, American Fire Journal, Fire Engineering, 9-11 Magazine* ("For the Emergency Response Community"), *Rescue-EMS* ("Serving Pre-Hospital Field & Medical Control Professionals"), *NFPA Journal* (official magazine of the National Fire Protection Association), *JEMS* (Journal of Emergency Medical Services) and *Training* ("The Human Side of Business").

Obviously, if you have a strong general knowledge of emergency fire and rescue work, markets await your ideas. The same is true for virtually any field of work or play.

You'll even find some of these specialized publications under one roof, printed by the same company.

Just today, in my mailbox, writer's guidelines arrived from Equal Opportunity Publications, a publishing group in Hauppauge, New York, that produces five career-guidance magazines — *Career Woman, Careers & the disABLED, Equal Opportunity, Minority Engineer* and *Woman Engineer* — and one aimed at seniors, *Independent Living.* They are primarily quarterlies, paying only ten cents a word. But they are exactly the kind of publications where many writers get their start.

If you concentrate your market search on only the biggest publications, you'll go after the markets where the competition is the heaviest, the markets that need novice writers the least. Find the less visible publications, zero in on them, and you'll greatly enhance your odds of making sales, developing your skills and building credits. From there you can move up into midrange markets—and beyond.

Whatever level you aim for now, it's vital that you know these specific magazines and newspaper sections not just casually, but almost intimately.

One way to keep current is to send away for writer's guidelines, which many publications provide free (again, study *Writer's Market* and other sourcebooks for this kind of information). Writer's guidelines will not only give you a general idea of which kinds of articles a publication does and does not look for, but also information such as rate of payment, frequency of publication, how to approach the editors (query or submission), departments most open to freelance contributions and so on.

Writer's guidelines are a terrific help.

But they aren't enough.

Big Differences

Let's say you want to write in the field of women's magazines. Maybe you're female, which gives you an edge right there. You're well read on women's issues—health, history, politics, careers, alternative lifestyles and so on. Or perhaps you're a more "traditional" type, experienced and interested in cooking, parenting, home accounting and budgeting, etc. Or maybe your personal experience and interests span the spectrum. The important thing is that it's a field in which you are burning to write and make your mark.

So you study dozens of magazines in the "women's" field, such as *Woman's Day, Cosmopolitan, Essence, Mademoiselle, Working Woman, Working Mother, Entrepreneurial Woman, Virtue, Good Housekeeping, Ladies' Home Journal, Big Beautiful Woman, Redbook, Lear's, New Woman, McCall's, Savvy, Mirabella, Woman's World*—the list goes on and on. As you study them, you realize how different most of them are. You find that *Virtue* is aimed at Christian women, *Essence* at black women, *Cosmopolitan* at younger women, *Lear's* at "mature" women, *Big Beautiful Woman* at large women, *Working Woman* at career women, *Working Mother* at women juggling parenting with employment. (Even as I write this, *Lear's* has just broadened its target audience from women in their fifties and sixties to women thirty-five and up.)

They are all "women's magazines," but they are all different—which

STUDYING THE MARKETPLACE

You can't get around it: To make a living as a freelance writer, you must apprise yourself of a wide range of markets, keep up with their changes, find the ones that are right for you, and vice versa.

Few resources are more valuable to a freelance writer than a home library of newspapers and magazines. Certainly, you should subscribe to a fair number of newspapers and magazines — besides acquiring first-hand market knowledge, you'll support your industry and fellow writers. Few of us, however, can afford *that* many subscriptions, which means you'll need alternate sources.

Some suggestions:

Public libraries. Some have reading rooms where you can browse through newspapers and magazines, but they're rarely wide-ranging enough to serve the freelance journalist adequately.

Newsstands. Better newsstands carry as many as a couple hundred titles, but they are primarily the major national publications, which are often the most inaccessible for the unestablished journalist. Prowl these racks regularly, but consider them only as a supplemental source.

Office libraries. Many companies subscribe to a wide range of magazines and newspapers, particularly media-related businesses. If you have access to such reading rooms, utilize it.

Send for sample copies. *Writer's Market* lists hundreds of publications that will provide free back issues, or copies for a nominal price, and tells you how to send for them. *Writer's Digest* and other writing magazines do the same. Be aware, however, that many markets are not covered in these publications, and that market information is already old by the time it gets into print.

You must constantly update your market knowledge by sending for sample copies, and studying them rigorously, along with writer's guidelines, if they're available.

Scan trade and professional publications. *Magazine Week, Folio, AdWeek, Advertising Age, Columbia Journalism Review, Washington Journalism Review, Editor & Publisher* and similar publications regularly cover trends within the industry and occasional news on specific markets.

Mail order sweepstakes promotions. Don't laugh! Scan those sheets of stamps in Publisher's Clearing House and other competitions for possible markets for your work. One set includes magazines as di-
continued

verse as *Doll Life, Aloha, Snow Country, Old-Time Crochet, Southern Accents, Home Mechanix* and *Piano Stylist.*

Friends and relatives. Often a terrific resource, particularly for smaller and nonmainstream markets that you may not otherwise see. Don't be embarrassed to ask others to save old copies for you. You're a working writer; collecting and studying markets is part of your job. Recycle what you can't use.

Trade with other writers. Set up a swapping network through writing classes, writers' organizations and other personal contacts.

Liberate back issues from your doctor's office. Well, maybe you should ask first.

means that you must find a specific slant that's appropriate for a specific market. A query letter or article written for *Cosmo* is not likely to work for *Lear's.* A pitch to *Essence* must be different from a pitch for *Big Beautiful Woman.*

The same applies to magazines with primarily male readerships: *Playboy, GQ, Essence for Men, The Advocate, Men Inc., Gallery* and *Men's Health* are all distinctively different publications, with varied editorial needs.

You must know those differences, and how to slant your ideas accordingly.

There is probably no more valuable skill in freelancing, outside the writing itself, than slanting for the particular market. Yet how many naive writers take this aspect of the craft lightly! Time after time, they send out "generalized" ideas to a newspaper section or a magazine, without studying the market and thinking through their slant. One editor I know calls this the "bicycle syndrome," when a writer attempts to "bicycle" one article or query around to several publications, without retailoring it for the individual needs of individual markets.

Subtle Differences

Going through a publication, page by page, cover to cover, will help you accomplish a thorough market study. This will uncover a wealth of vital information, not only about readership and editorial slant, but even information such as the amount of freelance material purchased.

Let's look at what a page-by-page study can reveal:

Front cover. Sometimes you'll find an editorial theme description beneath the title ("Truth in Travel," "The Human Side of Business," etc.). The cover date tells you how often the publication is printed. Promotional blurbs, or "cover lines," indicate content. You can also learn a lot about the income level, sophistication, gender, and other demographic factors from the cover price, tastefulness of layout, language, color combinations, even the quality of paper stock used.

Questions to ask: Which types of articles are promoted the most heavily? What is the language and tone of the cover lines? Is the cover cluttered, splashy, screaming with exclamation marks? Or more tasteful and subdued? What does that say about reader taste?

Inside front pages. Advertising content and style, as well as placement, offer valuable clues about readership. What products dominate? In a magazine aimed at women, for instance, do you see a lot of ads for household products, or cameras and cars? Lipstick, or investment firms? What does that say about the income, independence, lifestyle and interests of the magazine's average reader?

Table of contents. This is a great place to survey a publication's style, subject matter and scope, and get a quick impression whether your idea fits into any of the magazine's departments. What is the general subject matter? Is it narrow or broad in scope? Which article types turn up? Are they more informational and practical, or more cerebral and topical? How many main features, departments and columns are listed? How many articles in all? Here's one way to find out how many are freelance written:

- Note some bylines on the table of contents page.
- Turn to the "masthead" or staff box.
- Check the bylines against names on the masthead. If they don't turn up, they are probably freelancers — a good sign of opportunity.

If the names turn up under "contributing writers" or "contributing editors," that indicates they are freelance but have a contract or long-term relationship with the magazine — a "club" of regular established contributors.

Masthead. Besides helping gauge freelance contributions, the staff box can also tell you how big the staff is, key titles (such as Articles Editor), correct spelling of names and so on. (Remember, these change constantly.)

Editor's page. This optional page usually presents an essay from the editor or publisher to the reader, tipping you to the magazine's philosophy and general outlook.

The well. This is the main editorial section of the magazine, opening up to longer features, with less advertising and occasionally shorter features ("well-breakers" to break up the longer ones). This is the editorial "heart" of the magazine. As an aspiring contributor, you should take it to heart.

ARE YOU READY FOR YOUR OWN COLUMN?

A regular column is a coveted goal of many nonfiction writers, and with good reason: A column brings you special respect and high visibility, and helps stabilize your unpredictable freelance income. Columns customarily go to writers who have something special to say, or a special way to say it, and have proven they can deliver consistently and on time.

Because most syndicated columns are short—in the 500- to 800-word range—craft is at a premium; columnists tend to be the most economical of writers. In addition, columns that run weekly or several days a week require the capacity to come up with lots of fresh ideas and meet deadlines religiously. Although such successful columnists as Ellen Goodman, Bob Greene, Liz Smith, Herb Caen, Carl T. Rowan and William Safire make it look easy, they all have substantial journalism backgrounds.

Some naive readers dismiss the work of columnists like Smith and Caen as lightweight, but the daily "item" column is an especially tough grind that's entrusted only to those with excellent contacts and reporting skills; such columns often require support staffs.

"The pressure of having to deliver a daily syndicated show-business column never lets up," says Marilyn Beck, who writes an entertainment column with Stacy Jenel Smith that appears in 300 newspapers. If the two reporters can't deliver fresh, exclusive items that have "some sort of edge," Beck says, "the papers have no reason to buy our column—they can get announcements off the wires."

Because publicists and others plant so many false leads, Beck and Stacy Jenel Smith spend roughly half their time checking out information; they must come up with half a dozen exclusives every day, five days a week, supported by interviews and substantial detail, on strict deadlines.

Stacy Jenel Smith likens the experience to that of "a short-order cook, because we work on so many story leads simultaneously. You have to be able to shift your focus instantly."

Most first-time columnists get their initial opportunities in less demanding situations by:

• Contributing regularly to a local newspaper or smaller magazine until they prove their dependability.

continued

> • Filing columns that come out only weekly or monthly.
>
> • Writing in areas of personal expertise, such as gardening, cooking, financial and automotive matters, with an emphasis on helpful advice for the general reader. (The practical advice column, along with humor, is usually the most in demand.)
>
> Often, columnists who become established in smaller markets are able to branch out later to additional markets through syndication or self-syndication. (More on syndicating material in Step Fifteen.) If you're considering proposing a column, syndicate and periodicals editors generally like to first see a query letter outlining your column idea, accompanied by a few clips and an SASE. If they're interested, they'll ask you to submit several sample columns on spec.
>
> *Writer's Market* and the annual *Editor & Publisher Syndicate Directory* are excellent sources for studying the syndication marketplace.

Photos and illustrations. Differences, as noted above, can tell you a lot about editorial style and content, and readership tastes. Are the illustrations creative or rather trite? Subtle or pointed? Tasteful or garish? And so on.

Headlines and decks. Are they straightforward or more "literary"? Stolid or more fun? Practical or more thought-provoking? What do they reveal about style, taste, editorial approach?

Article content. As you study the articles, note length, depth of information, viewpoint and so on. How much research is involved? How many experts are interviewed? How serious or light is the tone? Is there a discernible slant? Are there different formats? Lots of sidebars? Very few?

Writing style. Do the editors favor a simple, straightforward approach or allow a wide range of expression? First-person or third-person viewpoint? Anecdote and storytelling over a more dry, factual presentation? Does attitude come through boldly, or is it understated? Are leads short and to the point, or more leisurely?

Biocredits. If you see a lot of academic and professional "credentials," you'll know the editors favor experts over general freelance writers.

Page count. Is the magazine fat or thin? What does that say about its need for material and its economic stability?

Back cover. Like the inside front pages, the advertisements on the back cover are strong indicators of the income level, lifestyle and purchasing interests of the magazine's average reader.

That's how you conduct a page-by-page market study. It will reveal subtle differences between similar publications that a more cursory examination would miss. For instance, if you glance at two magazines, *Parents* and *Parenting*, on the newsstand, they look almost identical. Both are well produced, well edited national monthlies aimed at active, intelligent, caring parents, designed to help them raise happy, healthy kids.

They're also different magazines, for slightly different readers, and if you want to write for them, you must understand those differences. An in-depth market study of each reveals that:

• *Parents* tends toward splashier covers and more traditional illustrations. *Parenting* is generally more subdued and "tasteful" in appearance.

• *Parents* offers more "nuts-and-bolts" articles, heavy on practical advice. *Parenting* has those, but also carries more "think" pieces.

• *Parents* tends to be more "parent friendly" and oriented toward "control of kids," running to lighter features. *Parenting* is supportive of parents but also concerned with the "empowerment" of children. It contains larger issues involving the family, including politics and global concerns.

• *Parents* appears targeted primarily at traditional, mainstream, middle-class homemakers. *Parenting* seems geared to a slightly more educated, sophisticated, upscale reader, working moms but including dads, and couples where husband and wife share in the responsibility of major purchases.

• In terms of style and range of expression, *Parents* is more traditional and straightforward, *Parenting* more varied and adventurous.

• Both magazines are thriving freelance markets, with lots of bylined articles and smaller departments. *Parents*, with the greater page count, relies more on credentialed experts; *Parenting* favors general freelance writers.

I drew these conclusions by comparing issues of the two magazines page by page, cover to cover.

Because you write articles not for yourself, but for editors and their readers, that kind of market analysis will tell you a lot about how to slant your idea, write your query, do your research, and then plan and execute the article itself.

◆ ◆ ◆

Studying a single issue is not enough; examine several before pitching your angle, and continue reading a publication regularly, noting changes. (See sidebar on how to survey the marketplace and collect sample copies on page 49).

You can no longer afford to read a magazine or newspaper section as a *reader.* You must read it as a professional *writer*, seeing it as a possible market.

SLANTING OFF-CENTER

Not long ago, I was surprised to see an article on Thailand's tourism boom in *Sierra*, the magazine of the Sierra Club.

At first glance, it seemed out of place. As I read on, however, I saw that an enterprising freelance writer, Dana Sachs, had slanted the piece to the environmental impact of economic progress on the lush Thai countryside, and the response of Thai environmentalists to the growing crisis. It was different, yet fit *Sierra* perfectly.

That article reminded me that we can become so fixated on the general editorial makeup of a publication that our ideas become overly *predictable.* Writers who look at a market from many different angles will find surprising opportunities.

When Chris Caswell was editor of *Sea*, he told me, "We cross so many topics in boating—cooking, electronics, sewing, craftsmanship, engines, fiberglass repair. If I could find a good writer-plumber, I could almost guarantee three articles a year."

Plumbing advice for a boating magazine? When you think about it—*really* think about it—it's a natural. It's often the offbeat slant that helps you to get noticed and crack a new market.

Pat H. Broeske sold her first freelance article many years ago to *Psychic Magazine*, a serious, scholarly journal dealing with the paranormal. Pat, a film buff, pitched the editors a survey piece on how movies had treated the subject of psychic phenomena through the years, with lots of examples. They were caught off guard by her angle—they'd never run a movie-related piece—but they assigned it. That byline was the beginning of a bountiful freelance career: Today, Pat covers film for publications such as *Premiere*, *Entertainment Weekly*, *Rolling Stone* and *The New York Times*, and has a major book deal.

"I went totally against the grain," she says of that first sale. "It doesn't always work. Sometimes, you get stern letters back telling you to read their publication more carefully. But you can also surprise a more adventurous editor with an idea they might never have thought of on their own."

I once wrote an 800-word humor piece on how lovable felines can turn macho men into soft-hearted pussycats. It was unlike most of the serious issue pieces that ran on the op-ed page of *The Los Angeles Times*, but in my gut, I felt it would work there—the offbeat piece that could lighten up the section. I got a note from a surprised editorial assistant that said: "It turns out the editor of the page is a cat lover himself. He thinks your point of view is not only funny, but true. We're buying the piece."

Although editors are fond of telling writers what they're "looking for," most of them are waiting to be shown something fresh and unexpected. The key to going against the grain is to study the market, up close *and* from a distance, and perceive openings even the editors might not see.

THE MARKETS ARE THERE

Take a look at one *AdWeek* compilation of the country's "10 Hottest Small Magazines," based on revenue growth and other factors: *Compute, Country America, Walking, Cooking Light, Midwest Living, Longevity, Spin, Soap Opera Digest, Entrepreneurial Woman, Backpacker.* Ten markets covering subject matter as diverse as computers, lifestyles, recreation, cooking, health, entertainment, business and the outdoors. And together, these "small" magazines buy a couple thousand freelance pieces each year, if not more.

Like thousands of other publications, they are waiting for the right angles.

If you'll study those markets carefully before you sit down to write, your chances of breaking in will be infinitely increased, and your time wasted infinitely decreased.

"I make a speech to aspiring writers," Dwight Whitney told me when he was Hollywood bureau chief of *TV Guide*. "I tell them (to) sit down and ask yourself, 'If I were reading *TV Guide*, what would I want to see?' Then put together six ideas. If you're right for *TV Guide*, your first three ideas will already have been done; the fourth will be in the works; the fifth, they'll dislike; but the sixth may be the golden one they're hungry for."

If you feel you know a market well and have an appropriate angle, it's time to make your pitch.

Which just happens to be our next step.

Onward!

Step Four

Making the Pitch

A close friend died several years ago at the age of fifty-nine. He led a full and rather colorful life. A pioneering surfer, he spent much of his time in Mexico, read voraciously, loved jazz, had marriages, children, passionate love affairs. He was expert at carpentry and fishing, and his photos were displayed in galleries and museums. He was also a writer, much more adept with style and language than I. But when he died prematurely of lung cancer, nonfiction writing was his single, great frustration.

He was only marginally successful at it, and the reason, I think, was that he lacked the willingness and discipline to write query letters.

"Waste of time," he used to grumble, between puffs on the cigarettes that would eventually kill him. "By the time I do the research and write one of those letters, I might as well just sit down and write the whole damn thing."

And so he wrote article after article, sending them out as unsolicited submissions. Over many years, he tasted just enough success — a nostalgia piece on surfing in *Sports Illustrated*, a how-to in *Salt Water Fisherman*, a few others — to keep him sending out all those other manuscripts to cold desks and unwelcoming hands. In the last years of his life, frustrated by so few sales, he gave up trying.

Meanwhile, I knocked out query letters right and left, rarely writing manuscripts without an assignment or a strong sign of interest from a publication. For every article he completed and shotgunned into the marketplace, I aimed five or ten queries at carefully chosen targets. Gradually, those queries helped me establish relationships with editors and eventually make a living from freelancing, while my stubborn friend watched with undisguised envy.

The difference was that I queried, and he didn't.

Each time I urged him to switch to an organized system of volume querying, he'd mutter that he just "didn't have the time."

The irony was that, all told, I spent less time writing queries than he did writing complete manuscripts, but I probably outsold him twenty-five to one.

THE ETERNAL QUESTION

To query, or not to query? It's the subject of debate and a source of great consternation for many writers.

Here are ten good reasons for sending proposal letters (in most instances), rather than uninvited manuscripts:

1. Most editors prefer queries.
2. Queries are a concise calling card; they not only outline and advertise the article you wish to write, but give editors a quick look at your skills, style, level of professionalism, even your character and personality.
3. They keep your proposal out of the deep slush pile of unsolicited manuscripts.
4. In the long run, queries save you time.
5. They're an excellent way to find the focus for your subject *before* you get into deeper research and writing.
6. They enable you to slant carefully for specific markets, then work with an editor to further tailor your article to the editor's needs.
7. They can be written relatively quickly, to get your timely angle "out there" ahead of competing writers.
8. They allow you to market your ideas in volume, reslanting for multiple markets with minimal extra work.
9. Even when queries fail to generate assignments, they are a useful writing tool with which to practice craft.
10. Editors remember sharply written queries, while they quickly forget unwanted manuscripts—if they bother to read them at all.

There are certainly (1) times when it is *not* appropriate to query, (2) editors who prefer the complete manuscript, and (3) drawbacks to querying, such as queries that get no reply. But by and large, most successful nonfiction writers prefer to query, particularly when trying to break into new markets and establish relationships with editors.

What It Is

A "query" is a proposal letter, customarily limited to a page, that pitches your angle to an editor. It can be conversational in style, but not so casual and "off-the-top-of-the-head" that it has insufficient substance or detail. A good query is succinct, yet gives an editor enough on which to base an assignment.

The biggest mistake less-experienced writers make when writing queries is to take them lightly, to dash them off as if they don't matter. Nothing could be more self-defeating. The query letter, combined with the clips you attach, is all that an editor knows about you. It represents your skills as a researcher and writer, and indicates how well you know the target publication.

The less experience you have, and the fewer samples of published work, the more vital that query becomes in terms of showing an editor what you can do.

Robert Epstein, then executive arts editor of *The Los Angeles Times* and a former editor of the paper's lifestyle section, once visited my classroom and offered a number of suggestions regarding queries:

- Get right to the point; sell yourself in the first fifty or sixty words. Because "an editor only has so much time to read these things."
- Start off with something "compelling, intriguing, dramatic, meaningful," to get the editor's attention and keep him reading.
- Give the editor a "shopping list" of the article's highlights or main points, "without trying to throw everything in."
- Throw out "all your big adjectives and adverbs. You have to sell yourself by constructing an excellent query—but don't sell too hard."
- Give your query "the cliché test." Get rid of every tired and trite phrase.
- Don't query unless you've read six months of your target publication— "if you haven't, you're wasting your time."
- Know your subject *better* than the reader does; an editor looks for evidence of the writer's keen knowledge.
- Include clips, even though "an editor will be skeptical of how much editing went into them. The trick (in overcoming that skepticism) is to write an excellent query letter."

Where's the Beef?

What's the element queries most commonly lack? That's easy. Substance.

The *style* of a query is important; it can go a long way toward catching and holding an editor's interest. But if the query doesn't deliver some goods, the editor won't deliver an assignment.

"Before you ever contact the magazine, do a certain amount of prelimi-

QUERIES: TWENTY DOS AND DON'TS

Here are twenty tips for writing more effective queries:

1. If possible, keep your query letter to a page.

2. Target the appropriate editor. Verify exact title and spelling of name. If necessary, call the publication; don't trust outdated market listings or mastheads.

3. Be sure you pitch an angle, not a broad topic. Have you given your idea the "angle test" (see page 33)?

4. Open strongly enough to grab the editor's attention, then get to the point quickly.

5. Provide enough detail and substance to indicate what kind of article you plan to write, its scope, sources, etc.

6. Convey *implicitly* why your proposed piece will serve the reader, without directly saying, "Your readers will really benefit from this article," or words to that effect.

7. Use anecdotes and examples to support your pitch, if appropriate, but don't crowd your query with too many.

8. Include only the pithiest quotations. Eliminate long-winded ones; paraphrase them tightly and to the point.

9. Use bullets in place of long, rambling paragraphs, but don't overdo it. Four or five should be plenty.

10. Include a title for your article only if it serves the query, is appropriate to the market and is fairly succinct.

11. Don't overpromote yourself; keep biographical data to a line or two. Let your query and clips do the selling.

12. Include the most appropriate clips to prove you're the one to write the article; three should be enough.

13. Craft your query as carefully as you would the final draft of your article. Proofread meticulously.

14. Include an SASE, with postage sufficient to cover all returning materials, including clips, photos, etc.

15. In general, let the editor suggest article length; that's his job. Ditto payment, deadline and so on.

16. In the case of timely or seasonal angles, allow for lead times and time for replies, research, writing.

17. Suggest sidebars only when they seem necessary and helpful to the piece.

continued

18. Avoid foolish or amateurish questions, such as, "Have you run an article recently about . . . ?"

19. Don't tell the editor his business ("This is the kind of story your readers will love," "this kind of article would greatly benefit your readers"). Let that be implicit in your well-chosen idea and its presentation.

20. *Never* apologize ("I know that this idea isn't fully developed, but . . ."). If you must apologize in any way for your work, you're not ready for an assignment.

nary research," says Lorraine Fletcher Farrell, an editor with *Modern Maturity.* "Don't just send off a vague, half-baked query letter. Know what you're talking about. Too many writers think they can just sit at home and spring material off the top of their heads."

One way to put meat on the bones of your query is to emphasize *what* and *who*:

- What do you plan to write about?
- What specifically will be covered?
- What do you intend to prove, show, teach, etc?
- What is the thrust and purpose of the article?
- Who are the experts or other sources you intend to interview and rely on?
- Who should write this particular article, and why (meaning you, mentioning your pertinent credits)?

Here's a sample query that covers the basic "whats" and "whos":

MY LETTERHEAD HERE

Pamela Abrams   December 5, 1992
Articles Editor
Parents Magazine
685 Third Ave.
New York, NY 10017

Dear Pamela Abrams:

With continuing economic instability and urban turmoil, more Americans are packing up and moving than ever — nearly 50 million are expected to hit the road this year alone.

For many families, changing homes will be a physical and emotional ordeal. But it doesn't have to be. With the right planning and outlook, the transition to a new home can be largely stress-free — even inspiring.

"It can be a time for profound change, a chance to start over," says Ilene Val-Essen, Ph.D., a family and marriage counselor. "The key is a positive, creative attitude."

For an article on how to take the trauma out of moving, I'd include concrete tips from moving experts, psychologists and experienced parents, including:

- — As a family, make a list of new activities that await you, such as gardening, hiking, ballet, Little League.
- — Condense a lifetime of memories into a photo album, then thin out burdensome mementos and "junk" with a garage sale or charitable donations. Envision who will benefit — "see the joy on their faces," suggests Dr. Val-Essen.
- — Utilize the special resources of professional movers. Bekins, for instance, offers a free, computerized "school match" program that helps you select the school district most appropriate for your family's needs.
- — Visit your new city and school *before* you move, so your kids feel more comfortable when they arrive.
- — Prepare your new residence thoroughly, *prior* to moving in. "Make a place that is really yours, the way you want it," advises one savvy mom. "Fulfill your fantasies."

I'm a former *Los Angeles Times* editor and widely published freelance writer who recently turned a painful move into a happy one. (Sample clips and SASE are enclosed.)

If you'd like to make an assignment, I'll get "moving."

Regards,
John M. Wilson

◆ ◆ ◆

I created this query as a sample for this chapter, but I also put it into the mail to test the marketplace (we'll get to the results in a moment). It's fairly typical in form, following the traditional beginning-middle-end structure: It summarizes the angle up top, makes its main points, and concludes with reasons why I might warrant the assignment. If it has a built-in problem, it's that the subject, family moving, has been covered so many times.

I got the bulk of my information from several sources: Bekins Moving & Storage; a mover's trade association; a psychologist with whom I was working on another writing project; and a friend, the savvy mom. Several quick telephone calls and a newspaper clipping or two gave me all the "research" I needed for this particular query.

Let's break it down and examine it section by section, to see how and why I put it together as I did:

Addressee. The articles editor is usually the appropriate choice, but not all magazines have one. Check the masthead or, better yet, call the publication and ask. While you're on the telephone, ask for the appropriate name, correct title and spelling. Remember, even mastheads are sometimes outdated.

Salutation. Not as cut-and-dried as it might seem. Do you refer to a female editor as "Miss," "Mrs." or "Ms."? Any one of those could be offensive, depending on the editor's feelings about such things. I avoid the problem by using a female editor's full name. Generally, I use "Mr." with male editors. I might use a first name with either gender, if the magazine has a more casual feel to it, and certainly if we're acquainted. Decide what feels right to you.

First paragraph. I chose to open with a general statement suggesting the urgency and topicality of the subject, supported by a statistic that indicates a broad potential interest, with millions affected. I could have opted for a different lead and tone, such as a humorous or dramatic anecdote.

Second paragraph. I narrow quickly to my angle. This is my "billboard" graph. It sums up what the query letter is about and the thrust of the proposed article.

Third paragraph. A quote from an expert source, to support and develop my main point and to indicate my ability to do research, interview, spot a useful quotation.

Fourth paragraph. This lets the editor know exactly what kind of article I intend to write, with a one-line, capsule summary ("how to take the trauma out of moving") that could almost be a title. It suggests the scope of my research and interviewing and sets up the "bullets" — the list of tips.

Bullets. These comprise the substance of the query, demonstrating to the editor that I'll provide specifics, not generalities. Without these concrete tips, the editor really has no idea if I can come up with "the goods."

Bullets can be a terrific tool in queries (and articles) because they allow you to say and show a lot, in organized and succinct fashion. Three or four bullets is usually enough, but because I'd never written a piece quite like this, I felt the need to provide a little more.

Closing paragraph. I mention my credits briefly and without detail, because the only how-to experience I had at the time were articles on the craft of writing; I also lacked credits in parenting or related publications. If

I had credits, say, from *L.A. Parent, Working Mother* and *Good Housekeeping*, I would have mentioned them.

If you have special experience or credentials that enable you to better write the article, include them. Don't tout unrelated credentials, such as a degree in a technical field, or nonprofessional credits, such as letters to the editor, or give any other indication that you're inexperienced. Promote yourself appropriately but with restraint, using common sense. Nothing tips an editor more quickly to an amateur than someone who heavily self-promotes.

Length. This query runs about one typed page; queries that run much longer test an editor's patience. Forcing yourself to keep it to a page will also force you to find your focus, stay on track, and craft your queries more cleanly and tightly. It's especially important to keep bullets tight and to the point. A long, complex bullet defeats its purpose.

Clips. Three clips is generally plenty. Choose them for their pertinence to your subject matter and how they reflect "the current you." There may be times when you include the offbeat clip, a published sample that may not fit the general subject area but may demonstrate your sense of humor, say, or your ability to handle a certain type of article. Again, common sense is the rule.

SASE. Your self-addressed, stamped envelope should include sufficient postage to cover a return letter *and* your clips. Some writers, rather than lick their stamps, attach them to their SASE with a paper clip, so they can be saved and used at the editor's end in case the SASE is not needed. Some editors appreciate this, others find it a nuisance.

So what happened to the query when I sent it out into the real world? It went first to *Family Circle* magazine; it was there nearly four months before a form rejection letter came back. At this writing, a revised version has been at *Parents* magazine for six months; I'm still waiting for a response. This kind of lag time is disheartening, and seems to be increasingly common, particularly with the high-profile national magazines.

According to *Get Published*, by Diane Gage and Marcia Hibsch Coppess, *Family Circle* receives 70,000 queries and unsolicited manuscripts each year, which tells you the kind of odds you face with the bigger, more coveted markets. Does that mean I wasted my time querying? Not at all. I can continue to keep this basic idea and query moving, reslanting it for other markets. It may eventually pay off. The *real* waste of time would have been in writing an entire manuscript, only to have it rejected.

In fact, if I'd submitted a complete manuscript, I'd probably still be wait-

HOW LONG SHOULD I WAIT AFTER SENDING MY QUERY?

You've sent your query letter, complete with clips and SASE. A week goes by. Another week. You're getting antsy. What should you do?

In most situations, wait. At least another week or two.

All editors would like to reply to queries in one or two weeks, but details such as work load, illness and having a life seem to get in the way.

Exactly how long you should wait is up to you. If it's a small publication with a limited editorial staff, the editors are undoubtedly overworked, and you may want to give them more time. If the publication buys a large amount of freelance material and has a larger staff, you'd think it would be better equipped to deal with queries, and more promptly. But those are also the markets that get the most flooded with queries and unsolicited manuscripts, and often take the longest to respond.

Some writers wait only two or three weeks before sending a follow-up note, reminding the editor of the initial query, perhaps enclosing a photocopy of the original. Others pick up the telephone. Some editors don't mind calls, but most don't like them; it's easier to deal with a piece of paper when they're able to clear the time, even if it means weeks or months down the line. Editors, just like writers, can be great procrastinators.

If you feel you must call, it's probably better to wait until the afternoon (after the day's deadlines and meetings are past), and toward the end of the week. (Additional tips on using the telephone with editors are in Step Fourteen.)

More patient writers give an editor four to six weeks before considering a response overdue. If the idea you're pitching is dated, however, and time is of the essence, you may have to prompt an editor sooner.

Recommended tactic: Find out who is the most efficient and appropriate assistant below the editor who might be able to help. Enlist that person's aid. A contact like that within an editorial staff can be invaluable. Such a person should be able to tell you the status of your proposal, whether it's appropriate to call or follow up by mail, how long to wait and so on.

Some writers also like to include a stamped postcard with their

continued

query for quick and easy reply, or a "form letter" of their own, with boxes the editor can check, such as:

☐ We like your article and we're accepting it for publication. A contract will follow shortly.
☐ We like your article, but we're overstocked at the moment. Pitch it to us again in ＿＿ months, when we'll also be open to other ideas.
☐ This doesn't fit our needs because:

_____
_____
_____
_____

Be prepared for editors who reply months after your pitch, or never respond at all. Some editors have a policy of never replying to a query unless they're interested; they claim their work load is so heavy and they are so understaffed, there just isn't time. (If there isn't fifteen minutes in the day when an assistant or intern can stuff form rejection letters into SASEs, it would seem the editor needs some serious training in management skills.)

When enough time has passed and you still have not heard back, you may want to send one last note informing the editor politely that you are withdrawing your proposal on such-and-such a subject sent to them on such-and-such a date, and pitching it to a competing market. This will clear you of any obligations to the first publication—and, sometimes, it will finally wake an editor up to respond or may even generate an assignment.

ing for *Family Circle* editors to find it somewhere in their gargantuan slush pile.

Find What Works for You

In *Get Published*, Gage and Coppess refer to our sample letter as a "summary query," which summarizes and pitches the idea up high, introducing the writer toward the end. They also identify other common query forms, such as:

Proposal query. A brief, "grabber" cover letter, strong on personality and style, which introduces a more detailed and substantive proposal that follows.

Outline query. Similar to a summary, but a bit more cut-and-dried, with a one- or two-paragraph synopsis of your idea at the top; a list of main points set off by numbers, dashes or bullets in the middle; and a summation of your sources, credentials and final, pertinent details at the end.

Short-take query. A query that pitches several angles at once, usually with each idea limited to a single paragraph, perhaps set off by bullets. The short-take query is especially useful, Gage and Coppess suggest, for proposing news briefs and other short items.

Forms for queries may work well for some writers in some markets. In fact, they are probably valuable guidelines for most writers most of the time. But they can also work against you if you adhere to formulas so rigidly that your query letters feel lifeless and predictable. Often, it's the query that reflects your personality and expressiveness that gets you noticed.

When I began pitching ideas to *The New York Times*, I didn't think about the "form" my queries took; I just wrote enthusiastic letters, with sharp viewpoint and lots of details; Guy Flatley, then the Sunday Arts and Leisure editor, responded positively to that enthusiasm. Pat H. Broeske, who never seems to be without an assignment, writes queries that tend to be chatty, breezy, funny, sometimes "off-the-wall" (she even affixes stickers of cute cat faces on every letter and envelope, so go figure). My friend Lee Green, who writes consistently for top markets, takes a more conversational approach in his queries. (Seven successful queries, including one of Lee's, are reprinted at the end of this chapter.) While guidelines can be useful, beware of hard-and-fast rules about how you must put together a query, except that it must be accurate, well written, professional and sincere.

As a writer, you must find what you're comfortable with, what feels right. That may mean taking the best from the suggested forms, then writing in your own, special way.

When to Query, When Not to

With certain types of articles, querying is *not* necessarily appropriate. Take my humor piece on cats, for instance (I went ahead and wrote it up). There was no way I could convey, in a query, the tone, nature and purpose of the essay I planned to write; with humor, it's all in the attitude and the writing. Additionally, my cat piece was only 800 words (most op-ed page pieces are short); a query is roughly a third of that. So it made no sense to query.

The same often goes for essays, think pieces, first-person or personal-experience pieces and the like. Their value is essentially in the personal thinking, viewpoint, tone and style — not in quotations, statistics, anecdotes and other journalistic elements that a query can convey.

In addition, some editors state publicly — in market reports, writer's guidelines and the like — that they prefer unsolicited manuscripts to queries. When contacting these editors, you may want to skip the query and go straight to the submission. But even when an editor requests unsolicited manuscripts, I'd still query on most articles, particularly those requiring much research. And here's why: You can go to all the work of writing a complete manuscript, and an editor can decide in the first few lines whether he wants it. And that's not fair to the writer. But it happens all the time.

The editor of a motorcycle magazine once told me why he preferred complete manuscripts to queries. "Saves me lots of time," he said. "I can usually tell in the first couple of graphs, sometimes in the first line, if it's right for us."

Bad spelling, inaccurate use of a technical term, weak writing, or any number of other flaws cause editors to stop reading unsolicited manuscripts. Yet some, like the "biker" editor, prefer unsolicited manuscripts, because it saves them time spent on reading and correspondence. "I just have 'em write the whole manuscript up and if I don't like what I see on the first page, I shove it into the SASE and send it back to 'em with a form rejection slip."

It may save *him* time, but it costs the writer countless wasted hours on a manuscript destined for rejection.

You can write a query in a fraction of the time. If it's a good one, no editor will ignore it — not even the ones who prefer completed manuscripts.

THE "ASSIGNMENT" YOU GIVE YOURSELF

A common complaint in my classroom is what students call the "Catch-22" of freelance writing: You can't break into decent markets without polished skills — but you'll never polish your skills unless you get the opportunity to write. How can you practice and develop nonfiction skills, they ask, without assignments?

My answer: *The query letter is one of the most valuable tools with which to practice craft.* Make it the regular "assignment" you give yourself when you don't have real assignments.

Structure, clarity, style, voice, viewpoint, et al; are a part of most effective queries. Indeed, because queries are so short yet must convey so much, they force you to write with *more* attention to craft. Even if you write in a

"PROTECTING" YOUR IDEAS

Two questions every writing instructor hears from students: "Do editors steal ideas?" and "How can I protect my ideas?"

Answers: *Sometimes* and *you can't.*

It's extremely rare that an editor deliberately "steals" an idea that comes in via a query letter or unsolicited manuscript, but it happens. There are unethical editors just as there are unethical writers, lawyers, doctors, car mechanics. More often, however, when a writer feels ripped off, what actually happened was:

• More than one freelance writer came up with the same idea and it was assigned to the one with the earliest or best pitch.

• When the pitch came in, an editor or staff writer had already thought of it.

• The subject falls within the territory or "beat" of a staffer, who lays claim to it, insisting (truthfully or not) that he had been noodling such a piece himself.

• The editor doesn't feel you have the credentials to handle this particular assignment and gives it to a writer he's more comfortable with.

In the latter case, the ethical move would be for the editor to offer the freelance writer a "finder's fee" for his idea. If you get such an offer, you'll know that you're dealing with a considerate and aboveboard editor, because there's no legal obligation to extend such a deal. You may be able to use your leverage in such a situation to get a different assignment, or at least to open a relationship with the editor.

Even then, a writer has no fast hold on an idea; you can't copyright an idea, only a completed manuscript that's distinguished in a literary way by the writer's personal execution.

If you wish to go to the trouble and expense, you can copyright your manuscripts with the Library of Congress, and confront a publication if plagiarism occurs. However, there's a danger in obsessing about such possibilities; it can be distracting, negative, stifling.

As in any creative field, it's probably more productive to just take your chances and get your ideas into the marketplace, hoping they land in honest hands.

More times than not, they will.

more conversational style, your query shouldn't waste words; polish it as carefully as you would the article itself.

In a sense, query letters are miniarticles that often make use of basic nonfiction techniques and devices, such as leads, kickers, billboard paragraphs, bullets, transitions, quotations, anecdotes. So until you have bona fide assignments, assign yourself a query—many queries. Make deadlines for them; take them as seriously as you would an assignment from an editor.

If you write and polish one query a week, with two weeks off for good behavior, you will have completed fifty queries by year's end.

That will be fifty pieces of polished writing, an enormous step forward in terms of practicing craft. And none of it will be "make work." You will have fifty queries out in the mail, to a wide range of publications. As some of them come back, you will reslant and rewrite them for other markets, getting better and better at it. Out of fifty attempts, well written and properly targeted, some assignments are bound to be waiting.

Query letters are both the writing tool you can use to develop your craft and stay busy until assignments come, and the very device that will generate those assignments.

◆ ◆ ◆

Let's look at some queries for both style and content. They come from various sources: my students; colleagues from around the country; and one or two from me. Each led to an assignment. You'll find some better than others; in a few cases, I've performed some editing, including lopping off letterheads for privacy's sake, and deleting addresses of publications. Each letter, though, is pretty close to original form.

I lead off with a proposal written by Brenda Day, a former student in one of my UCLA Extension classes. At the time, her clips were limited (one published article), so her query had to do most of the work. It has everything a good pitch letter should: angle, specifics, good target market, and clear, energetic writing. (Note the clever way Brenda concludes, keeping the tone consistent right to the end.)

Mr. Rodger Claire   Date
Senior Articles Editor
Los Angeles Magazine

Dear Mr. Claire:

Shadowing suspicious characters down the mean streets of Marlowe's town, putting away $5 pints of Scotch on stakeouts, bantering with a sexy cohort in crime-solving—what else is there to being a great gumshoe?

Plenty, according to Milo A. Speriglio, Director-and-Chief of Nick Harris Detectives, Inc. Its offspring—the Nick Harris Detective Academy in Van Nuys—has been wising up aspiring P.I.'s since 1907.

"So You Want to Be a Private Eye," the article I'm proposing for the Front Page section, would focus on the academy, answering questions such as:

- Who are these would-be sleuths? (Students run the gamut from house-keepers to process servers to doctors.) Why do they enroll?
- What kind of information does your $1,650 buy? (The 14-week course covers skip tracing, fingerprinting, undercover work, background checks, photo surveillance and more.)
- What's the employment outlook? How much can you make doing other people's dirty work?
- What's the job really like? ("Chasing cheating spouses is not the bulk of our work," says Speriglio. Nor do detectives dodge bullets daily. So what do they do?)

I'm an armchair detective myself—a member of Mystery Readers of America. I came across the Nick Harris Detective Academy while writing the enclosed article for *The Los Angeles Times.* I think it warrants further investigation. Can you use me on the case?

Sincerely,
Brenda Day

◆ ◆ ◆

Another of my former students, John E. Merryman, sent the following pitch to the lifestyle section of a Copley, California, newspaper. He got the assignment, the sale, and this note from the editor: "Yours is the best query letter I've seen in quite a stretch. Happy to see the art form isn't lost."

Ms. Jennifer Cray   Date
Lifestyles Editor
The Daily Breeze

Dear Ms. Cray:

The topic is the primaries. The authoritative comments come fast and thick, crisscrossing the room like verbal lasers:

"Super Tuesday finally worked just the way the Democrats designed it: It gave a big push to a Southern moderate. . . ."

"But Jerry Brown has tapped into a wellspring of resentment that will definitely make him a factor. . . ."

"No! His flat-rate tax will hurt him. . . ."

But this isn't TV's "The McLaughlin Group" or "The Capital Gang." It's a meeting of avid readers of *The Nation*, one of the country's oldest publications of liberal thought, who have been convening regularly in Manhattan Beach for over two years to discuss contemporary issues.

I'd like to profile the group, covering:

— How the group predated the current salon revival trend, but sprang from the same human need: people wanting a place to hold a serious discussion of issues.

— Why the group has not just endured, but grown.

— How the group has become a template for other fledgling *Nation* groups in Albany, N.Y., and Eugene, Oregon.

I've been published in numerous magazines, including *Los Angeles*, *Playboy* and *California*. My next piece will appear in the *L.A. Reader* in June. (Clips enclosed.)

Interested in hearing more about the South Bay's premier discussion group?

Sincerely,
John Merryman

◆ ◆ ◆

Lee Green sent the following query to Playboy's *West Coast editor after a telephone conversation discussing the idea. Lee combines a conversational style with plenty of details and a strong viewpoint; he also lets the editor know exactly what questions would be asked.*

Steve Randall   Date
Playboy Magazine

Dear Steve:

As I mentioned the other day, Los Angeles holds the dubious distinction of being the stalking capital of the world. The LAPD is the only police department with an antistalking unit.

In 1989, California became the first state to pass an antistalking law. More than twenty other states have followed suit; several others have legislation pending.

Passage of the California law was not in response to the 1989 stalking and murder of actress Rebecca Schaeffer, which would have been my guess, but in horrified reaction to five Southern California cases in a six-week period in early 1990, each resulting in the murder of a woman by a male stalker.

Stalking is an exploding phenomenon in this whacked-out society of ours. The majority of cases involve former lovers or spouses, but there are plenty of exceptions. And it's not just the John Lennons and Jodie Fosters who become objects of this sick obsession. Some 200,000 ordinary Americans, according to one expert, are being stalked at any given moment.

A leading forensic psychiatrist told *Vanity Fair* last year that in Hollywood being stalked "has become a form of status." It's difficult to take that remark seriously given the chilling, invasive nature of the act and the frequently violent consequences. If being stalked was an honor, David Letterman didn't appreciate it. Nor did Michael J. Fox or Janet Jackson or Olympic figure skater Katarina Witt, who was stalked across two continents by a Westminster, California man recently sentenced to three years in prison.

I'd like to propose a story on LAPD's antistalking unit. How do they know which complaints to take seriously, which cases to pursue? What are their investigative methods? Can stalking be headed off before it results in tragic violence? What characteristics do stalkers share? Is there a "stalker's profile"? Are most stalkers dangerous? Are there things that someone being stalked can do to discourage the stalker? What are the weirdest, sickest, cleverest, etc. stalking acts they've observed or heard about?

I hope this interests you. Let me know.

My Best,
Lee Green

◆ ◆ ◆

With the following query, I did not include credits or clips, because this editor knew my work. The article ran on the section's front page, with staff photos. The lead in the query was also the lead in the published article.

Mr. Art Berman   Date
View Editor
Los Angeles Times

Dear Art:

O. Robert Levy's artwork is more valued by its owners than the most prized Picassos. Hundreds of Southern Californians display Levy's art publicly — but secretly. His pieces are simultaneously copies *and* originals, of such quality that they go virtually unnoticed. Which is just the way Levy wants it.

Levy, a pioneering Los Angeles oculist, creates prosthetic eyes. To Levy and his colleagues, creating real-looking plastic eyes is an uplifting profession, not a morbid one.

"We deal with a lot of heartbreak when we see new patients who have just lost an eye," says one of Levy's assistants. "But we also get tremendous satisfaction helping people to feel whole again."

Levy has created ocular prostheses for some 30,000 persons since he began developing them during World War II to replace the traditional glass eye. The result was the safer, more durable, less expensive plastic eye—a new American art form. Today, Levy is one of only 150 oculists serving roughly a quarter of a million patients in the United States.

In addition to his local human clients, including Sammy Davis Jr. and poverty-stricken kids (who are treated at no charge), Levy has made eyes for a horse, a pedigreed dog and E.T., the movie extraterrestrial. Current price: $800.

Would View be interested in a behind-the-scenes look at Levy's unusual craft, including some history, and a visit to the lab to observe just how a plastic eye is made? I'd interview Levy, of course, as well as his assistants.

Best,
John M. Wilson

◆ ◆ ◆

The writer first sent the following query to a publication for retired military officers, where it was turned down. She then reslanted for a publication aimed at active Air Force sergeants, and it published her article, entitled, "Second Careers: Writing a Resume."

Mark L. Ward Sr.   Date
Executive Editor
Sergeants Magazine
Air Force Sergeants Assoc.

Dear Mr. Ward:

When we ask children, "What do you want to be when you grow up?" we're perpetuating a myth.

It's the rare individual who is employed in just one place and just one capacity, throughout his or her career. Most of us accumulate numerous titles, employers and job descriptions during our lifetimes.

That's particularly true for individuals who enter the military in their twenties. Eventually, they leave the service and frequently enter civilian employment — even when retiring after thirty years — an often difficult transition to a different kind of working world.

As a professional writer of resumes — for more than 3,000 clients — I can help make that transition easier for your readers with an article titled, "For a Second Career, You Need a First-Rate Resume."

I would outline a resume format that has been proven successful for individuals in the process of retiring, or who have already retired, from the military. I will show readers how to "translate" their military background into format and language relevant to civilian employment — while giving the military highlights their deserved attention. Resume samples will be provided as illustrations.

My published credits include *Christian Home & School* and *Licensed Practical Nurse* magazines, the latter with a piece on resume preparation, slanted to the needs of nurses.

I look forward to hearing from you.

Sincerely,
Ellen E. Behrens

◆ ◆ ◆

Prior to a speaking engagement in Phoenix, Arizona, I called the area's Chamber of Commerce and asked for fresh magazine ideas. A spokeswoman told me, "The All Arabian Horse Show in Scottsdale is one of tourism's best-kept secrets." I knew instantly that I had a marketable angle, and pitched it successfully to an inflight's special Southwest section.

Ed Dwyer   Date
Editor
Western's World

Dear Ed:

More than 2 million tourists a year visit Scottsdale, and it seems like there are as many articles written about the Arizona resort. So why should you want another one?

Because the popular desert city features one of tourism's best-kept secrets: Over the last decade, Scottsdale has become the capital of Arabian horse training and breeding in the United States, and each February hosts the spectacular All Arabian Horse Show for horse fanciers from around the world.

Open to the public, the weekend event culminates in an auction that brings an average of $115,000 for each of these magnificent animals. Filled with pomp and spectacle, the show is one the lone traveler or whole family can enjoy.

I'd like to put together a Scottsdale piece for your Dateline section, focusing on the horse show but including some of the area's more offbeat attractions, perhaps in a sidebar. I'll be in the area in May, with all expenses covered, and can provide photos as well. The Chamber of Commerce has offered to provide a local guide to escort me on a tour designed expressly for *Western's World*.

We'll go to an Arabian horse farm, Frank Lloyd Wright's Taliesin West, the Paolo Soleri Cosanti Foundation (world famous "earth sculptures"), a Native American reservation museum, and The Borgata, a luxurious new shopping complex fashioned after an Italian Renaissance village.

That mix of attractions should add fun and flavor to just about any visitor's stay in the fabled Valley of the Sun.

Interested? We've worked together before, and you know my credits. I hope to hear from you soon.

Best,
John M. Wilson

◆ ◆ ◆

The next query proposes an angle spun off from research done for two previously published articles. The magazine purchased the article, a sidebar and several color slides.

Christopher Batin   Date
Editor
Alaska Outdoors

Dear Mr. Batin:

Alaskans, I have found, are generally a hospitable people. Not so, the land. Rather than inviting us, the Alaskan wilderness *dares* us to venture into its endless, untamed stretches.

What better place then for the National Outdoor Leadership School (NOLS) to put down new roots?

NOLS, which *Outside* magazine calls "the largest and most successful of the nation's wilderness schools," has recently become Alaska's first state-certified outdoor school and is buying its first permanent site not far from Anchorage. Last summer, on assignment with *Western's World*, I spent two weeks on a NOLS kayaking trip into Prince William Sound, and later accompanied two NOLS instructors for a week of backpacking among the grizzlies in the vast Denali.

What sets the nonprofit school apart from so many outdoor organizations is its emphasis on educating participants — aged fifteen to sixty — about the natural environment. NOLS instills deep respect for the wilderness, teaching minimum-impact techniques for backpacking, mountaineering, kayaking, etc.

I'd like to profile NOLS, asking such questions as:
— How will this activist environmental school fit into a region known for its individualism?
— Are NOLS' rules for outdoor recreation too regimented?
— Will the school steal business from local guides?
— What is the school's safety record?
— What about cost? Is it only for the wealthy?

In addition to outdoor pieces for *Western's World*, my work has appeared in *The New York Times*, *The Los Angeles Times*, *TV Guide* and numerous Sunday magazines. Clips are enclosed.

Sincerely,
John M. Wilson

◆ ◆ ◆

The following query breaks lots of rules, including the cardinal sins of gushing with praise for the target publication and emphasizing writing inexperience. Yet the letter has such sincerity, charm, nifty details and a wonderfully straightforward style, I had to include it. It generated the writer's first sale ($650).

Washington   Date
1500 Eastlake Ave., East
Seattle, WA 98102
Attn: K. Gouldthorpe

Dear Mr. Gouldthorpe:

I would like to write an article for your lovely magazine on fresh water fishing in Washington. What I have in mind is an overview of some popular rivers and lakes on both the wetside and the dryside — the type of fish, successful lures and methods, and what the locals have to say about fishing.

I would also like to include information on popular fishing resorts, camp spots and some "secret" holes. For instance: The fishing in Curlew Lake near Republic (I really enjoyed that article on Republic, by the way. One can really get "tucked in" there, all right.) is great, but few people know that by going to the end of the lake, lifting your motor, and scooting through a shallow channel between the tall grasses, you will find yourself in tiny Roberta Lake, where the fishing is even better. I caught more rainbows than my husband there last summer, although I had some trouble reeling them in as I was pregnant, and my reel was tied to my pole with shoelaces and kept falling off.

I am the sort of fisherman who never has the right gear, or even soda pop, on hand. Therefore, although I plan to include a great deal of mechanical information, I plan to emphasize colorful descriptions of fishing areas and brief profiles of interesting people.

I am a Newaukum River buff; my husband only fishes dryside. Through our business we know people across the state who also enjoy fishing, including one man who "limits out" every year during opening day at Cascade Lake on Orcas Island.

I have no book or magazine publishing credits, yet. I have a teaching certificate in secondary English education, and I worked for two years as a writer for a privately owned newspaper in the San Juan Islands.

I am looking forward to your reply.

Regards,
Mary Baker

◆ ◆ ◆

These queries vary widely in quality, style and form; fault could probably be found with each of them. Yet they demonstrate enough detail, substance, craft and enthusiasm to have warranted assignments.

Suggestion: Read through each query again. Think about what more you would have put in each one—or what you would have left out—and how you might have written them differently.

QUERYING IN VOLUME

Many of your queries, even the best ones, will meet with rejection, at least when you start out.

There are certain factors over which you have no control: Another writer got there ahead of you, your angle has already been assigned to a staff writer, a competing magazine published a similar piece, the editorial direction of the publication just shifted, pages shrank because of a drop in advertising revenue, the freelance budget just got cut, the editor has a migraine, et al.

Accept the fact that rejection is part of the game, that editors are constantly bombarded with hundreds, even thousands, of ideas, and they can only assign so many.

That's why it's so important to *prioritize* your markets, then query *systematically* and in *volume*, to increase the probability of making a sale.

Step Five tells you how.

Playing the Odds

W hen *The Doors* was shooting on location, Pat H. Broeske filed a story on the film with Sunday Calendar in *The Los Angeles Times*. But she didn't stop there. She sold essentially the same article throughout Europe, where Doors lead singer Jim Morrison lived during the last years of his short life. Pat also fashioned a piece for *Fame* magazine looking back at Morrison's "dark side," spun off an article on the revived interest in his poetry for a newspaper lifestyle section, and peddled several short *Doors*-related items to *Entertainment Weekly*. She even sold some of her notes to *People* for $750.

From an original assignment in the $1,000 range, Pat earned thousands of extra dollars, and will continue milking her material for more angles — and more income — in the years ahead.

There was nothing unethical, or even unusual, in what Broeske did. Reslanting for secondary markets is just smart business.

THE MULTIPLE MARKETS GAME

You don't have to wait until you start getting assignments before reslanting for multiple markets. The sooner you start reslanting — with query letters — the sooner those assignments will start coming in.

The more queries you fire into the marketplace, the better your chances of hitting a bull's-eye. The fewer queries you have out there, the fewer your opportunities of scoring.

Combined with a system of market prioritization, volume querying also lets you take risks by shooting for the more coveted markets, while simultaneously targeting smaller markets that may be more within your range. (Before continuing, take a look at sidebars on two important issues: overlapping readerships, page 90; and simultaneous submissions, page 81.) Some writers feel the smaller, lower-paying markets are beneath them, even when they start out. They aim straight for the top and won't settle for less.

THE SIMULTANEOUS SUBMISSION ISSUE

Writers and editors constantly debate the practice of simultaneous submissions — sending an unsolicited manuscript or query on the same essential idea to more than one publication at the same time. Some editors don't mind simultaneous submissions — they turn up in *Writer's Market* listings saying as much — but many consider them unethical and duplicitous.

Their argument goes something like this: If an editor takes the time to read a query, to decide if it warrants an assignment, to possibly fight for it at an editorial meeting, then takes more time to put through the assignment, she doesn't want to find out it's been submitted to competing publications, perhaps even assigned at one.

Many freelance writers counter that simultaneous submissions are a practical necessity. Since so many editors take months to reply, or never reply at all, these writers argue, it's not fair to ask the writer to be patient, contacting a new market only after the last one has responded. Simultaneous submissions, this argument goes, are prudent and productive. You pitch your idea or submit your article widely, and if more than one market goes for it, you sell to the first or highest bidder.

The chief risk with simultaneous submissions — some would call it wonderful luck — is that two or more markets might say yes, forcing the writer to choose and therefore alienate the "losing" editor or editors (a definite possibility).

To be completely aboveboard, some writers note in their queries or cover letters that the same material is going simultaneously to other markets, yet that in itself may alienate some editors.

You must decide for yourself what's fair, and what's worth the risk. You're clearly operating in a buyer's market, with the odds stacked against you, and you need to find ways to change the odds.

One approach is to *reslant for markets that don't directly compete*, avoiding the complicated issues of simultaneous submissions and overlapping readerships.

If you happen to feel that way, more power to you. I don't want to discourage anyone from chasing their dreams, professionally or creatively. Taking chances, stretching, challenging ourselves is part of the excitement of freelance writing, a big part. But I would also advise you to consider a different approach, especially if you're still developing or sharpening your basic skills.

I'm talking about prioritizing and targeting markets, not based on their prestige and high payment rates, but on *sales probability*.

Prioritizing Inversely

When Russell Baker or Amy Tan or Carl T. Rowan or Richard Rodriguez get ideas for nonfiction pieces, they probably think *Vanity Fair, Playboy, Ladies' Home Journal, Mademoiselle, The New York Times Magazine* and, down the road, a lucrative reprint payoff in *Reader's Digest*. And their agents probably take care of the marketing for them.

But if you've never made a sale, you're wise to think: local newspaper, small trade journal; department of "shorts" in a mid-sized magazine. Even if you write for free at first (as I did), it's worth it if it gets you started. To get established, you don't need money. You don't need fame, prestige or a million readers.

You basically need three things: *credits, clips* and *experience*.

And your best chance of acquiring those career building blocks is to reverse normal priorities, targeting less-illustrious markets. Put the smaller, more accessible markets on the top of your list and the bigger, less accessible markets at the bottom.

Market prioritizing—*realistic* market prioritizing—will keep your feet planted firmly on the ground, while allowing you to still dream big, to display your most dazzling wares to the highest bidder (I'll show you exactly how in a moment).

Some factors to consider, when prioritizing inversely:

High or low profile. The more visible and widely distributed the publication, the more competition you face.

Payment. The more it pays, the choosier it can be. The less it pays, the more it needs you.

Frequency of publication. Does it come out daily, weekly, monthly, bimonthly, quarterly? What does that tell you about your chances of selling there?

Volume of freelance material. Do you see plenty of freelance bylines? What does its profile in *Writer's Market* indicate, if it's listed there?

General reputation. What do you hear about a particular market from other writers and writers' organizations? How has it been evaluated by sources like *The Writer, Writer's Digest* and *Writer's Market*? What do interviews with editors reveal about their willingness to work with less-experienced writers?

In choosing the most accessible markets, take them as seriously as the higher-paying markets; never look down on them. When querying or writing for a smaller market, write with all the concentration and skill you can muster, as if you're going after the Pulitzer Prize. Even if it's a small local newspaper that's paying you nothing, write to your highest standard and acquire the kind of clips that will help you move up fast.

GETTING ORGANIZED

To prioritize your markets and query in volume effectively, you must find many angles from a single idea. And you'll need to market your queries *systematically*.

Let's consider that idea I had on "taking the trauma out of moving" in Step Four.

Suppose I'm just starting out. Let's say I'm a resident of Kansas City, Kansas; mother with two kids; churchgoer; employed part time in a florist shop; with a husband who drives a truck for a living. I worked on my high school newspaper fifteen or twenty years ago. In the years since, I've taken a few writing classes, done some volunteer work on the newsletter for a local nonprofit organization, and helped my children with their class papers. I might even have written a few articles for my local newspaper, for the byline, but no pay. So I have some basic writing skills and a bit of experience. But I'm years behind my professional contemporaries who have gone to J-school, staffed on newspapers, written for a variety of magazines, completed dozens, even hundreds, of articles. While they're selling to midrange markets and up, I've got a lot of catching up to do.

OK, that idea on "moving."

Hypothetically, I've done some basic backgrounding. I've clipped articles on the subject, done a brief telephone interview or two, sent for brochures and other material from some of the big moving companies or related trade associations, like the American Movers Conference. I've jotted down notes from my own experience changing homes, and those of friends, including a black male friend in management who's experienced racial animosity in his new neighborhood. As I've conducted this preliminary research, I've run into some unexpected leads, such as a former athlete, now disabled, who runs a moving business from a wheelchair; and my boss, the florist, who works through a local real estate association to make contact with potential new customers. Before I've done any in-depth research, my file is already filling up, much of the material coming from my own interests and daily life experience.

Now I'm ready to start querying.

As a relative beginner, I aim not for *Parents*, at least not at first, but for the lifestyle section of my local metropolitan newspaper, *The Kansas City Star*.

The angle for *Parents* — "How to Take the Trauma Out of a Family Move" — may also work for a metropolitan daily; or I may want to localize it, something like: "Should You Use a Local Mover for a Long-Distance Move?" Or: "Ten Tips for Choosing a Reliable Local Mover."

That market and angle go at the top of my "marketing log," which is simply a graph or chart that helps me prioritize my markets and keep track of queries, responses, assignments, deadlines and so on.

I then develop different angles for a wide range of markets, prioritizing publications inversely, for my greatest chances of breaking in, and filling out my log.

An example of such a log follows, using "packing and moving" as a general topic.

◆ ◆ ◆

This "marketing log," with its twenty-five prioritized publications, is strictly hypothetical, and only a beginning. It illustrates the almost-endless possibilities for stretching basic source material into multiple opportunities. This approach lets you target prestige markets (those at the bottom) while covering yourself with queries to more accessible markets (those at the top), simply by reslanting. Obviously, you could never contact this range of markets unless you were querying. To try to write complete manuscripts on spec for all these publications, or even a fraction of them, would be sheer folly.

The marketing log you use doesn't have to be exactly like this one. Adapt this model, or create a whole new one that feels right for you. Then prioritize depending on your personal circumstances — the depth of your writing experience and skill, your confidence and personality, the geographical area you live in, your available time and so on. The system you develop should allow you to see at a glance where your queries are, to keep them circulating to other publications if they get turned down, and to add suitable new markets as you become aware of them.

You may feel you're ready to move into the top rungs of the marketplace. Terrific — put those big markets up top, and go for it. But cover yourself with midrange or more accessible markets below, to keep your business calendar filled with active assignments.

Reslanting for Resales

The multiple markets game isn't just for nonfiction writers getting started. Those who have freelanced successfully for awhile, even for many

MARKETING LOG

Topic: Packing and Moving
Angle: how to find a reliable local mover
Market: *Kansas City Star* (real estate section?)
Potential: works with new writers, prints six days a week

Queried: Reply: Deadline: Pub. date: Paid:

Angle: disabled man who operates moving firm from wheelchair
Market: *Kansas City Star* (lifestyle section)
Potential: buys several short "people profiles" each week

Queried: Reply: Deadline: Pub. date: Paid:

Angle: how to find the right school when your family moves
Market: *Kansas Parent* [hypothetical parent newsletter]
Potential: low pay, needs material, publishes monthly

Queried: Reply: Deadline: Pub. date: Paid:

Angle: disabled man who operates moving firm from wheelchair
Market: *Careers & the Disabled* (emphasize how-to tips)
Potential: only quarterly, but needs role-model profiles

Queried: Reply: Deadline: Pub. date: Paid:

Angle: disabled man who operates moving firm from wheelchair
Market: *Grit* (change angle/approach from newspaper pitch)
Potential: buys lots of "upbeat" articles, good reputation

Queried: Reply: Deadline: Pub. date: Paid:

Angle: disabled man who operates moving firm from wheelchair
Market: alumnae magazine, his college (he was sports star)
Potential: quarterly, buys "where are they now" shorts

Queried: Reply: Deadline: Pub. date: Paid:

---

continued

Angle: how a disabled athlete got his life "moving" again
Market: *Celebrate Life* (inspirational, if *Grit* says no)
Potential: quarterly, but 75% freelance written

Queried:　　　Reply:　　　Deadline:　　Pub. date:　　Paid:

Angle: tips on how to pack and move, from a wheelchair
Market: *Paraplegia News* (for wheelchair users)
Potential: monthly, buys only a few freelance pieces yearly

Queried:　　　Reply:　　　Deadline:　　Pub. date:　　Paid:

Angle: "I Trusted in God When I Packed the China" (humor)
Market: *Virtue* (for Christian women), first-person dept.
Potential: fair, works with some new writers, bimonthly

Queried:　　　Reply:　　　Deadline:　　Pub. date:　　Paid:

Angle: your new church can help brighten a lonely move
Market: *Today's Christian Woman*
Potential: only fair; bimonthly, 25% freelance written

Queried:　　　Reply:　　　Deadline:　　Pub. date:　　Paid:

Angle: free flowers to new homeowners for future profits
Market: *Flower News* (trade journal to florists)
Potential: weekly, established since 1946

Queried:　　　Reply:　　　Deadline:　　Pub. date:　　Paid:

Angle: how to turn your truck into a part-time moving van
Market: *Overdrive* (magazine for independent truckers)
Potential: monthly; 50% freelance; solid, established market

Queried:　　　Reply:　　　Deadline:　　Pub. date:　　Paid:

Angle: how to safely pack your most precious breakables
Market: *Home* (shorter feature)

continued

Potential: bimonthly, buys 200-plus freelance pieces yearly

Queried:　　　Reply:　　　Deadline:　　Pub. date:　　Paid:

Angle: your first home: how to get started romantically
Market: *Bride's* (specific tips, related to new couple)
Potential: discriminating market, bimonthly, worth a shot

Queried:　　　Reply:　　　Deadline:　　Pub. date:　　Paid:

Angle: ten tips for handling toddlers during a family move
Market: *Parents*
Potential: 25% freelance, selective, but lots of pages

Queried:　　　Reply:　　　Deadline:　　Pub. date:　　Paid:

Angle: moving doesn't have to be traumatic for your kids
Market: *Parenting* (if *Parents* says no)
Potential: buys only 25-30 manuscripts a year, but pays quite well

Queried:　　　Reply:　　　Deadline:　　Pub. date:　　Paid:

Angle: don't let moving put you on the road to divorce
Market: *Redbook* (slant very differently than for *Bride's*)
Potential: top market, 80% freelance, wants strong research

Queried:　　　Reply:　　　Deadline:　　Pub. date:　　Paid:

Angle: don't let moving put you on the road to divorce
Market: *Ladies' Home Journal* (only if *Redbook* says no)
Potential: elite market, lots of freelance but picky

Queried:　　　Reply:　　　Deadline:　　Pub. date:　　Paid:

Angle: how to meet the right guys when you arrive
Market: *Cosmopolitan*
Potential: good freelance market, needs "Cosmo girl" style

Queried:　　　Reply:　　　Deadline:　　Pub. date:　　Paid:

continued

Angle: leaving a lifetime home can be a bright new beginning
Market: *Modern Maturity* (aimed at those fifty and older)
Potential: high standards, but excellent freelance market

Queried: Reply: Deadline: Pub. date: Paid:

Angle: make your new home a renewed commitment to ecology
Market: *Sierra* (Sierra Club magazine)
Potential: specialized, only bimonthly, but 80% freelance

Queried: Reply: Deadline: Pub. date: Paid:

Angle: surviving the pain of changing schools
Market: *Seventeen* (for teenage girls)
Potential: very selective, 80% freelance, seems friendly

Queried: Reply: Deadline: Pub. date: Paid:

Angle: moving blues: dealing with racism in your new 'hood
Market: *Essence* (for upscale African-American men)
Potential: some freelance, no current *Writer's Market* info

Queried: Reply: Deadline: Pub. date: Paid:

Angle: high-quality moving company that caters to the elite
Market: *Esquire* (for "Man at His Best" shorts section)
Potential: reputation for not responding, real longshot

Queried: Reply: Deadline: Pub. date: Paid:

Angle: high-quality moving company that caters to the elite
Market: *New York Times* (Sunday feature, if *Esquire* says no)
Potential: top newspaper market, buys freelance, need clips

Queried: Reply: Deadline: Pub. date: Paid:

years, can also benefit, reviewing their files and reviving dormant material for additional profits.

Here are some tips:

Plan ahead. If you query on an angle within a general topic area, or receive an assignment, don't stop there. Try to come up with other hooks on the same general subject—*before* you begin your deeper research. Find noncompeting markets for those new angles.

Some years ago, a friend nailed down an assignment from a runner's magazine to cover the running segment of a triathlon in Hawaii, for something like $2,000. He then queried an inflight magazine, focusing on business executives in the race and how triathlon training improved their career performance. The inflight guaranteed $1,000 or thereabouts, plus plane fare.

My friend next pitched *TV Guide* on the difficult logistics of covering the event for television. *TV Guide* offered another $1,000, and picked up food and lodging expenses.

The writer notched a fourth assignment with a women's sports magazine that wanted profiles of top women athletes in the race.

By knowing the marketplace and reslanting carefully for noncompeting markets, he landed four assignments—all *before* he went to Hawaii.

Expand your research. Again, think ahead. When researching or interviewing, even at the preliminary stage for a query, broaden your scope. Ask questions that might generate quotations for spinoff pieces or spinoff queries. If possible, plan photos or illustrations for use in secondary markets. And, by all means, keep all your material.

Scan the categories. Run through the *Writer's Market* list of publication categories, from consumer publications on animals, art and architecture to trade journals on travel and veterinary medicine, and the more than 100 genres in between. Do these categories trigger new ideas, suggest appropriate ancillary markets? As I scan these categories, for example, all kinds of possibilities loom up for my files on wilderness travel: health and fitness, ecology, self-improvement, teen and young adult, camping, photography.

Brainstorm. Look at your topic, then jot off a list of every conceivable angle you might wring from it; discard the ones you don't want to do or feel might be beyond your scope. Now, find markets for the new hooks you want to develop. Or work the other way, glancing over individual markets to see what new angles they suggest; scan those tables of contents, particularly the departments, and watch marketable ideas spring to mind.

Think "article types." Concentrate on each article type—profile, roundup, travel, historical, nostalgia, personal experience, essay, investigative, how-to, service and so on. What new possibilities do they suggest?

Think "shorter." In your ongoing market study, be aware of magazine and newspaper sections that use shorter items—they may suggest nuggets you can mine from your lode of material. Sometimes a pithy quote or two

MAKING SENSE OF OVERLAPPING READERSHIPS

Overlapping readership refers to markets that duplicate subject matter and compete for the same target audience, or at least similar enough core audiences that the publications share many of the same readers.

Some obvious examples:

- *Playboy* and *Esquire*. Both are aimed at sophisticated, upscale male readers.
- *Ladies' Home Journal* and *McCall's*. Fairly sophisticated but more "traditional" women.
- *Virtue* and *Today's Christian Woman*. Mainstream Christian women.
- *Us* and *People*. Both cover entertainment and personalities.
- *Outside* and *Backpacker*. Angled at wilderness enthusiasts.
- *Florist* and *Flower News*. Two trade journals that go to florists.
- *The Detroit News* and *The Detroit Free Press*. Major newspapers that blanket the same market.

The simple definition of overlapping readership is *publications that directly compete for many of the same readers*. But it can get a bit more complicated.

Because *McCall's* and *Savvy* are both aimed at sophisticated women, they also compete, although the publications are quite different in content and tone. In fact, *McCall's*, *Savvy* and *Today's Christian Woman* all overlap, if less directly, because they are all women's markets.

Esquire and *Sports Illustrated*, though vastly different, also compete; their core readerships are adult men. Ditto, to some extent, *Sports Illustrated* and *Backpacker*, because of the subject matter.

To get even more complex, a men's magazine like *Esquire* or a woman's magazine like *Ladies' Home Journal* also overlap a regional general-interest publication like *The New York Times Magazine* because of their high profiles and large New York City readerships. This is a blurry area of overlapping readership; the ethics and rules are less clear-cut.

What does this mean to the freelance writer?

It means you can't sell the same article, or something too close to it, to publications with overlapping readerships, unless they are willing to buy second rights. And few high-level markets want second rights;

continued

---

they generally expect an article tailored exclusively for them.

It means you cannot write an article on spousal abuse, for example, for *Esquire* or *Ladies' Home Journal* and also sell it to *The New York Times Magazine*, unless your approach with each article is different.

Very different.

---

from the right person, a useful anecdote or factoid, can be enough for a brief item.

Update. Look over your files or published articles; can you find a current take for a topic, perhaps updating a subject with only a few telephone calls and some new research?

James Joseph, for example, writes prolifically on engineering and related matters for publications like *Popular Science*. Bicycles, which are popular around the world, are one of his favored topics; each time there's a new development in the industry — mountain biking, for example — he's able to spin off a new piece. He reslants, does new research and meticulously re-packages these articles worldwide (more on foreign markets in Step Fourteen).

Think topically or seasonally. Do upcoming dates, holidays and special events suggest ways to rejuvenate or stretch your material? Be aware of trends, because they tend to be cyclical, making old material useful again.

Pat H. Broeske first profiled actor John Travolta for *The Los Angeles Times*'s Calendar section, focusing on his career decline, when he was making the film, *Look Who's Talking*. When the movie came out and was a hit, Pat reworked her material for an *Us* piece on his career *comeback*. As the picture was released abroad, she sold an updated Travolta profile in overseas markets, because she was well known there. She even resurrected her material when the sequel, *Look Who's Talking Too*, came out nearly two years later. She estimates her overall take at close to $10,000.

Change viewpoint. If you've completed an article for a target readership, can you flip the viewpoint for a contrasting audience? Gender bend an angle for the women's market into one for a men's magazine? Retool a piece aimed at one age group for another? For example, if you've written a self-help piece for a seniors' magazine about communicating with grandchildren, can the viewpoint be switched for a teen publication?

Think "regional." Start locally and expand your market survey outward, from city to region to a national scale. What new markets does this suggest? Does your regional peg suggest a piece with national scope? Or, conversely, can you localize a national topic?

Using a national peg, Broeske sold a survey piece on America's top ten amusement parks to several noncompeting Sunday supplements around the country. She went historical for a look at turn-of-the-century amusement parks for *Minnesota Motorist*. Then she used a regional angle for the inflight, *Air California*, examining the Golden State's top thrill rides.

Reader response. Was there a reaction to your published article that suggests new spins on the same subject? New leads, contacts, sources?

Keep in touch. Maintain communication with subjects, publicists, related organizations and the like. Not only can they keep you current, they'll often have ideas for stretching your material into other markets.

Extract and remix. Are you able to take bits and pieces — quotations, anecdotes, statistics, other details — from a number of your existing articles, find a new theme and create a new piece? A couple of years ago, I got to reminiscing about the handful of celebrity interviews I'd done over the years that had ended in kill fees for one reason or another. From that throwaway material, I put together an anecdotal humor piece for Calendar about a freelance writer dealing with rejection and frustration.

As much as I've earned through multiple sales over the years, I've thrown away thousands of dollars more by not paying keen attention to resale possibilities.

Broeske is particularly adept at wringing multiple sales from primary source material. Her tips:

- Keep everything, especially related clippings from other publications.
- Maintain voluminous files by subject ("action heroes," "amusement parks," "women directors," etc.).
- Build relationships with editors.
- Network with other writers.
- Read a lot, keeping an eye on new and changing markets.

Every time you find a new market for your existing material, it's like finding an extra paycheck.

QUERIES: YOUR "REGULAR ASSIGNMENT"

Your ability to study and evaluate individual markets is a key to successful volume querying; so is your skill at finding marketable angles and crafting effective query letters. As I emphasized before, craft, technique and marketing are all related.

Remember, too, that queries are the "regular assignment" you give yourself.

Maybe Saturdays are query-writing days. Perhaps it's the entire weekend, or several evenings a week. The important thing is to assign yourself queries steadily, put the deadlines on your calendar, and follow through.

It's possible, by reslanting for multiple markets, to have literally dozens of queries out in the marketplace at once, without selling quality short. Most of us may not be that enterprising; we may have regular jobs and supplemental incomes, writing only part time. But at the very least, if we're serious about freelancing, we need to set quotas for ourselves well beyond the occasional query.

Not every pitch will land an assignment; it may take a while for even one to find the right market and the right editor at the right time. But if you keep at it, making a determined effort to improve each new query that you write, some will eventually pay off.

At this point, it seems appropriate to explore the nuts and bolts of writing craft, specifically writing the lead—Step Six.

Step Six

Those First Crucial Words

An article landed on my desk one morning at *The Los Angeles Times* written by Don Chase, one of our regular freelance contributors. Don was an established writer with hundreds of articles to his credit, as well as a highly respected book, *Filmmaking: The Collaborative Art*. This time out, he'd written a location piece on a movie in production overseas.

I began reading:

> PARIS — A perruqued, pear-shaped castrato is trilling the "Largo" from Handel's opera *Xerxes* in the Grand Salon of the suburban Parisian chateau designed by Francois Mansart, he of Mansard roof fame. But the singer (played by the ungelded, but testosterone-deficient Brasilian, Paolo Abel do Nasciemento), and the setting (crystal-and-gilt chandeliers, walls hung with blue-and-gray tapestries) are just background.

I forced myself to read on:

> The focus here on the set of director Stephen Frears' film version of *Les Liaisons Dangereuses* is on *Les Jeuz D'amour* — the love games — being played by the Marquise de Merteuil (Glenn Close) and the Vicomte de Valmont (John Malkovich). Merteuil has just seen Valmont, her former lover and current partner in perversity, exchange a glance with Madame de Tourvel (Michelle Pfeiffer). Tourvel is the devoutly religious and indubitably faithful young matron whom Merteuil has egged Valmont on to seduce both for the sheer nasty thrill of it all and to gain a prize: one more night with her. Except now it's clear from Valmont's glance that he has fallen in love with Tourvel, violating the cardinal rule of . . .

Enough already!

Never mind the obscure references to architecture, history, literature, et al., that went right over my head. Never mind the film's convoluted story line, jammed into the second graph. Never mind the distracting parentheses. Just tell me what the heck this article is *about*! Give me some itty-bitty indication where it's going! Or why subscribers to a general-interest newspaper should want to read it!

I grabbed the telephone and called Don in New York. "Your lead boggles the mind," I told him.

He'd tried to write a terrific lead, he explained, but jet lag and a quick deadline, combined with the "dizzying material," caused him to turn in his article before it was ready. Being the pro that he is (also a good sport, to let me tell this story), Don performed an expeditious rewrite, giving us a lead that was literate, full of colorful detail, yet considerably more succinct and to the point.

By the time he sold reprint rights to *The New York Daily News*, Don had revised further, for an even tighter, livelier opening:

PARIS—"Oh, no—I turned too quickly and made eye contact with Michelle. We're going to have to do it again!" Glenn Close lamented.

To me, this little story underscores two points:

1. how important leads are, and
2. how we sometimes *place too much importance* on them, trying too hard to write "great" ones.

THAT ALL-IMPORTANT OPENING

Can there be anything more crucial to the success of your article than its opening lines, particularly in this age of declining literacy and short attention spans? After all, a good lead must be provocative enough to grab the reader's attention. It must set the tone for the article. It must provide enough information to get the story going, but not take too long doing it. It must have an entertaining style that infuses the piece with vigor, energy, personality. It must *sell* your subject to the reader.

That said, leads may also be the most overrated aspect of nonfiction writing.

Let's repeat our initial argument, but from a different viewpoint:

A good lead catches the reader's attention, but doesn't call attention to itself. Simpler is generally better. Those opening lines set the tone for the article, of course, but that's pretty much a matter of knowing your material and writing in a relaxed, natural way.

The lead should provide enough information to get the story going, but you don't need to reveal everything in the beginning, or rush into things. Have some fun with your leads; be creative. They shouldn't feel tight and overworked. Just make sure they are comfortable and appropriate. Nothing turns a reader off faster than a pretentious or overly tricky lead, written for show.

In a sense, leads act like a flag, catching our attention; but they shouldn't flap so loudly or flamboyantly that they look silly or out of place.

Don't try to make your leads do more than they need to.

"Finding" Your Lead

Some writers are more natural lead writers than others, but I suspect all of us tighten up and agonize over those first crucial words at one point or another. Here are some questions you might ask yourself if you find yourself faltering at the beginning of an article:

- What attracted me to this story in the first place?
- What is it really about?
- What will the reader respond to most strongly in this material?
- What's my single best anecdote, one that captures the essence of the story? Best quote? Statistic? Etc.
- Am I trying to work with an anecdote or other element that's not pertinent to the material? Am I forcing a beginning on my story that's inappropriate just because it's clever, or because it came to mind?
- Is it possible I've buried my lead deep in the copy? Likewise, am I trying to save a terrific bit for the end, for my kicker, when I should be using it up top?
- Is my approach plodding and stilted when I ought to be using power words, strong verbs, vivid phrasing?
- Am I trying to say too much in my lead, cramming my opening with facts and meaning, when I'd be better off with a brief sentence or two? Am I rambling when I should write to the point? Does my lead feel sufficiently *focused*?
- Am I writing from a place of involvement and enthusiasm with my material? Or am I intellectualizing, writing from my head rather than my heart?
- Am I trying to be too "cute"? Am I more concerned with showing off than just giving the reader the start of a good story?
- What is the theme of my article? The message? What tone do I want to establish at the outset?

OVERCOMING WRITER'S BLOCK

A period of procrastination before writing can be useful; like athletes who warm up with various rituals and excercises, "creative procrastination" can be the writer's way of getting mentally prepared, working up to the act of writing the way a diver visualizes the dive or the sprinter fidgets purposefully in the starting blocks.

Too much procrastination, however, can become a habit, deepening to the point that it renders a writer dysfunctional—the so-called "writer's block." It's a kind of mental rut that has a way of feeding on itself, winding a writer tighter and tighter with the fear of creative impotence.

Over the decades, writers have practiced various techniques to avoid or break free of this kind of mental paralysis. Here are a few:

Develop options before sitting down to write. As you research and collect your material, make note of possible elements for openings, such as anecdotes, statistics, quotations, images and so on. Have a list of possibilities before you ever start writing.

Hit the ground running. Lay in bed in that creative "twilight time" just before fully waking, and let ideas come to you. Carry the best one with you, straight to the writing desk, and start writing.

Go with your gut. Suspend intellectualization. Follow your heart, vision, hunches. Write what bursts out of you right now, regardless of anyone's judgment, including your own. Takes risks. Be silly, adventurous, uninhibited.

Try writing in the first person. It often helps a writer to find his "voice" more easily.

Take the category test. Try to write an opening for every one of the lead "types." See what happens.

Bang 'em out. Write a slew of leads, all widely varied, and do it quickly. Look them over and see if one works for you. Retype it, and keep going.

Spin a fairy tale. Start out with the words "once upon a time." Then tell a simple story, not unlike the fairy tales you read as a child. Forget about structure, technique, details, etc. You can always rewrite later.

Perform a "spinal tap." Find the spine of your story with a brief outline. Nothing formal, just a fast step outline, listing your main points

continued

in the order you'd like to develop them. Try to find a key element within one of those points that might be a good place to start.

Play the card game. Jot down main points, scenes, quotations, anecdotes and other elements on three-by-five-inch cards. Arrange them in a logical order. Glance at the first card and start writing whatever it suggests. If you hesitate at any point, go back to the cards.

Picture a movie. Pretend you're in a darkened theater; close your eyes and envision your material as a vivid film. What is the first image you see, the first scene? Open your eyes, write it down and don't stop. If necessary, close your eyes at the end of every section and envision your next scene before writing again.

Write anything. Just start writing, even if you have to write, "I can't seem to get started. I'm trying to write about such-and-such, but I freeze up every time. Maybe I'm blocked because. . . ." Find out where it takes you; it may take you right to your opening.

Don't start; finish. Write the ending to your piece, a wonderful, inspiring kicker. Or start somewhere below the lead, such as a billboard paragraph, and keep going from there. Go back later and write your opening.

Read other writers. Keep on hand favorite pieces of writing by others. If you're stuck, look them over. Or read inspirational how-to pieces on the craft of writing. See if they don't move you to get your own piece underway.

Change environments. Leave the rut of the workroom or office. Find a bench at a park or museum, corner table at a quiet coffeehouse, someplace pleasant where you wouldn't ordinarily work. Relax, open your senses, let anything come into your head. Write.

Once you're going, leave your writing open-ended. At the end of each working day, write a line or two, or a few graphs, to start the section you'll work on tomorrow.

Writer Maya Kaathryn Bohnhoff has a different view of writer's block. Discussing the problem in a *Writer's Digest* piece, she says that she sees not writers block—a solid barrier to be knocked down—but writers *gap*: a trackless waste to be crossed. Her solution is to let her imagination go, coming up with story elements she uses as bridges or stepping-stones across that vast wasteland, filling it in creatively.

However you look at it, don't let writer's block—or writer's gap—stand in your way of telling stories.

- Am I writing a lead that promises more than it can deliver, because I'm so determined to attract readers?

Don't get too cerebral about your leads. Try lots of them, play around with them, get the juices going. An effective lead should *feel good*, like the booming kickoff of the football or the popping of a cork. Even the downbeat lead must be compelling.

Close your eyes. Listen to your inner voice. What first few words do you hear? What images do you see? Do they make you smile? Grimace? Cry? Scoff? Jot them down; one may grow into your new lead sentence.

Or go outward: *Open* your eyes. Keep your antennae up and your senses raw for every bit of stimulus. A good lead can come to you in someone's glance, a snatch of laughter, a vivid image, piece of music, anecdote, quote, fact, number, moment of human interaction or understanding.

All the leads you will ever need are all around you, inside your head and out. The more open you are to the world and the humanity around you, and its connectedness to your own humanity and to your writing, the more you will be flooded with possibilities for opening your article.

When one feels right, snatch it and try it out.

Types of Leads

Over the years, students have asked me to draw up a list of lead "types," with examples of each. I balked, because I worried about laying down formulas, the quickest route to dull writing. With that warning, I've put together that aforementioned list, not to provide you with easy answers, but to show you how many possibilities there are for opening an article. All the leads on my list, though hypothetical, are obstensibly written to open an article on bed-wetting, probably aimed at parents.

(*Note:* Names, facts, statistics, etc. in these leads are made up, strictly for use in these samples; do not consider them real or accurate.)

These "types," by the way, are arbitrary; other writers or teachers may use other categories and names, or none at all. But they are all fairly common.

Anecdotal:

The screaming wakened Susan at 3 A.M. She leapt from her bed and raced down the hall. The plaintive wailing continued — unmistakably her son Jimmy. He sat up in bed, tears streaming. He'd wet his bed for the third straight night, and she knew she had to find a solution.

Quotation:

"I don't want my son to feel any worse than he does," says Susan Johnson, a thirty-five-year-old single mother. "But it's becoming critical. I'm up changing sheets and calming him down almost every night, and I go to work exhausted.

"It seems like such a small problem, but it's making me crazy."

Or:

"There's got to be an answer!"

Or:

"Momma!"

Paraphrased thought:

If Jimmy wets his bed one more time, Susan thought, I'll break down and cry.

Descriptive:

The sheets hung on the clothesline almost every afternoon. Out behind the pleasant two-story house with the picket fence, between the roses and the vegetable garden. Flapping in the breeze like flags.

Only in this case, they were flags of shame.

Telltale yellow stains reminded the neighborhood that Jimmy Johnson was a bedwetter.

Or:

Jimmy Johnson is a skinny, freckled, blue-eyed towhead. An average-looking kid of twelve, with holes in his jeans, dirty sneakers and a T-shirt at least a size too big. Look him in the eyes, though, and he averts them. That's when you notice the fingernails chewed to the nub.

Summary:

Bedwetting may seem like a small problem, but it can seriously affect a child's self-esteem and leave parents angry, exhausted and confused about what to do.

Thankfully, help is on the way: New approaches to this old problem are providing parents with practical, effective solutions.

Or:

According to figures compiled by the National Child Psychology

Institute, as many as 10 million American children may be afflicted with chronic bedwetting syndrome, and the numbers appear to be growing.

Delayed revelation/surprise:

Jimmy's a model student: straight A's, perfect attendance, plenty of extracurricular activities, including sports. He's healthy, popular, an exemplary son and an all-around good kid. Maybe too good, trying too hard to please.

Beneath that perfect exterior, Jimmy harbors a secret: He's a chronic bedwetter.

Teaser:

Your child does it alone in his room at night. He's so ashamed, he engages in elaborate deceptions to keep it secret. It's ruining his self-esteem, his social life, his study habits. And you probably have no idea what it is.

Contrast/comparison:

Every night, twelve-year-old Jimmy turns his home into hell, screaming, crying, tormenting his parents and siblings. But Jimmy is no sociopath, and he doesn't do it deliberately. He's simply a chronic bedwetter, who needs more understanding and emotional support than he's getting.

Or:

Imagine a night when you sleep all the way through, without interruption. Imagine your child smiling happily the next morning, then coming home from school without suffering the taunts of neighborhood kids. Imagine a family dinner that night, without averted eyes and shameful silences. You may take such a day for granted. To the parent of a chronic bedwetter, however, it's only a fantasy.

Humor/irony:

If Jimmy wets his bed one more time, Susan thought, I'll put him up for sale — at a discount price!

Metaphor/figure of speech/play on words:

Susan Johnson goes through clean sheets the way soap opera addicts go through Kleenex.

Or:

If urine-stained sheets were hundred-dollar bills, Susan Johnson would be laughing all the way to the bank.

Parody:

Once upon a time, there were three bears: mama bear, papa bear and baby bear. Alas, baby bear was a bedwetter, and had to sleep by himself.

Single Word:

Shame.

Shock/emotional impact:

Bedwetting is a hidden tragedy that's tearing apart thousands of families.

First person:

I was Jimmy Johnson's eighth grade teacher, and I knew something was wrong. I just couldn't put my finger on it right away. Then an offhand remark by my father reminded me that I had been a bedwetter at Jimmy's age.

I'd found out his secret.

Direct address:

Needed: Several million sensitive mothers and fathers, with the patience of Job. Assignment: care for the several million preadolescent bedwetters who need parental understanding and patience.

Factoid:

Last night, according to an estimate by the National Child Psychology Institute, 3.7 million American kids wet their beds.

Stage setting:

It was a typical night in the Johnson household. Jimmy worked on his homework on the living room carpet, Susan and Jack finished up the dishes, and the cat slept curled up near the heater. Susan put on a classical record, and as the melody wafted through the house, everything seemed in order. Perfect, really.

Clustering:

Screams at 3 A.M. Terror. Relief. Anger. Tears. Reprimands. Guilt. Another sleepless night, another self-help book, another psychologist. Another frustrating day, trying to find an answer.

Tabulation:

Bedwetting doesn't end with sleeplessness and a busy washing machine; it can have serious side effects, including:

- Emotional trauma.
- Disrupted education and socialization.
- Child abuse.
- Family conflict and tension.
- Lifetime self-esteem problems.

Declarative statement:

Several million children suffer from the shame of bedwetting, but it's the parents who should be ashamed — because many of them only make the problem worse.

Narrative:

Jimmy started wetting his bed not long after his fifth birthday. Although his mother, Susan, read all the right books and tried all the techniques, the problem got worse. At age eight, he wet his bed almost every night. At twelve, despite regular sessions with a psychologist, it was such a problem that it eroded his self-esteem and drove Susan to tears.

Speculative/hypothetical/fantasy:

Suppose you had three children. Suppose you were determined to love each of them equally, without favoritism. Now suppose one of them was a bedwetter who disturbed your sleep every night, showed no signs of stopping and disrupted family unity.

Composite:

Jimmy Johnson is twelve years old, and he's pretty normal in most respects: an average student, fair at sports, shy with girls, a big eater. Yet one thing sets Jimmy apart from most of his friends — he still wets his bed. Jimmy isn't a real person, but he could be, because there are thousands of twelve-year-olds just like him in the United States.

Sensory:

Cries shatter the stillness, lights blast the darkness, footsteps thunder down the hallway, cupboard doors slam, curses punctuate the chaos.

Question:

If your child wets his bed tonight, do you know how to handle it?

◆ ◆ ◆

Consider these examples as a guideline that illustrates the wide range of possibilities for opening your story, and as a form or pattern if one seems useful. But don't try to copy and force them into your articles. Let them be an inspiration, not a substitute for creativity. There are many more possibilities — inside *you.*

Most professional writers don't categorize their openings at all when sitting down to write. They just *write.*

For example, look at this "hybrid" lead from a business profile by Christopher Knowlton in *Fortune*:

> Sir Peter Holmes has a way of brushing death aside. He stepped on a land mine while serving with the British Army in Korea forty years ago but escaped with minor injuries. Last summer he walked away from the crash of a small plane on a riverbank in Zambia, then fended off crocodiles and lions by lighting fires until help came sixteen hours later. A good resume for a man? Sir Peter, fifty-eight, is in an even more dangerous business — oil.

This lead combines declarative statement, anecdote, question, narrative and delayed revelation to introduce the subject. It defies formula, yet it's well crafted and satisfying on many levels.

WHAT'S APPROPRIATE?

Your lead cannot just be well written. It must also be suited to the editor, reader, publication, article type and angle you've chosen.

Four essential qualities — *length, type, tone* and *style* — come into play when you consider what's appropriate and what's not.

Length

Plenty of factors can influence the length of your lead, such as:

The length of the article itself. A long lead on a short article would make it top-heavy and use up too much precious space needed for the body of the piece.

An editor's personal taste. Some editors just don't go for long leads, long being roughly a hundred words or more, or several paragraphs.

Article types. How-tos, for example, are almost always to the point, because their primary purpose is providing useful, concrete information. Likewise, business articles rarely feature leisurely leads.

The editorial style of a given magazine or section. In a general way, it will clue you in about style and about how much freedom you have to write leads of varying length.

If you write for *The New Yorker* or *The New York Times Magazine*, you get to write long creative leads. The same is true for other more "literate" publications, such as *Vanity Fair*, *Harper's*, *Texas Monthly*, *Rolling Stone* and so on. But if you write for more mainstream publications such as *USA Today*, *Popular Science* or *Horse Illustrated*, you'd better get started pretty quickly. Different readerships, different purposes, different editorial styles.

Generally, the longer your article, the longer your lead can be. But that's not always true. Sometimes, an editor simply wants a lead that gets more quickly to the point. Editors tend to read manuscripts like readers do; if they get bored, they figure the reader will get bored. Even with a longer piece, they may demand a punchier opening.

When I turned in my Jane Fonda profile for *The Los Angeles Times*, the initial draft ran something like 7,000 words; my editor, Irv Letofsky, told me not to worry about the article's length. My lead went like this:

> Jane Fonda faces a dilemma: Once a self-righteous star of the radical Left and critic of big business and class privilege, Fonda has made a stunning metamorphosis, emerging as the multimedia Wonder Woman of the 1980s. She's amassed wealth, power and material comfort far beyond the reach of the oppressed and disadvantaged for whom she has so often taken public stands, putting her in an awkward spot.
>
> For some, she's having her slice of the American pie and eating it, too. Opportunities to generate vast amounts of money pop up right and left, and she has seized many of them. . . .

It went on and on like that: A long summary lead that led to an investigative look at business problems Fonda faced within her multimedia empire, and how she personally reacted to these issues.

Letofsky liked the article. But he also told me: "Give me a new lead that doesn't put the reader to sleep." I fiddled with a number of possibilities, then changed my verbose and rather ponderous opening to a funny line, quoting comedian Joan Rivers:

> "Jane Fonda didn't get that terrific body from exercising—she got it from lifting all that money!"

The new lead was more fun, helped lighten and brighten my opening, but kept the edge I wanted—and got to the point.

I also used a quote to open a profile of performer Suzanne Somers for *The*

Detroit News Magazine when she first hit it big and was being merchandised profitably as a sex symbol. This quote, which was from the subject herself, summarized my theme:

"We have a business now, and the business is me."

Quotes can be useful ways to jump start articles, but beware those that run on too long; they unfairly demand that readers read on and on without understanding the context or meaning of the quotation. Usually, the shorter, the better.

"Lies! All lies!"

That was my lead for a story on the filming of *Torch Song Trilogy*, screamed across the set in jest by the writer and star, Harvey Fierstein, as I interviewed actress Anne Bancroft. I liked the lead because it captured Fierstein's sense of humor and irrepressible need for attention, while enabling me to grab the attention of the reader — all in three words.

Generally, good quotation leads are those that have impact, that are brief, revealing, and meaningful.

Shorter Is Harder

When you need to get to the point quickly, summary and declarative leads are especially useful; they can capture the essence of the story in a sentence or succinct paragraph.

This declarative lead by *Los Angeles Times* writer Jesse Katz, about a grieving father who committed suicide at the site of his son's murder, is both brief and intriguing:

In the end, the bullet that killed sixteen-year-old Jesus Perez claimed two lives.

If you write features for departments, there's usually little room to waste. When Amanda Gardner penned a profile for the Ink section of M, she chose a delayed revelation lead, but kept it tight:

Most of us don't know his face. But we know his sadistic bent. He humiliates us every day, calling on us to know arcane facts and obscure words in a prescribed number of letters. His name is Eugene T. Maleska, editor of *The New York Times* crossword.

Gardner had some fun with her opening, teased us a bit, but also managed to tell us exactly who her subject was and what he did — all in forty-seven words.

Items for news brief sections, shorts departments and other tight formats require special economy and craft. Look at this direct address lead for a sidebar item on the snack downsizing trend, from *Newsweek*:

> Go ahead, grab a handful.

The next two sentences pay off that opening sentence:

> Those mini chocolate-chip cookies are only the size of a quarter, so they can't be too fattening, right? The logic might be flawed, but the strategy isn't: Marketers are shrinking cookies and crackers to morsel size, hoping to sweeten their own balance sheets.

Three sentences; crisp, active, clever writing; few wasted words—and we're into the story quickly.

Type

Next to overwriting and dull writing, perhaps the most common problem editors encounter in openings is a lead type that's inappropriate for the material. A student in one of my classes turned in an article that began:

> Breast cancer. These two words strike fear into any woman. They can mean surgery of the most personal, invasive kind, which is never fun. They conjure up the horrors of losing one's pride and self-esteem, not to mention their relationship with her husband or mate. Of course, they also mean possible premature death, ending a life long before it would happen naturally.
>
> My cousin Leslie faced all these fears and terrors when she found a lump in her breast. Thankfully, the lump was benign and she came through her ordeal with flying colors. She was lucky, but many women who wait too late to have a breast exam are not so fortunate.

What's wrong with this lead? That is, besides clichés, redundancy, word clutter, incorrect pronoun reference, inappropriate understatement and weak structure?

Answer: The writer is working with material full of potential drama, but she's not writing *dramatically*.

In the first paragraph, she tells us information we already know. What we don't know about is *Leslie*; she's new to us and we want to know her story. But in the second graph, the writer reveals there's no cause for alarm, Leslie is just fine—end of drama. Just when the suspense should have been building, the writer destroyed it. For a story that was potentially engaging, the writer chose a declarative lead that diffused the drama and suspense.

LEADS, NOT CLICHÉS!

The danger in heeding "rules" about good leads is that we may start to place limitations on ourselves.

There's only one irrefutable sin regarding leads: the use of a cliché, unless it's given a new spin, for deliberate effect.

Here are several successful leads that shine with originality and creativity, just to remind us how much those qualities count in getting published:

> For me, all hope for New York died on the day I read about the arrest of a young man out in the borough of Queens. A special kind of murder. *DAD HELD IN KILLING*, said the page-three headline in the *Daily News*. Another neat summary of a familiar New York story, reported in the matter-of-fact tone of an aging war correspondent. You know: The cops say this, the neighbors say that, and, uh, pass the jam, will ya, honey?
> — PETE HAMILL, *Esquire*

> I have been married to an Episcopalian, a Jew, two fallen-away Catholics and a nondenominational. I have been married to a Paul, a Greg, two Bills and a Dick. I have had two divorces and two annulments.
> Could looking for the right husband be my life's work?
> — LOU SAATHOFF, *Lear's*

> I was sitting near a clam bar on a southwest Florida beach when I saw 60 billion or so Lycra molecules writhing in pain. Lycra, the miracle fiber that wraps all of sporting America — and most of its rock stars — can stretch 500 percent before it snaps. Beside me, an abundant woman, packed into an orange bathing suit, was reaching toward a wicker basket. I estimated that the Lycra at this moment was stretched about 497 percent. It was an amazing sight, just the kind your mother told you not to stare at.
> — PENNY WARD MOSER, *Sports Illustrated*

> Nearly every season a new movie nuzzles onto the scene, promising to be the next exit to Nirvana — a mind-body meltdown that will massage us like Aldous Huxley's "feelies" and make our eyeballs egg out. Whether it's a southern-fried *noir*, like *The Hot*

continued

Spot, or a dew patch, like *Wild Orchid*, this new honey offers to take us past peroxide down into the deep dark roots of things. All that, plus naked babes!

    —JAMES WOLCOTT, *Vanity Fair*

Where men and phones are concerned, I've got my rules. Never put a man in your phone book unless it's on a Post-It note. Never commit a man's number to memory. And never, *ever* sit around the house, waiting for a man to call.

But, hey, rules are made to be broken. So for Groovie Mann, dimpled dreamboat and lead vocalist for My Life With The Thrill Kill Kult, I make an exception. After all, this is business. Besides, the boys are on the road, I've got to cut them some slack. Groovie will call me sometime between 10 A.M. and 3 P.M. on Saturday. Or so their publicist assures me.

Over breakfast, I take a gander at the press clips:

"As S&M-fixated, gay, Satan-worshipping drug fiends go," says *Sounds* magazine, "the TKK are hard to beat." Wow, what can I hope to add to that? I make a note to ask Mr. Mann if the magazine left anything out.

    —BRENDA DAY, *L.A. Village View*

It's not likely that I will ever be mistaken for a true Texan, even though I have lived nowhere else since the sixth grade. I don't know how to dance to country music. I haven't made it past page 47 of the 843-page Pulitzer-Prize-winning classic *Lonesome Dove*. On trips to the country, I still find it amusing to roll down my car window and stick my head out in order to moo at cattle.

    —SKIP HOLLANDSWORTH, *Texas Monthly*

"The matches are under the moose."

    —RICHARD OLSENIUS, *National Geographic*

◆ ◆ ◆

What distinguishes these leads from thousands of other less interesting, more formulaic openings? Imagination, attitude, personality, energy, wit, style—plus the ability to arouse the reader's curiosity. They feel unique, and they prove that if a lead "works" for the article and the publication, as these did, editors will give you wide latitude to be creative.

She put her article through several drafts and came up with this anecdotal lead, which was considerably tighter and more polished:

> When Leslie found it, it was no accident, but the shock left her reeling. It happened as she self-examined her breasts, which she routinely did while soaping herself in the shower. This time, she felt a lump, the size of a lima bean and unmistakable, in her left breast. She stood there shaking, as steaming water mixed with her uncontrollable tears.

In this case, an anecdotal lead was ideally suited to her dramatic material. An anecdote, when it's vivid or revealing, involves us immediately with a human subject; statistics, declarative statements and other less-involving elements can always be worked in later.

Certainly, there were other choices. The writer might have tried a quotation lead, such as:

> "My god," Leslie cried, standing in the shower with tears streaming, "it's finally happened to me."

A paraphrased thought, such as:

> I have breast cancer, Leslie thought as she felt the lump, and I'm going to die.

Or a first-person lead, like this:

> I've known my cousin Leslie since we were kids, but I never saw her so frightened as she was the day she discovered a lump in her left breast.

There are an infinite number of ways to open your article, as long as it suits the material.

Tone

Like the opening scene of a movie, your lead establishes a feeling, an atmosphere, from which the rest of your story will grow.

When *The Chicago Tribune Magazine* asked me to profile romance novelist Judith Krantz, I wanted to open with a breathless energy and gossipy quality, suited to my subject. So I wrote:

> One expects her to be different. Taller. Somewhat overbearing. Elegant, or at least glossy, like her latest book. But Judith Krantz, the highest-paid author in the history of book publishing, pads across her

plush Beverly Hills living room in stockings, almost smothered in a
purple turtleneck sweater, a tiny blonde pixie who tucks her feet
under her on a floral-print sofa and starts chatting away like she's
known you since way back when.

"I was at a party recently, and someone asked me if I had really
had a hysterectomy, or if it was all just a cover while I had a facelift,"
she blurts out, referring to recent surgery and a new hairstyle. . . .

I felt this descriptive lead set the right tone for a visit with a famous
writer of romantic sagas and a peek into her posh personal world.

When I went to Manila during the last months of rule under Philippine
dictator President Ferdinand Marcos to report on film censorship there, I
had a far different world to capture. I again opened with a descriptive lead,
but the style was distinctively different:

It was a steamy evening, punctuated by thunderstorms. Destitute
figures, emaciated and clad in rags, slept under the remote porticoes
of the government's luxurious Manila Film Center. Soldiers stood
guard against possible terrorist attack, while inside, civic leaders in
formal dress piled their plates high with delicacies from a lavish buffet.
Nervous anticipation charged the air — tonight's film event was the
hottest ticket in town.

This time out, I needed to establish a tone reflecting the economic
disparity and ironic contradictions, constant themes of the article.

Establishing attitude, viewpoint or "edge" at the outset is vital for certain
publications, departments or types of articles.

For an *Entertainment Weekly* piece about a publisher exploiting the legacy
of a famous author, Kelli Pryor used metaphor:

Laura Ingalls Wilder used to wake up in the little house in the big
woods and hear the wolves outside. Now, thirty-five years after her
death, the wolves seem to be circling again. This time they smell
money.

For a *TV Guide* star profile, Mary Murphy and Frank Swertlow used a
stage-setting lead to instill a sense of suspicion and paranoia:

Sound Stage 44 at Universal Studios usually has a guard or two
to prevent overcurious fans from wandering in. But today it looks like
a fortress, guards at every door — big, mean-looking guards wearing
guns. No audience, no fans, no press, no one is allowed onto this set.
It's the rehearsal for the pilot of "Delta," the new fall series starring

Delta Burke. Somebody at the studio, or at ABC, the network, must really want to keep this set under tight control.

That's detailed, colorful writing that says a lot economically — exactly eighty-three words.

Style

The more personal a style, the more distinctive the writing.

Some publications favor a more traditional, simple approach, but others, like *Rolling Stone*, thrive on individual style. Consider this offbeat lead for a profile of Marlon Brando by Chris Hodenfield:

> Marlon Brando's body was going through the motions, awaiting the return of his personality. It was miles away. He was reeling it in like a dancing sailfish.

Not too many publications would let you get away with such an esoteric lead. Yet it somehow suited a profile of the moody, eccentric and elusive actor, particularly in *Rolling Stone*.

For Calendar, Irv Letofsky once assigned me to go to Emporia, Kansas, to research the chilling true story of murder involving a church minister and his mistress, focusing on the scramble by Hollywood producers to acquire the dramatic rights for filming. I wanted my lead to match the dark, Gothic quality of the events:

> The countryside here is lush, vibrant green, vast and nearly empty beneath an unpolluted, cloudless sky. Almost too placid for murder.
>
> But at night, as a visitor drives along shadowy gravel roads outside town, passing farmhouses that are dark by 11 P.M., he can imagine death sprouting as easily as the stalks of corn and milo that waltz in the humid summer breeze.
>
> Deadly violence did come to this town of 29,000 people and forty churches, germinating in a mix of lust, greed and ambition.
>
> And then Hollywood came, descending like the proverbial plague of locusts to pick clean the dramatic rights.

In writing that lead, I alluded purposefully to both farming and religion, and wrote in a deliberately overwrought style. Letofsky grumbled that my lead was "writerly," preferring that I go with a more conventional summary up top, emphasizing the television production angle. He didn't hate it so much, however, that he made me change it.

Style does not necessarily mean lots of literary flourishes and other "writerly" techniques. For a *Ladies' Home Journal* "as told to" piece about an incest survivor, the writer, Karen Surman Paley, and editors used a first-person lead that was purposely simple, detached and a bit ironic. It went like this:

> As a biochemist and scientist at a Harvard-affiliated research institute, I study how microorganisms adapt themselves to harsh environments. It's a survival process I'm all too familiar with; in fact, it's a process I had to go through myself.

Detachment and irony, in a grim account of terrible child abuse? It wasn't an accidental choice but one, I suspect, that allowed the writer — and the reader — to better handle the horrifying subject matter. (More on "style" in Step Eleven.)

KEEPING A "LEAD FILE"

As you read magazines and newspapers, try to identify leads by "type," but don't be bothered if you can't categorize them. Decide which ones you like, which you don't, and why. File them, and update them with leads you find particularly effective. Use them for reference as you write your own leads, both for query letters and then for assignments as they come in.

Then, when you write your lead, turn off your intellectual powers and switch on your emotions, your instincts; quit being analytical and simply write, letting your lead pour out of you.

◆ ◆ ◆

Now that we've covered getting started, it's time to think about where we're headed — organizing your material and developing and structuring the rest of your article.

Please head with me to Step Seven.

Step Seven

Knowing Where You're Going

I reread an article recently, a cover story published years ago in the *L.A. Reader*, about a serial killer's twentieth victim. The teenaged boy, Davey, was the pivotal victim who brought the killing spree to media attention. He was also a cousin of one of the writers, giving them access to inside information on the case.

The writers told the story chronologically, from the second Davey ran away from school one afternoon, frustrated by his poor performance in class, to the moment he hitchhiked away from home, angry and frightened by his allegedly violent stepfather. The story followed the teenager, chillingly and almost inevitably, into the deadly hands of his murderer.

Gradually, *too* gradually, a theme emerged: how abuse at home can drive children into the streets and into waiting danger, with boys at special risk because we so often assume males can instinctively take care of themselves. While much of the material was poignant and compelling, the piece needed something more. It seemed to meander from story point to story point, without focus or perspective until the end.

The article, I decided, was an admirable failure, but a failure nonetheless.

And since I was the more experienced writer on that article, working with Davey's cousin, the failure was mine.

THE MISSING LINK

When Jon-Noel Orestes and I put that piece together years ago, I suggested we try something I'd never done: tell the story in exact chronology, intercut with italicized news announcements of the deaths of other victims, to give the sense of the victim and killer getting closer and closer, drawn to each other by tragic destiny (a structural device known as *parallel narratives*). We wrote in almost documentary style, letting the story unfold without comment or intrusion, just as it happened.

As I read that piece now, it seems a calculated risk that didn't pay off, because many readers probably put the story down long before it ended. It ran on and on, with no sense of where it was headed, of what it was essentially about.

How often have you had this same experience, either with your own rough draft or a published piece? You begin reading the article. The lead captures your attention, but five or six paragraphs later you begin losing interest. You try to stick with it, but it seems to be going nowhere in particular. Finally, you give up, moving on to another article, hoping it has a better focus and sense of direction.

Often, an article is just one rewrite short of finding its sense of unity, of feeling "of a piece." Sometimes, it's a case of reorganizing the material, moving paragraphs or blocks of text around into a new and more logical order. Or trimming chunks of material, streamlining the piece. Perhaps an outline is called for, to help the writer give an article more structure, keeping it on track. (More on structure and outlines in Steps Eleven and Twelve.)

In the case of my *L.A. Reader* piece, though, I believe I know what was missing: *a billboard paragraph.*

The "Sign" of Strong Writing

I learned about the billboard paragraph almost two decades ago when a *New York Times* editor said to me, "Your piece is pretty solid, but you need a billboard graph to pull it together."

At *The Wall Street Journal*, it's called the "significance graph." Elsewhere, writers and editors refer to it by various other names: summary graph, focus graph, nut graph, theme graph, thesis graph, guidepost graph, essence graph, signal graph and so on.

Whatever you call it, the billboard paragraph is a valuable writing tool that can help turn a rambling article into one with focus and direction.

It's simply a paragraph — sometimes two — that appears high in your piece and sums up what your article is about. It tips readers to your theme, guides them on their way, enabling them to decide if they want to read on and, if they do, to better assimilate the information that follows, reading with a sense of perspective.

If I'd written a billboard for the *L.A. Reader* piece, it probably would have followed three or four graphs describing Davey's anguished day at school, and looked something like this:

> Davey cut the rest of his classes, as he had several times before. This time, however, he didn't go home. Fearful of another argument

with his stepfather, he headed for a freeway on-ramp, thumb out.

Violence and psychological abuse at home had finally driven Davey into the streets, which social tradition and stereotyping tell us are a threat to girls, but not to boys. Like so many boys, however, Davey was tragically unprepared for what awaited him on those dark, dangerous streets, from which too many young men never return.

Certainly, not every story requires a billboard. But I believe a signpost like the one above would have pulled Davey's story together near the top, making it a more effective article and satisfying read.

Finding the "Significance"

Billboards are particularly useful when you write about a serious or complex issue and need to crystalize it for the reader early, before moving into deeper territory.

Kathleen Doheny opened a *Los Angeles Times* piece on male victims of sexual abuse with a disturbing anecdote about a young man who kept his story secret for thirteen years until he saw his abuser targeting a younger family member, and put a stop to it. Then, Doheny wrote:

> Estrada's story isn't rare. Childhood sexual abuse, once believed largely a trauma of girls, cuts across gender lines, researchers know now. Some estimate that as many as 15 million American men may have been sexually abused as children.

That's a classic, straightforward summary graph, something many veteran journalists rely on. Many nonfiction writers add their special paragraph *after* they write their first draft, helping build structure and find focus during their rewrites.

The Wall Street Journal seems particularly fond of significance graphs, such as this one in a piece by Laura Bird:

> Before Nissan Motor Co. rolled out its Infiniti line two years ago, it ran the Zen-like ad campaign that showed no cars and pictured plenty of rocks and trees, creating suspense and appeal for affluent luxury-car buyers.
>
> The daring campaign is gone, but Infiniti's aura of inscrutability lingers — in a logo that reminds some people of a pizza.
>
> Corporate logos, plastered on almost every package, mailing envelope and advertisement, are the signatures companies use when they talk to consumers and shareholders alike. But a new study finds they can do more harm than good, undercutting the corporate image.

In fewer than 100 words, Bird led off her roundup piece with a clear-cut example, then used her billboard paragraph to tip the reader to the theme. *WSJ* reporter Suein L. Hwang did the same, but even more quickly, with this exclamatory, two-word lead, followed by a nut graph:

> "Prices Slashed!!!"
>
> It's the Christmas message of many big-name retailers this year as they confront a shorter holiday shopping season, sinking consumer confidence and an army of discount competition. But the constant hype and dizzying array of preholiday promotions are signaling desperation to some consumers, who say the stores often promise a lot while delivering very little.

That second graph, which provides an effective summary and points the way ahead, is especially helpful to the reader who can't read the entire article but may want to come back to it later.

It Takes All Kinds

The danger in using billboards, of course, is in following form too rigidly—forcing one into your copy when it isn't needed or doesn't feel right, or writing summary graphs that are predictable and formulaic.

As long as they serve their purpose, guideposts can be as varied as you want them to be. Let's take a look at several disparate examples, and how they work:

They can take the form of a summary lead. Sometimes, with tighter articles such as how-to or business roundup pieces, you'll see a billboard in the first paragraph—a summary lead, serving the same function as a billboard. Here's an example from Larry Miller's *Writer's Digest* piece, "How to Think Like an Editor":

> I had little success as a freelancer until I realized that thinking like a writer is the worst way to get magazine writing assignments. Success came when I started thinking like an editor.

Miller obviously wanted to get right to the point, to let readers know quickly where the article was going. With the hook set, he could then slow down and develop his theme.

They can establish strong viewpoint and tone. Some billboards are sharply opinionated, suddenly changing the tone of an article or giving it edge. Consider an article on racism in professional sports by Lynn Rosellini of *U.S. News & World Report*. The article opened matter-of-factly with a

SEEING EYE TO EYE ON THE ASSIGNMENT

Before you start writing, even before you start researching, it's important that you see eye-to-eye with your editor on the assignment. Are you both clear on the type of article you plan to write? The angle? The viewpoint? Have you reached a consensus on the scope of the piece, such as the depth of research or number of interviews?

If you plan to use devices such as composite characters or anonymous sources, is the editor aware of this, and in concurrence? If you have a special format in mind, such as a list or diary structure, should you run it past the editor?

Do you have a specific deadline for turning the piece in? Has the editor given you parameters, such as word length? Are questions regarding supporting materials, such as photos or illustrations (if applicable), answered to your satisfaction?

Most editors will give you a fair amount of leash, but some will be more demanding and dogmatic. An editor can't, and shouldn't, lay out exactly how you are to write an article. That's what you get paid to do, in your own special way. However, if you are unclear about any important aspects of the assignment, telephone or write your editor and get your questions answered. Many articles become derailed because a confused writer is timid about contacting an editor and clearing up cloudy issues.

Better to do it before than after writing your article.

couple of seemingly innocent, race-related anecdotes, followed by this sharply-worded billboard:

> Welcome to baseball, 1987, the reverse Time Warp where it's Jackie Robinson vs. the color barrier all over again. Only this time the weapons aren't racist epithets and rotten tomatoes but attitudes so subtle — yet systemized — that it took Al Campanis, with his shot-heard-round-the-sports-world-assessment of blacks' fitness for management, to articulate what no whites wanted to believe: Racial stereotypes persist in American sports, barring all but a few blacks from front-office jobs and "thinking" playing positions.

That outspoken billboard lets you know exactly where the writer stands on the issue.

They can be offbeat and colorful. Here's a less traditional two-paragraph guidepost from a piece by John Dreyfuss in the travel section of *The Los Angeles Times*:

> Guests sleep in a Cadillac convertible. A former Ping-Pong champ makes balloon sculptures in the bar. You can't locate the bathroom until you find a secret door. A guest describes the owner as "kind of like the illegitimate son of Woodie Guthrie and Howdy Doody," and nobody argues that.
>
> Welcome to the 1880 Union Hotel and Victorian Annex, the delightful, bizarre, romantic and incredible dream-come-true of Richard Wilkes Langdon, a sailor turned piano salesman turned ink salesman turned meat wholesaler turned hotelier.
>
> His *pièce de resistance* is the Victorian Annex, a bed and breakfast push-button fantasy land. Life was never like this.

Written with energy and a twinkle in the eye, those two graphs that follow the lead give the article focus before the writer moves on.

A quotation can serve as your billboard. Here's an example, appearing in the fifth paragraph of a *Los Angeles Times* piece about the reluctance of many Latina immigrants to use birth control:

> "We are a community that is still just beginning to learn how to talk with our husbands, with our lovers, with our children and with our church about issues as intimate as birth control, family planning, and the spacing of our children."

It's important, when using a quotation as a focus graph, to set it up and place it effectively for context and maximum payoff.

A billboard can help advertise and sell your subject matter. In an age of lazy readers, nonfiction writers must work extra hard to attract and hold their attention. In that vein, it's not unusual to follow a billboard immediately with a supporting paragraph, or a quotation for validation and impact.

Here's an example, from a *Washington Post* piece by Howard Kurtz:

> Beth Darnall, a University of Missouri journalism student, didn't exactly go undercover to get the big story. She went topless.
>
> Darnall worked as a singing-telegram stripper for a local costume store before turning the experience into a first-person expose for the student paper, *The Columbia Missourian*.
>
> "I worked in a whorehouse a block off Broadway," she wrote. "I didn't turn tricks, but the other girls did. College girls."

That quotation gives punch and power to the relatively low-key lead and billboard preceding it.

Billboards don't exist alone; they support what comes before and after, acting as a linchpin.

It's possible without an obvious billboard to make your subject and theme clear to the reader. By weaving together a number of elements—details, quotes, anecdotes, etc.—you can create an "invisible" billboard that can get the job done as well as or better than the more blatant. A sample, from a roundup piece by Michael DiLeo in *Mother Jones*:

> "We are definitely the illegal aliens of American lit," says short-story writer and poet Sandra Cisneros, who lives in San Antonio, Texas. "The migrant workers, in terms of respect." For years Chicana writers labored in the shadows. Now Cisneros and others are changing that. For her upcoming collection of short stories, Cisneros has received the first major publishing contract ever awarded a work of fiction by and about Chicanas; this after winning a Before Columbus American Book Award for her previous collection, *The House on Mango Street*. "I'm excited about this whole generation of Chicana writers . . . ," Cisneros says.

The quote continues, discussing gender- and class-consciousness, finishing out the paragraph. While the graph singles out a particular writer, it also serves the purpose of a thesis graph: It conveys a strong sense of what the overall piece is about, but without resorting to formula.

TAKING A PIT STOP

You might think of your billboard as a "breather" for your reader near the beginning of a long trip.

Often, shortly after embarking on a journey, we like to take a pit stop, not only for relief, but to consult the map, make sure we're properly oriented. A billboard serves a similar function for readers, so they don't have to drive on with only a vague sense of their destination. Give them a good guidepost, and they can move on confidently, relaxed and able to absorb the sights along the way.

This is especially true for longer features, or articles with lengthy, more leisurely leads. Back in 1990, I profiled two up-and-coming filmmaking brothers for *The Los Angeles Times*. The piece opened like this:

> Reginald and Warrington Hudlin are behind schedule in the great Hollywood tradition of "running late."

The two brothers, both Ivy League film school graduates, relay their apologies to a waiting reporter by car phone as they scoot from a studio meeting to the office of New Line Cinema. With New Line about to open the Hudlins' first feature, *House Party*, the filmmakers are cashing in on the stuff of "buzz": favorable early reviews in the trade papers; strong audience reception and a prestigious award, the Filmmakers Trophy, at the recent Sundance United States Film Festival; and good word-of-mouth following industry screenings.

It's a Friday evening, the end of a week the Hudlins have spent pitching projects across power desks to the kind of executives who make and break deals, sometimes careers.

Just one more writing-directing-producing team hustling a dream . . . but with a distinction: Reggie and Warrington Hudlin are black.

The New Yorkers are the latest in a continuing wave of African-American filmmakers — Spike Lee leading the charge — who are trying to get their foot in the proverbial Hollywood door without compromising their personal visions.

Without those last two graphs serving as a pit stop, restless readers might have wondered just who these two unknown filmmakers were, why we were writing about them, what the piece was about, where it was headed.

The billboard not only gives the reader a useful pause, it enables the writer to give her story a strong beginning, laying the foundation for good organization and structure.

Think of it as the end of Act I, a solid base from which to develop Act II (the middle) and Act III (the end).

TESTING FOR FOCUS

If you feel your piece can benefit from a billboard, it's essential that it come relatively quickly. I've found that most editors prefer to see a thesis graph within the first half dozen paragraphs. If it's beyond the first quarter of your text, it's much too late — by then, you've lost many readers, and a billboard would feel awkward, out of place. In general, the shorter the article, the higher your billboard should be.

A billboard can be as brief as a good, pithy line, or broken into more than one paragraph. But if you find your "signal" spread out beyond a couple of graphs, chances are that:

- You've lost your focus;
- You don't know what your angle is;

- You're trying to cover too much ground in the article (too *broad* a topic); or
- You're being verbose.

Sum up the thesis fairly succinctly, leaving subthemes and qualifying points to be dealt with later.

How can you tell if you need a guidepost graph? Here's a simple test: Read the first third of your article, then stop. If you were a reader who wanted to recommend the article to friends, could you sum it up in a line or two so they understood what it was about? Are you able to underline a particular section — no more than two or three paragraphs, say — that captures the essence of the piece? Does that section do justice to the scope or complexity of your subject? If not, you may need to create a billboard, or write a better one.

Now, finish reading the article. As you read along, do you find the article going off on tangents that don't pertain to your nut graph? Do you stray from your main theme? As the piece develops, does it feel at odds with your focus graph? At the end, do you feel you've covered all of the points suggested by your billboard? Delivered what you've promised?

Another step: Write a headline and "deck" for your completed article (strictly as an exercise). Do you have an essence graph that is at least as helpful, coming high enough in your story to be useful to the reader?

Billboards are among the nuts and bolts of nonfiction writing, part of the craft. Some stick out like the proverbial sore thumb. Others are disguised, woven deftly into the material. Look for them as you read newspapers and magazines. Clip and study them for their variety and effectiveness. Ask yourself how you might have written them differently — or better.

Don't be surprised to find published articles without billboards. Some writers are unaware of them as a writing tool. Others may feel that such a conscious device intrudes on the flow or style of a particular piece of writing. There may be types of writing for which billboards don't feel right. By and large, though, editors are thrilled to see a strong billboard when it's appropriate, because it gets readers started safely on their journey, pointing them in the right direction.

◆ ◆ ◆

Our own journey now takes us to other useful techniques in the writer's toolbox — Step Eight.

Step Eight

The Writer's Toolbox

When I was a high school senior, my well-meaning English teacher asked students to contribute entries to a "national writing competition." The winning essays were to be printed in an "anthology"—actually a cheap booklet of shamefully shoddy quality—that would then be foisted on the parents of the "lucky" students at a couple bucks apiece.

Naturally, I jumped at the opportunity to show off my budding talent. I selected "Virtue" as my theme, and loaded my 500-word sermonette with metaphors, literary allusion, fancy transitions, and every big word I could find in my dog-eared thesaurus. I wrote with great earnestness, in a style I was certain displayed what a fine writer I was, but that was actually pompous, riddled with clichés and ludicrously overblown.

I was out sick when the class selected the top submissions, but upon my return, was delighted to learn mine would be among those published. For a day or two, I basked in glory, feeling validated as a brilliant writer, before a fellow contestant inadvertently burst my bubble.

Pam, one of the brighter students in our class, congratulated me enthusiastically on my winning entry.

"I thought it was absolutely hysterical," she said, quite sincerely, from behind her horn-rimmed glasses. "It was a great parody of bad writing. When the teacher read it, we were all laughing like crazy. I had no idea you could write such funny stuff!"

I swallowed hard, maintained a stiff smile, and expressed my relief that the other students had "gotten it."

If there's a lesson to be gained from my humiliating experience, it's that we should relax when we write, not try to show off; use what works; don't throw everything we've got into the stew just to throw it in. The secret to effective writing is to write naturally and well, using techniques at our disposal, but appropriately and with care.

I offer that caveat as we prepare to dig deeper into the nonfiction writer's toolbox.

THE TELLING ANECDOTE

There's a good reason so many articles (as well as some chapters of this book) open with an anecdote: Anecdotes tell a story. They are the tiny tale that draws us into the larger one, illustrating its meaning. There is nothing more involving or revealing than human drama, and anecdotes capture that drama succinctly and with impact.

For her *Los Angeles Times* profile on John Travolta, written twelve years after *Saturday Night Fever* had made him a star, Pat H. Broeske opened with an anecdote about a group of star-struck teenage girls asking the now-husky actor to "point for us." Reluctantly, the thirty-five-year-old Travolta struck his familiar disco pose from the movie that had made him famous, pointing his finger "at an imaginary mirrored disco ball," as Broeske described it. She ended it:

> The girls erupt in squeals and giggles and collect his autograph. Then they walk off—without even asking about the movie he's filming now.

In a deftly told, real-life anecdote, Broeske captured the plight of a former heartthrob struggling to revitalize a declining film career, but trapped, a bit sadly, in the past.

Anecdotes are particularly useful when you deal with poignant or disturbing subject matter. A former student of mine, Muriel Schloss, recounted her struggle to accept her granddaughter's autism for *The Exceptional Parent*. Muriel used a pivotal moment in her life to capture the pain she felt when reality suddenly shattered her illusion and denial:

> Meravie flew into Los Angeles on Monday escorted by airline personnel. I was to meet her at the terminal door. I waited, then watched with horror as flight attendants tried to take her off the plane. Kicking, screaming, even biting, Meravie wrenched herself out of everyone's grasp, and flung herself to the floor.
>
> The split second it took for me to get to her seemed like hours. I knelt beside her and whispered in her ear. I forced myself to smile and tried to calm her. All the while, autism—that terrifying word— careened from my head to my heart and back again, splintering and crashing every dream I ever had for her.

Anecdotes can be touching, funny, shocking, heartwarming—*anything*—

SOME GUIDELINES ON ANECDOTES

Here are some questions and answers to help you as you try to find, select and shape anecdotes for your articles:

Can I make up an anecdote to illustrate a larger point?

You can, but be careful. If you create a composite character and concoct an anecdote, it's best to notify the reader with an advisory, such as, "Mary Beth is not a real person, but there are a million women like her who face the problem of. . . ." In recent years, editors have frowned more and more on the composite creation; after all, they figure, if you must rely on a bogus character and anecdote to make a point, what other shortcuts to the truth might you be taking? Besides, made-up anecdotes usually ring false. Better to search for the real-life incident.

Must I get permission to use an anecdote from someone else's life?

If he is a public figure, and it's not a private or defamatory anecdote, you're usually safe. And if it's revealed during a formal interview, you can use it without worry. But if it pertains to an ordinary citizen, you'll probably need his OK. There's a simpler solution, however: Tell the story without identifying the party or parties involved, blurring enough details to protect their identity. Writers do this all the time, including anecdotes in which the writers themselves are involved.

How much can I alter the anecdote?

Like any other element in your article, every anecdote, and the related quotations, will be subject to revision. If you blur or omit identities, you have more leeway to be creative. Also, many anecdotes come from memory and will be filtered through time and personal perspective. Your primary obligation as a journalist is to hold to the *truth* of the actual events, while tailoring the anecdote to fit your piece.

How long should an anecdote be?

Long enough to tell it well, but not a word longer. Like all stories, an anecdote has a beginning-middle-end structure: Introduce it, amplify and build in the middle, then end with your tag or punchline. It helps to keep events in straight, narrative order; keep description spare; and exclude any extraneous details. Write your anecdote with all the panache and economy that a skilled comic tells a joke: with deft timing and not a wasted word.

continued

How many anecdotes are effective in an article?

That depends on the length and nature of the article, and its general style. Too many anecdotes, however, begin to call attention to themselves; instead of being the little gem that illustrates a point, yet another anecdote will seem repetitious and distracting. As you read nonfiction writers you especially admire, see how — and how often — they use anecdotes in their work.

Where do I find anecdotes?

Everywhere. Certainly in interviews, although subjects are generally hard pressed to come up with an incredibly funny, exciting or revealing moment from their existence. You'll often come across anecdotes in other writing — articles, books, brochures, press releases, radio or TV news accounts. If you re-create the anecdote in your own words, so that it's uniquely yours, you can use it; otherwise, give attribution. And if you keep your ears open, as all writers should, you'll overhear good anecdotes on the bus, in a restaurant, wherever you happen to be.

as long as they reveal at that moment in your article exactly what you want to reveal. They are among the most difficult bits of information to ferret out in your research, especially during interviews, when they may not spring readily to your subject's mind. (Tips for mining anecdotes during interviews appear in Step Ten.) Sometimes, a reporter discovers them only firsthand, by being there, one reason I like to "hang out" as much as possible when I'm researching a story.

When I interviewed Denzel Washington on the set of a film called *Heart Condition*, I found the actor imposing and a bit cool, partly because I was asking some questions he wasn't thrilled about. The atmosphere wasn't hostile, just tense. In the midst of our conversation, a friend of the actor delivered a freshly baked pecan pie to his trailer, and Washington graciously offered me a slice.

"Is this a bribe," I asked, good-naturedly, "to get the reporter to ease up?"

"Not at all," Washington responded, breaking into a grin. "Everyone knows the pen is mightier than the pie!"

The chill lifted, and the interview thawed.

When I wrote my article, I used that anecdote — and, of course, the quote — to inject some humor into a somber, rather edgy, meeting, and to reveal another side of the actor, to humanize him. Just as the pie incident lightened the tension in our conversation, it performed a similar function in my article.

A writer can write page after page trying to make a point about a subject's character or experiences, but without a telling anecdote or two to back it up, all the words don't mean much.

When I profiled a teenage paraplegic, I wanted to capture the spirit of independence and zest for life that had survived the paralysis of his lower limbs. But I was nearing the end of the piece, and didn't have much room to get it said. This thirty-eight-word anecdote helped:

> Last summer, longing for an ocean swim, Roland hitched a rope to his wheelchair and rolled off a pier in Marina del Rey; while his friends hauled the chair out of the water, he swam to shore on his own.

If a picture is worth a thousand words, a good, succinct anecdote must be worth at least that much.

◆ ◆ ◆

Suggestion: As you read and clip articles, circle the anecdotes. Decide which ones work best, and which are less effective. Try to figure out why. Are too many anecdotes cluttering up the story? Are they too long? Too short, with not enough detail? Poorly constructed, without a proper build to the punchline? Believable, or farfetched? Appropriate for the material, or shoehorned in?

THE QUOTABLE QUOTATION

Many years ago, I interviewed actress Tatum O'Neal when she was filming *The Bad News Bears*. She had just won an Oscar for *Paper Moon* and, at age eleven, was now earning $350,000 for her second movie—big money in those days. I was fairly green at celebrity interviewing, and had made up a list of oh-so-serious questions.

"Are you concerned that there aren't enough women's roles?" I asked, putting forth a stock question of the time.

"No," she replied frankly. "I'm concerned that there aren't enough *children's* roles!"

It was a terrific response, and a wonderful quote.

Here's the kicker: I never used it.

Why? Because I didn't recognize a good quote when I saw one. I was so intent on turning in what I thought was a proper, serious piece (the assignment was my first for *The New York Times*) that I overlooked a gem.

Sometimes, in searching for the ideal quote, the clean and tidy one that says "something important," we miss the offhand, ragged or otherwise unconventional quotation that is more interesting and more revealing.

Here's a tidy one, the kind that sums up a lot of information in a short space, from an article titled "Train Wreck" in *Soldiers* magazine:

> "At first she seemed to be doing okay," Fischer recalled. "The German medic told me the ambulance was coming and he left. I don't know what happened, but within two or three minutes she died. I covered her up and stayed there until the ambulance arrived. I'll never forget her eyes," he said quietly. "They'll haunt me for as long as I live."

That's a good, solid, expositional quote, which also captures some feeling. Now, here's one that's much messier, but original, expressive and revealing, from a *Rolling Stone* profile of hard rock drummer Keith Moon:

> "I get accused of being a capitalist bastard, because, you know: 'How many cars you got?' 'Eight.' 'Big 'ouse?' 'Yes.' Well, I love all that; I enjoy it. I have lots of friends over and we sit up, drinking and partying. I need the room to entertain. I enjoy seeing other people enjoy themselves. That's where I get my kicks. I'm kinky that way. I have the amount of cars I do because I smash them up a lot. . . . They're always saying I'm a capitalist pig. I suppose I am. But ah . . . it's good for me drumming, I think. Oh-hoooo-ha-haha!"

Though wildly different in sound and style, both are good, useful quotations.

The Good, the Bad, the Unnecessary

As with anecdotes, getting a good quote depends on plenty of factors, not the least of which is the writer's interviewing skill (again, Step Ten). But a quote is often your best tool for breaking up and enlivening long stretches of text — if the quotes are *good* ones.

Some guidelines for effective quotes:

They have meaning and are pertinent to the subject. Not stuck in just because they are colorful or outrageous.

They reveal information, character or emotion. The best quotes are generally those from which the reader learns something important — about a subject, event, character's personality, etc.

They do not repeat information already provided. Just having a good quote is no reason to use it; it should serve a purpose, reinforcing a previous statement, changing the tone of the article or presenting new information, but not just filling space. *There is such a thing as too many good quotes.*

They say something better than you can say in your own words. Again, paraphrase when you can explain something more effectively than a source.

They are relatively lively and "pithy." If they are dull and flat, excise and paraphrase.

They do not run on endlessly. Even the most informative quotes get boring if they run on for pages. There is a time to break up a quote and bridge the best pieces together. Expositional quotes—"I was born and raised, etc."—tend to be particularly apt candidates for paraphrasing.

They sound "real." Not as if they've been concocted beforehand, or too carefully edited afterward.

They are placed judiciously and usefully within the copy. They may be used as leads or kickers, or within the main body of text. In general, they're most effective when sprinkled throughout the copy to add spice and variety, not served up as the main course.

The Power of a Good Quotation

Like a good anecdote, a strong quotation backs up a point you want to make. John Powers's *Boston Globe Magazine* piece on a standout Louisiana State University basketball team and its coach, Dale Brown, included the following paragraph—a declarative statement, followed by a supporting anecdote and quote:

> Brown would go anywhere for players. He turned up at Cook's high school, in New Jersey, wearing a yellow sport coat in the middle of a snowstorm. "Dale went some places where the taxi would take him only so far," says Jones. "The police had to take him the rest of the way."

Nothing fancy about that, just good, succinct, straightforward writing using a couple of key nonfiction writing techniques.

Sometimes, you'll get a quote so good, it will become the seed of an entire article. A legendary *Sports Illustrated* piece by Jack Olsen on the status of the black athlete opened with this almost matter-of-fact statement from the white athletic director of a major university:

> "In general, the nigger athlete is a little hungrier, and we have been blessed with having some real outstanding ones. We think they've done a lot for us, and we think we've done a lot for them."

TAMPERING WITH QUOTATIONS

Quotations rarely appear in print exactly as they came out of a subject's mouth. That's because they tend to be too long, rambling, boring or ungrammatical for direct transmission to the printed page. Interviewees don't talk in perfect "bites," and a writer's need and space for quotes varies widely from section to section of a given article.

Before publication, most quotations get tightened, excerpted, re-arranged and paraphrased. Also, deliberately or accidentally, writers sometimes change the words and meaning of quotations, and lift them out of context. This is the greatest danger in "cleaning up" quotations. One of the foremost responsibilities of a nonfiction writer is to pay careful attention to and maintain the original meaning and context of words exactly as they are spoken by the subject. Never arrogantly assume that you know what the source intended; if in doubt, ask — or leave the quotation alone.

Some common questions regarding a journalist's use of quotes:

Can I paraphrase quotes? Absolutely. It's done all the time. In fact, every time you print information gleaned from an interview that is not in quotation marks, you "paraphrase" the source. It should be done — again, with careful attention to accuracy — with any quotes that are long, rambling or dull.

Should I fix poor grammar in quotes? Purists might tell you to leave a quote as it is, because it's a more honest and revealing approach. But quotes are customarily cleaned up, not only as a favor to the source, but for more readable copy. Sometimes, however, poor grammar helps convey the personality or background of the subject and the flavor of his speech.

Do I have the right to rearrange wording or insert words for clearer meaning? Quotes are frequently "fixed," especially if an important point is garbled, but you might want to clear the rewritten quote with the source (they're usually pleased to sound more intelligible). If you insert a word, place it in parentheses or brackets, depending on the style of the publication you're writing for.

Do I have the right to condense quotes by trimming unnecessary verbiage? Again, it happens, but must be done with the utmost care not to alter meaning or context. Use ellipses to indicate where trims

continued

have been made.

What's the difference between "not for attribution" and "off the record"? "Not for attribution" means a source is giving you the quote, but his name should not be associated with it; if used, it must be attributed to an anonymous source. "Off the record" means the source is giving you information that is is strictly for background and not to be quoted.

Often, when sources say "This is off the record," they really mean "not for attribution," and you can talk them into giving you the quote if you promise to protect their anonymity.

After writing my rough draft, should I check quotes with my source? If you use a tape recorder (and it works), you won't need to. If you take notes and feel unsure of yourself, you should. But checking quotes can open up a can of worms: Sometimes, upon hearing their words read back, subjects will get nervous and recant them, putting you in a tough spot. Solution: Always tape, or check only those quotes about which you are uncertain.

Can I lift quotes from copyrighted material? Fair use generally allows you to "borrow" a quote or other excerpt up to a certain length, particularly for criticism, research or educational purposes. The rule of thumb is 100 words, which I've used in excerpting printed matter for this book. If you do use a copyrighted quote, credit the publication and, if possible, the writer.

For a more extensive discussion of fair use and copyright, see *Writing A to Z*, edited by Kirk Polking (Writer's Digest Books).

That quote led off what became perhaps the most famous series of stories ever published in *SI*, lending it special credence.

I don't think I realized how important a single quote can be until I profiled a world-champion boxer for *The Los Angeles Times*, an addict whose troubled relationship with his alcoholic father led partly to his own downfall inside and outside the ring. I interviewed the dad, but got almost nothing from him; a shy, recovering alcoholic, he was only comfortable when talking about boxing. Although we talked for nearly two hours about his son's boyhood, when I wrote my story, I used but two brief quotes, including this one:

"I've never told this to anyone, and I'm so sorry I did things like that, but instead of talking to him, I'd slap him around. I know now that was wrong. A father should talk to his son. Later, when he'd sober up, maybe we'd talk."

A friend of mine, also the son of an abusive alcoholic, read the piece and said to me, "I'm really glad you included that quote. It made a big difference when you got the father's voice into the story."

It reminded me how important it is to work hard for good quotes, and to use them well.

KICKERS: THE FINAL TOUCH

Kickers, those last lines or words that conclude an article, are nearly as important as your lead. A lead entices your readers, gets the story going. Your kicker finishes that story; it's your last chance to have an impact on your reader, to drive the nail home.

Just as there are no rules for the form a good lead must take, there are no magic formulas for effective kickers. They can be as simple as a quote — one of the most common types of kickers — or as creative as elaborate wordplay.

One thing that many effective kickers have in common: They help the article to "circle back," bringing the reader back to your original theme, established in your opening. At the very least, they find a "winding up" point that feels right, leaving the reader with a distinct impression, message, feeling, or important piece of information. What a kicker should *not* do is let a story just trail off, ending nowhere in particular. Although there is such a thing as a "natural close," in which an article ends fairly abruptly, and even "off-the-wall" kickers that seem to come out of nowhere, they usually bring the article to some meaningful summation, or make a point.

The Last Word

Quotes are frequently used as kickers because they seem to suggest themselves naturally — after all, they are already *written*, ready-made. Also, for reporters, they allow someone other than the writer to have the last word.

When I wrote about Sierra mule packers trying to survive in modern times — again, for *The Los Angeles Times* — my story focused on a soft-spoken young packer named Luke Messenger. Despite his college education, Luke was considering a rigorous, low-paying "career" as a mountain guide, like his boss and mentor, Walt Schober. I wrapped up my piece like this:

Messenger knows it will be a hard life, that it may leave him partially crippled in old age, and that he will have to make his real living in the off-season, working at something else. Yet it's a line of work that sets him apart, and he holds on to the dream.

"It's something about being up in the mountains," he explained, while the sunset's glow struck the granite peaks behind him. "And I really love the mules. Also, a lot of it has to do with Walt Schober, with the way he is — patient. He taught me all I know about packing.

"I guess there are a lot of reasons, but what it mainly is, I just love the way of life."

No flashy ending. Just an honest, straightforward conclusion for a story about an honest, straightforward young man.

My profile of the alcoholic ex-boxer, however, was charged with emotion, conflict and sordid detail. I wanted a poignant, inspiring close. For me, this quote did the job:

"Being sober is a totally different experience, and it isn't always easy. But I'm enthused about this program. I want sobriety, I really want it. The first time I went down to AA, the people there, they had a glow in their eyes, such serenity. Like they're at peace with themselves.

"I want that kind of peace."

Even now, that ending brings a lump to my throat, which is one of the reasons I used it in the first place.

Endless Possibilities

There are many ways to end your article besides quotes. Here are a few:

Anecdotal. "Tiny tales" can work as well for kickers as they do for leads.

For a *TV Guide* piece on comic actor Tim Reid, I needed an ending that probed the source of his humor, which came partly from a tough childhood, in which he learned to laugh through his tears. For my close, I used an anecdote in which Reid took me back to his days on the road as a stand-up comic with partner Tom Dreesen, just after the funeral of Reid's father:

"I was grieving. I walked into the hotel room, and Tom said, 'OK, did you put the dude in the ground? Can we go do some comedy now?' It was about getting on with life, and it made me laugh, and the laughter turned to tears and it became a very cleansing thing.

"And we went out and did our act."

I can hear a few readers already squawking, "But that's a *quotation!*"

Yes, it is. It's also an anecdote. It could even be a quote, anecdote, summary, and a bunch of other things all rolled into one.

Don't worry about the label; these are just guidelines, and these kicker "types" often cross over into each other's territory.

Off the wall. This catchall covers lots of territory — those "freak" endings that have some fun but still relate to the preceding text. These include what I call "fantasy" conversations, a device that Charlotte Allen and Charlotte Hays put to clever use in a *Spy* piece on Vice-President Dan Quayle. It ended with an imaginary scene — Marilyn Quayle waking in bed to find her husband in a cold sweat:

What is it, honey? Is it that Lloyd Bentsen dream again?

Kickers don't have to follow the straight and narrow; when it's appropriate, you can have lots of fun with them.

Play on words. This kind of kicker depends on the clever use or rewording of a familiar phrase. Brenda Day, stood up for an interview by a raunchy rocker named Groovie Mann, ended her piece (about being so rudely stood up) by announcing she had waited long enough and was going to take a shower. Then:

And while I'm at it, I'm going to wash that Mann right out of my hair.

Literary allusion (in this case, a song lyric), metaphor, and other figures of speech often inspire effective conclusions to an article.

Looking ahead. Prediction or speculation about what is to come, tied to your theme, is another way to end your article with a lasting impression.

Back in 1987, for *The Los Angeles Times*, I wrote a roundup piece about the response — or lack thereof — of the film and television industry to the AIDS crisis. A producer's forward-looking quote provided my ending:

"It's like the early years of the Vietnam war," he says. "When sons and brothers and boys down the street started dying, people started to be troubled by it. It's the same with AIDS.

"More and more of us will be troubled in some way, and attitudes will change."

Finding significance. With this kind of kicker, the writer finds special meaning and tacks it on to the ending in the form of a final comment. It might be speculation, the pointing out of irony, a declaration of feeling; but it's stated in the writer's voice.

My profile of a mother faced with her teenage son's sudden paralysis emphasized how she had risen to the challenge and pulled the fatherless family together. I closed the piece as the young man announced his engage-ment to be married. Then, this final line:

> Nine days later, the family gathered at the house to celebrate. Fittingly, it was Mother's Day.

By finding significance in the timing and the date, my kicker gave the story back to the mother, and left the reader thinking about my main theme.

Editorial. Exactly what the tag implies — a statement of opinion or view-point, such as this one winding up a piece by Kathleen Sharp in *Savvy Woman* on an S&L gone bust:

> Whoever the "real" North America Savings & Loan villain was — Doc, Jan, the North America board or lax government regulators — it is certain that the American taxpayers — you and I — have been left holding the now quite empty bag.

Summary. This kind of kicker attempts to tie up loose ends or sum up main points, usually through a statement of facts or a quotation. An exam-ple, from a profile in *Sea* by Neil Rabinowitz of a high-performance yacht named Katherine:

> Katherine looks chiseled, lean and mean, yet classically propor-tioned and appealing. The result of Garden's efforts is a boat that is both intimate and performance-oriented.

Advisory. This ends with a warning — about the dangers of smoking, need to invest quickly, et al. — straight at the reader. Here's one, from "Buy Now, Avoid the Rush," an *Inc.* piece by John Case:

> So it might be wise to look around — at your company, your indus-try, the marketplace you do business in — and ask yourself where, among all those seemingly sleepy companies, the entrepreneurial op-portunities lie. Because it's a safe bet that, sometime soon, the new breed of business buyers are going to come looking. When they do, you may wish you had gotten there first.

Here's another advisory: Don't worry too much about classifying your kicker.

Like most professional writers, I've written hundreds of kickers, but never tried to figure out what "type" to use, or even to think much about my conclusion as I moved toward it; as with good leads, my kickers usually sprang naturally from the research and writing process. Often, the most effective ones are not those you *try* to write, but the ones that surprise you in the writing.

Whatever emotion a kicker arouses in you, the writer — be it laughter, surprise, outrage, tears — it will probably have a similar effect on many readers.

If it feels right for your piece, use it.

THINK FORMAT

Subheads and section breakers are not the only devices you can use to structure and format your article. A number of format techniques may be right for one of your particular projects, giving it a distinct look and feel. As you study publications, be aware of how many different ways there are to put an article together. You may even want to keep a file of varied formats to give you ideas as you start your next assignment.

For now, here are a few to consider:

Bullets. We've already discussed bullets in Step Four, and you've seen examples in a number of the query letter samples (you're also reading through a set of bullets right now). Bullets allow you to pull together, organize, and make several points in quick order. Beware of doing too few — two bullets can look a little silly — or so many that they run on and on. If they encompass the entire article, it is technically a list, not a bullet, format.

Lists. The list article becomes more and more popular in this age of faster formats. It's simply an introduction, followed by a list of tips, arguments, facts and so on. *Forbes*, of course, has made lists one of its staples, coming out regularly with compilations of the top-earning companies, highest-paid sports figures and so on. *Ebony* also favors list articles, with such titles as "The Ten Biggest Myths About the Black Family" and "Forty-five Events that Changed You and Your World," two list articles that ran in the same issue.

The Diary. This is a chronological telling of a story, with each section separated by calendarlike time increments. It might be day-to-day, even minute-to-minute, providing your story with a strong narrative structure. (More on this technique in Step Eleven.)

Open letter. This is an article written in the form of a letter, often in a satirical vein. Critics like using it — in an imaginary letter to a film director or a star, for instance — but it also turns up as a format for straight articles. It allows the writer to make his points in a direct and personal way, and with wit.

Script. This format opens with "Fade In:" and then follows a screenplay format with scene or action description, character dialogue and so on.

A FEW WORDS ABOUT SIDEBARS

If you don't know what a sidebar is, you do now — you're reading one.

Sidebars are useful devices for separating a block of text, like this one, that slows down your main article but is worth highlighting in a short space. It's usually set off graphically in some way, such as in a box.

In general, editors assign sidebars either during research or after an article is turned in. But don't be afraid to suggest a sidebar if it suits the publication you target, and if you truly feel it will stand on its own, supporting your main story in a direct and pertinent way. It's a good way to save valuable material that might otherwise be trimmed.

In general, sidebars are succinct, packed with useful information, and often utilize bullets (of specific tips, resources, places to go, etc.) or another segmenting device.

Some examples that illustrate the wide range of sidebars and the purposes they might serve:

• "A Lunch Box Library," with recommended cookbooks, supporting an article on improving children's lunch box nutrition, in *Family Fun*. By including this sidebar, the magazine not only covered the value of good lunch box nutrition, but pointed parents to more detailed information on how to achieve it.

• "Six Ways to Make It Easier," accompanying a self-help piece on women learning to compete with other women, in *Working Woman*. This offered readers practical steps they could take immediately to make use of more general information found in the main piece.

• "Pizza Power," a bar graph charting the decline in meals eaten at home and the increase in eating out, illustrating an article on dining trends in *American Demographics*. This was an informative, visual way to underscore a primary point of the main text.

• "Another Type of Diabetes," a 500-word sidebar on adult-onset diabetes in an article about dealing with diabetes through vegetarianism, in *Vegetarian Times*. This was a case of salvaging a sizable block of important information that would have slowed the main story down.

If there were any doubts about the value and increasing popularity of sidebars, they were dispelled by *Modern Maturity*, when it ran a

continued

whopping ten sidebars with Michele Bekey's special consumer report on telefraud and other ripoffs. These included such information-packed sidebars as "The Twenty Most Insidious Cons Operating," "Ten Ways to Sidetrack a Scam" and "Where to Turn for Help."

Generally, editors pay extra if they use a sidebar or request you write one, or negotiate it as part of a package payment.

Sometimes, it's used just for the opening, before the article shifts to more traditional form. This format can also be adapted to imitate a TV script, stage play, radio play, etc.

Expect to see more articles of shorter length in the years ahead, with a wide range of more visual and "reader-friendly" formats. Along with *USA Today*, magazines like *Esquire*, *Spy* and *Entertainment Weekly* have been experimenting and leading the way for some time, and others will certainly follow.

WHAT'S IN A TITLE?

Two questions I hear frequently in the classroom: "Should I suggest a title for my proposed article in my query?" and "Should I include a title on my manuscript?"

I write titles on most of my articles before submitting them, because I like that extra opportunity up top to catch the editor's attention, let him know what the piece is about, and make a strong first impression. Even when it's assigned, an article goes into a pile to be dealt with later, unless it's top priority. An editor may take days or weeks getting to it and will often select a manuscript because a title catches his eye and gives him a reason to read that piece *now*.

If you're not confident in your headline-writing skills, however, skip it. A weak title may not be enough to get your manuscript rejected, but it won't help its chances, either.

Here are some of the most common mistakes I've seen in writer-written titles:

Flat. The dull, lifeless headline prepares the editor to read a dull, lifeless manuscript; fair or not, the "hed" can prejudice the reading, especially of those first crucial paragraphs.

Flat: *A Mother Pulls Her Family Together*

Better: *After Overcoming a Family Tragedy, She's Earned a Special Mother's Day*

Better Yet: *When Tragedy Struck, This Mom Responded*

Uninformative. A title doesn't have to convey the entire story. But unless it's a deliberate, off-the-wall teaser, it should at least tip the editor to the nature of the piece.

Uninformative: *Mountain Packers Face Challenge*

Better: *Mountain Packers Face Challenge of Changing Times*

Better Yet: *Sierra Mule Packers Buck Modern Times*

Long and convoluted. Unless it's purposefully windy for stylistic effect, the "KISS" rule applies: Keep It Simple, Stupid.

Long and convoluted: *He May Be Devoted to His Church and Young People, But Jesse Jackson Never Lets His Political Goals Get Too Far Out of Sight*

Better: *Jesse Jackson Tends His Youthful Flock — and Looks After His Political Future, Too*

Better Yet: *Jesse Jackson's Still Pushing Heaven, Hard Work — and Himself* (actual headline used by *Today*, the magazine of the *Philadelphia Inquirer*)

Inappropriate. Make sure your title not only conveys what your article is about, but stays in the appropriate tone. You wouldn't use a wiseacre pun in a headline for a story of poignancy or tragedy. Likewise, a humor piece should probably be slugged with something punchy or witty.

Inappropriate: *One Man's Disturbing Story of a Life Nearly Destroyed by a Faulty Car Alarm*

Better: *A New Car Owner Who Encountered the Alarming Side of Life*

Better Yet: *How a Paranoid Yuppie Learned to Live Without a Car Alarm — And Sleep Soundly Again*

Clichéd, too cute or simply "lame." Puns and other clever wordplay are a favorite headline-writing device. But beware the strained attempt at wordplay or the clichéd phrase that doesn't say much — or, worse, that starts your editor off wincing and groaning.

Lame: *Rain, Sleet or Snow, Willard Scott's In the Know*

Better: *Willard Scott — Raindrops Keep Fallin' On His Smilin' Head*

Better Yet: *Willard Scott — A Weatherman for All Seasons*

My Style — or Theirs?

Freelance writers are often advised to write their titles in a style that conforms to that of their target publication. However, published headlines, particularly those in flashier magazines, tend toward the succinct and cute (puns proliferate), or the wild and wacky; they're supported by decks, photographs and other visuals to let readers know what they're getting, which is not true of your manuscript.

For example, "You Don't Know Jack" was the brief title of an *Entertain-*

ment Weekly cover story on Jack Nicholson, with a head shot of the famous actor coyly raising his famous eyebrow. That was enough, apparently, to catch the attention of readers and sell copies of the magazine. The title of another *EW* piece, an update of a popular television show, went to the other extreme: "What Has 10 Legs, 30,000,000 Viewers, 2 New Faces and a Southern Accent? *Designing Women*."

I'm not sure either one of those published titles would have served the best purpose at the top of an incoming manuscript, though the second one is certainly eye-catching.

The answer, of course, is to write in the style of the target publication *and* convey what's in your manuscript, prompting an editor to pick your article, rather than another, from the teetering pile.

A FEW WORDS BEFORE STARTING

When we see the word *precede*, we tend to think of the verb meaning "to preface, to come before." But *precede* (pronounced *pray-seed*, accent on the first syllable) is also a noun and journalism term, referring to a unit of text that prefaces the main body of an article, used to provide preliminary information, tweak curiosity, set tone, establish theme and so forth.

Time magazine's Nancy Gibbs used a biblical quotation to set up her story about an elderly convict — a God-fearing model prisoner — about to be freed from a prison for a crime committed forty-five years earlier:

> And, behold, the angel of the Lord came upon him, and a light shined in the prison . . . . And his chains fell off from his hands.
> — ACTS 12:7

Judith Newman found a powerful precede for her first-person piece in *Gentleman's Quarterly*, about the problems women can have dealing with the mothers of boyfriends and husbands:

> The mealy look of men today is the result of momism and so is the pinched and baffled fury in the eyes of womankind.
> — PHILIP WYLIE, *Generation of Vipers*

Many writers, finding precedes to be a nice "literary" touch, are tempted to use them more than some editors would like. Most of my precedes were deleted before publication, but a few got through, and I've since learned to be more judicious with them.

For my profile of the troubled boxer, Mando Ramos, I found a precede in the clip files at *The Los Angeles Times*:

Mando Ramos . . . a teenage phenom who has everything—looks, personality and great natural talent. He's the Elvis Presley of the boxing ring.
—SID ZIFF (sports columnist), *Los Angeles Times*, June 2, 1967

I used this precede because Ramos had been out of the public eye for nearly two decades, and because the profile appeared on the lifestyle page, which is heavily read by women; I wanted to sell my subject to less sports-minded female readers, right at the start.

We're all tempted to dress up our articles as much as we can, showing off how clever and well read we are. Before pinning a precede on your article like a piece of costume jewelry, ask these five questions:

- Does it serve a purpose?
- Is it appropriate for this material and type of article? For the publication or section it's headed for?
- Do I "pay off" the precede later, either directly or indirectly, by the story I tell?
- Is my precede so off-the-wall or obscure that it will only distract or confuse?
- Is it so long that it discourages the reader from getting to the start of my story?

DOT, DOT, DASH, DASH (ETC.)

Now, for the truly tiny devices that can sometimes spice up your writing: style marks that can have an impact on pacing, rhythm and readability.

A few examples:

Ellipsis points. Those three little dots known as an ellipsis are most commonly used to bridge quotations that have been tightened up, indicating excised words ("I wish I could have been at the train to meet her . . . I might have warned her"). But ellipsis points can also be used to indicate a trailing off of a thought . . .

. . . or emergence into a new one.

They can help pace bits of information clustered together, in this way:

I find myself procrastinating more and more instead of writing this book. You know, washing the dishes . . . watering the plants . . . scratching the cat . . . taking yet another nap!

Dashes. These little marks can also be used to set off material—something you want to highlight, like this—or merely to tighten up a sentence. Let's start out with this:

Writing is like any other craft, be it carpentry or cooking or surgery; the more you do it, the more natural it feels.

Now, some editing and a few dashes:

Like any other craft — carpentry, cooking, surgery — the more writing you do, the more natural it feels.

Used naturally, in the smooth course of your writing, dashes can be like mortar to a bricklayer, helping cement words and phrases. Used too often or inappropriately, they call too much attention to themselves.

Parentheses. The same can certainly be said for the parenthetical phrase. Parentheses are useful for slipping comments or bits of information into your copy that you don't want to intrude into your main line of discourse (providing they aren't too long or complicated), but too many of them will disrupt the flow of your copy, distracting and making the reader work harder.

My colleague, Pat H. Broeske, sprinkled her manuscripts heavily with parenthetical phrases until a reader sent a letter to the editor in response to one of Pat's articles:

Congratulations are certainly due (and how!) to Sigourney Weaver (the actress), who gave (or endured, more likely) three dozen (that's thirty-six) one-on-one interviews for her new (and rather remarkable) movie (known as *Gorillas in the Mist*).

But (isn't it always the case?) the real prize (what a trophy it should be) goes to Pat H. Broeske (the author of the article "Gorillas in the Press," Oct. 30) for using (so subtly too) parentheses (here I am again) a total of thirty-one times in her epic article . . .

And so on.

Pat, who provided the above letter for this book, still uses parentheses (but more judiciously).

However, you can use parentheses as a stylistic device to add humor and emphasis to prose. An example, from *Newsweek*'s George Will, on a scandalous government subsidy for the rich:

Oh? The wealthy travelers (few from Harlem or Watts) taking deductible trips (another subsidy) to a tony watering spot (three golf courses, stocked trout streams, skeet range, spa) will stay home and sulk unless taxpayers foot part of their travel bill?

Will, a writer who knows his craft, knew full well he was overdoing his use of parenthetical phrases; he did it deliberately, to reinforce his point.

◆ ◆ ◆

In Step Eight, we've covered some techniques that can add spice to your writing; we'll explore others in later chapters.

For now, let's take a break from writing craft, and examine writing *content*.

That's Step Nine: Getting the Goods.

Step Nine

Getting the Goods

After three weeks of attending class, one of my students dropped out. A working mother, she was bright, upbeat, and seemed to have some writing talent. I called her to find out why she'd quit.

"When I enrolled, I thought I wanted to write a book," she said, laughing. "I learned that I didn't want to *write* a book—I wanted to *have written* a book!"

She'd had the notion that she could write a fact-based book pretty much off the top of her head, not realizing that most nonfiction requires not just comment and opinion, but nuts and bolts—*specifics*. Although some humor, nostalgia and other "light" features can be written without much research, even they need *concreteness*.

Nonfiction writing isn't just writing; it's information-gathering and writing. If words and language alone are your passion, you'd better stick to poetry.

SHOW, DON'T TELL

We've all heard the basic points most articles cover: *who, what, where, when, how, why*. But covering these main points either skimpily or with generalities doesn't get the job done—not in your queries, your articles, your book proposals or your books. You'll need plenty of the aforementioned nuts and bolts that give substance to your articles.

Some nuts and bolts come in the form of the anecdotes and quotations already discussed. But it's not enough to just stick in the odd quotation or incident. Writing in a nuts-and-bolts way is partly a developed style, as William Strunk made clear in *The Elements of Style*, when he wrote: "Prefer the specific to the general, the definite to the vague, the concrete to the abstract."

Countless editors put it this way: *Show, don't tell.*

Don't tell us Michael Jordan is tall. Tell us how many feet and inches. Mention that he ducks when walking under awnings, looks *down* on Joe Montana, bumps his head in small cars. Don't tell us someone is nervous; tell us how many packs of cigarettes she smokes, if she paces, fidgets, has ulcers. Don't tell us California has a serious earthquake problem. Tell us how many earthquakes the state has had in the last ten years, how many to expect in the next ten. Tell us how many lives, buildings and dollars have been lost, how wide and deep the fissures were. Don't tell us that people suffered, *show* us — with an anecdote, figure, quote, vivid description.

Let's say you're profiling a rock star:

Telling: He makes a fortune singing and playing the guitar.

Showing: In 1991, his gross income from concerts and albums was $16 million, placing him on *Forbes* magazine's Top Forty list of highest-paid entertainers.

Telling: He loves his guitar.

Showing: He got shot trying to save his guitar from robbers.

Telling: He was inconsiderate, slovenly and rude.

Showing: He sauntered in an hour late, sneering, and spent the next hour blowing smoke in my face as he chain-smoked. The ashes fell on an unpressed shirt already stained with God-knows-what, and his chin stubble and sour breath suggested he'd been up all night. "Screw you," he snapped, when I asked if I might have a follow-up interview when he was more rested.

Which versions do you find more interesting?

Details! Details! Details!

From time to time, at some publications, you'll hear a copyeditor holler, "Adjective alert!" That means she has found another needless adjective with which a lazy writer is trying to take a shortcut instead of doing some real reporting.

An adjective or adverb now and then is no crime, and sometimes they can be laid on heavily for deliberate, exaggerated effect. But to convince and hold your readers, and satisfy your editors, you must come up with details. Some examples of showing, rather than just telling, right off the printed page:

• When *Parade* profiled oceanic scientist Sylvia Earle, it wasn't enough to say she was dedicated and brave. The writer made the point that, *at five-foot-three* and *110 pounds*, Earle had spent *6,000 hours* underwater, surviving *shark* and *lionfish attacks*.

- In covering abortion protests in Wichita, Kansas, a *Time* article mentioned the hostile reaction by some to a doctor who performs late-term abortions. To underscore that point, writer Jon D. Hull added that the doctor "wears a bulletproof vest to work and checks his car for bombs every morning."
- In her first-person piece for *Virtue*, "Giving Away the Fantasy When I Gave Away My Daughter," Debra Evans needed to say more than "my daughter and I were very different," which was central to Evans's theme. To make an effective comparison, she needed details:

> You see, I'm fairly quiet and serious; a woman who enjoys foreign films, reading in libraries and shopping at bargain stores for top-name clothing and china.
>
> Joanna, on the other hand, relishes memories of being the loudest varsity cheerleader on her squad, never reads *The Wall Street Journal* or C.S. Lewis, likes Jean Claude Van Damme movies and makes spaghetti Ragu-style. She also likes thrift stores but for a different reason: bargain-priced lingerie.

Without that kind of detail, no editor would have been interested in the piece, and probably would not have read past the first page or two.

- For my profile of the mother coping with the paralysis of her teenage son, it would have been pointless to state that she was "anguished"; the article demanded hard, convincing evidence. So I included this:

> She describes a nightmarish scene the first time she saw him in Northridge Hospital Medical Center: Roland immobile, with a device called "Crutchfield's thongs" fitted into holes drilled in his skull, weighted with sixty-five pounds to stretch his head and neck upward. When nurses turned him every two hours, his mother recalled, "I could only stand the screaming for a few minutes, then I had to get out of the room."

To me, that descriptive scene — seventy-one words — is worth a thousand words of vague copy about how painful the tragedy was.

- Statistics and other concrete figures are an excellent way to show, instead of tell. In its table of contents, *American Health* claimed that cancer survivors constitute "a growing army"; in his article, writer John Ritter supported that statement with these specifics:

> About 40 percent of the 1.1 million people diagnosed with cancer

this year will live five years or more. For people fifty-five and younger with certain types of cancer, survival rates are 90 percent or higher. Demographics alone will greatly expand the survivor pool. By the year 2000, the American Cancer Society estimates, there will be about 10 million cancer survivors.

• A telling document or other core piece of evidence can also provide your general statements with the support they need; indeed, the more serious your claims, the more you need to back them up.

In a *Los Angeles Times* opinion piece about the government's insensitivity to AIDS-afflicted people, I used this concrete example from the life of a friend, whose applications for supplemental social security income were repeatedly denied:

> The final rejection came in a form letter bearing the signature of President Reagan's Social Security Administration director, Dorcas R. Hardy. It stated simply, "We do not consider you disabled at this time," and suggested that Jon-Noel reapply in three months.
> The letter arrived two weeks after he died.

For me, that letter was the dramatic, concrete evidence, the smoking gun, that made my point.

• Even when your writing is more fanciful, details are crucial. In his column for *Condé Nast Traveler*, Simon Winchester wrote of the spectacular and sometimes "nail-biting" experience of approaching Hong Kong's Kai Tak Airport. But he didn't just tell us, he *showed* us, with these details:

> With the glittering skyline of Victoria to your right and the jungle green mountains of China to your left, you skim lower and lower over the tenements of Kowloon until it seems that your wheels are touching the very roofs themselves. For a few moments you are unbelievably close: Old hands say that engine blasts from passing jets dry the locals' wash famously and that observant and obsessive TV watchers on board the incoming plane can catch an entire sequence of Dallas as they flash past 10,000 televisions gleaming from 10,000 apartment windows.

Winchester writes wonderfully, mixing fact and fantasy, but he's also an excellent observer and reporter, who knows the value of details.

◆ ◆ ◆

Here's a simple exercise: Take one boring story and one you find unusually interesting. Go through both, underlining each fact, detail and anecdote. See which one has the most.

Now, go through an article you're working on. With a red pen, circle all your generalities, adverbs or adjectives, as in "painful experience," "wonderful personality," "incredibly fast," "beautiful scenery." Then underline each concrete fact, statistic, image, example, anecdote, revealing quote, etc.

Your piece should have plenty of the latter and relatively few of the former.

DEPTH, BALANCE, PERSPECTIVE

Back in the mid-1980s, *The Los Angeles Times* asked me to put together a comprehensive article on the cultural boycott of South Africa. This was a movement, instigated by an antiapartheid group within the United Nations and supported by other organizations, to pressure top-name entertainers not to perform in South Africa, to "isolate" the country culturally.

Ignoring the boycott became a serious stigma in liberal Hollywood; I had no problem getting interviews with such proboycott entertainers as Harry Belafonte and Goldie Hawn. But after three dozen interviews, I had no one on the record defending her right to perform and make a living wherever she pleased. Even as I put the piece through its final drafts, I continued calling publicists and managers, seeking someone brave enough to buck popular sentiment.

Finally, producer Saul Zaentz returned my calls and forcefully defended the South African tour with which he and director Milos Forman promoted their Oscar-winning film, *Amadeus*. I quoted and paraphrased him at length, up high in my story, including these words:

> "I don't have to defend my background. I would not apologize at all. Milos and I are totally against apartheid. But we would do business there the same as any other country. . . .
>
> "People tend to come up with facile answers to the problem. I don't know the answer, but isolation isn't the answer. I think isolation will *strengthen* apartheid. We all need a better education . . . does anyone feel we'll make progress by isolating them?"

Why had I worked so hard to get that single response, and to make so much of it? Because, to me, it was crucial to discuss free trade, free travel and free expression — the "other side" of the boycott issue that no one was talking about. The piece could have run without Zaentz's comments, but it wouldn't have had the same credibility or balance.

Digging Deeper

Some articles don't require so much research and "reporting." If you write lightweight features ("Ten Super Snacks for Super Bowl Sunday"), you can get away with relatively little. Likewise, if you write blatant, advocacy journalism, with a strongly slanted viewpoint or agenda—for example, my piece on the government's insensitivity to persons with AIDS—you probably won't spend much time telling the other side.

But if you intend to write articles of much scope and substance, you must dig. Anytime you read a roundup or survey piece on a serious or controversial subject, and see half a dozen people quoted, it's quite possible the writer interviewed two or three times that many people, using only the most effective or appropriate quotations.

Some reporters assigned to substantive pieces concentrate on getting to certain sources; others go after documentation; and some want both.

When I wrote a multipart series for *The Los Angeles Times* on copyright infringement and plagiarism involving film and television, I investigated a number of separate lawsuits. It wouldn't have been enough with each segment to just state the basics, chat with both sides, and write it up. To do the series well, I had to get hold of the original scripts and treatments, affidavits and other records, look into the backgrounds of the principal parties on both sides, review legal books and talk to legal experts, and analyze it all—*before* sitting down to interview plaintiffs, defendants and related parties.

Likewise, for a survey piece on Hollywood's response to the AIDS crisis, my interviews numbered nearly fifty, including AIDS experts and activists, actors, producers, directors, writers, and network and studio executives. It was too important an issue to shortchange.

Even if you only intend to interview a handful of sources for a less-complex issue, a certain amount of planning, persistence and legwork is required. Here are some strategies for coming up with "the goods," and giving your articles depth and balance:

Brainstorm. When you get your assignment, think it through. In a general sense, what should it cover? How broad is its scope? Who are the essential interviewees? Bounce your angle off other journalists or media-savvy friends to come up with facets worth including and sources worth interviewing. Public relations people can be surprisingly helpful, especially when they talk off the record and strictly for background, because the good ones know a *lot*.

List every possible source. When you get your assignment, jot down the name (and telephone or fax number) of anyone who might be able to

DON'T JUST ASK A, B AND C

When he was Sunday arts and entertainment editor at *The Los Angeles Times*, Irv Letofsky was fond of telling his disciples: "Most writers ask A, B and C. Writers who are good reporters ask D, E and F." Letofsky was talking about several approaches that characterize a probing interview:

- Thinking beyond the predictable and expected.
- Asking questions that get beneath the surface of a topic or area of discussion.
- Asking questions that challenge.
- Developing interesting or experimental lines of questioning.
- Developing questions that take the reporter where she wants to go—not necessarily where the subject wants to go.

For example, let's look at a hypothetical interview between a reporter and a producer:

Reporter: "How involved were you in the TV series, 'Bimbo on Board,' which was spun off your movie, *Lethal Bimbo?*" (Question A, straightforward and innocent.)

Subject: "Not as much as I would have liked."

Reporter: "Why do you say that?" (B, nonthreatening but probing a little.)

Producer: "It could have been a better show."

Reporter: "In what way?" (C, still straightforward, but digging a bit more.)

Producer: "I think if the scripts had been better, and I'd kept a closer eye on it, it might have been successful, or at least of a higher quality."

OK, that takes care of questions A, B and C. Many writers would stop there, happy to have a confession from a producer that her TV series wasn't terrific. But a good reporter would continue, asking D, E and F, which might go like this:

Reporter: "What about the way the show treated women? Some critics, male and female, found the show sexist." (D, a challenging question.)

Subject: "As I said, I didn't have the kind of control I would have liked. I was off making feature films, which took most of my time."

Reporter: "I saw one episode where the female stars were cavorting

continued

and jiggling in negligees—pretty blatant T and A. . . ." (E, tougher and more specific.)

Subject: "I'm not proud of that, believe me, especially as someone who has supported feminism for so many years. It's certainly not what we intended or envisioned at the outset."

Reporter: "What would you do differently next time?" (F, giving the subject the ball to see where she carries it.)

Subject: "I learned that it's impossible to develop quality scripts under the time constraints of turning out a weekly television show. I'd like to be involved in TV again, but I'll never try to do another weekly series."

Conceivably, the reporter could continue in this direction, asking G, H, I, J, K, etc., taking the line of questioning deeper.

◆ ◆ ◆

The above "interview," by the way, is based closely on one that actually took place.

help you. These might be names gleaned from printed material, friends, associates, whomever. These people will not only provide you with many of your interviews, they'll frequently point you to other excellent sources.

See it from different angles. There are always conflicting sides to an issue, different ways of solving a problem and so on. You may write from a certain viewpoint, but seeing your story from different angles in the beginning will help you amplify your research and interviewing. And when you go into your research with an open mind, you'll be surprised at how often your viewpoint changes.

Discuss it with your editor. What does she expect you to deliver? If she has the time and seems amenable, discuss the article's range with her, without sounding naive or at a loss. Exchange ideas.

Think "article type." What type of article are you writing? What special qualities does this suggest? (See page 36 for sidebar on article types and how they serve the reader.) What does it mean in terms of fact-gathering?

See it as a reader. If you were a paying subscriber or newsstand purchaser, what would you expect from this piece?

Go to alternative resources. There are countless libraries, archives, data-base systems, etc., where experts can help you find valuable research material. Think of the librarian as a writer's best friend.

Put people into your piece. Gathering facts is fine, but getting the personal element into your article makes it not only more involving and entertaining, but gives it more dimension. Find the human story that helps tell *your* story.

Pay attention to detail. This goes back to our "show, don't tell" approach. Become a keen listener and observer, particularly of tiny and seemingly insignificant details. Learn to write down everything—from the color of the carpet to dandruff on a subject's collar—because you'll never know when or how it will help you tell your story.

Assume nothing. Go into your research to find out the facts, not just to verify what you think them to be. Then, double-check your facts meticulously, never assuming something to be correct. This will not only assure the accuracy of what you print, but open up your world of research at the outset.

One reward you'll discover as you do intensive research: how much people are willing to help you. If you're enthusiastic about getting your story, and getting it right, most people you contact for help will become enthusiastic as well. Indeed, you'll sometimes be embarrassed by how much strangers will go out of their way to be of assistance. Don't be. As veteran freelance writer Hayes B. Jacobs once advised: "Bask in it, revel in it, and be grateful for it."

FLEXING YOUR MENTAL MUSCLE

Except for the most simple fact-based or lightweight pieces, editors want something more: depth combined with viewpoint. Some call it "perspective."

When she was executive editor at *New West*, Rosalie Wright put it this way: "We're not looking just for reports, but for stories from behind the scenes, in depth, with point of view and analysis—*muscle*."

To put that kind of mental muscle into your articles, it helps to ask two questions: "Why?" and "What does it mean?"

For example:

• Why do some aspiring writers lack discipline and willpower? What does it mean to their chances of success?

• Why is so-and-so an erratic actor? What does it mean to the films he makes, and his career?

• Why is a serial killer still loose in such-and-such a county? What does it mean to the quality of life for local residents?

• Why do so many battered women stay with abusive husbands? What does it mean to the self-esteem of their children?

- Why do we allow so much toxic dumping? What does it mean to world health and the future of the planet?

Not long ago, two friends, both seasoned journalists, asked me to read their book proposal, the biography of a famous business tycoon and his lifetime of obsessive relationships with women. I told them I thought the information was fascinating, but lacked a crucial element that would help elevate it to a more serious level.

"What's missing is the *why*," I said. "You've put together some terrific anecdotes and details, but you never suggest what it all means, why he had such troubled relationships and lived his life the way he did. Find out the why, and you'll have a book with something special."

They dug more, uncovered important revelations about the man's relationship with his mother, and wrote a proposal that had considerably more perspective and dimension. It got them a six-figure advance.

Tough, Not "Puff"

Premiere once ran a profile of Dustin Hoffman that made clear from the outset that the writer, Peter Biskind, greatly admired the actor. At first glance, it appeared the profile was probably a hopeless "puff piece."

The term *puff piece* applies to an article that treats a subject with the softest kid gloves, adopting a tone that is adoring and reverential, not unlike a publicist's typical "puff job."

Biskind's article, however, turned out to be a rich, well-rounded profile, an excellent piece of entertainment journalism. What saved it was its depth and balance: Biskind went to great lengths to interview people who had worked with Hoffman, getting a broad cross-section of opinions and anecdotes, including some that characterized him as fussy, temperamental, egotistical, infuriating. Overall, the profile was a tribute to a dedicated, perfectionist actor, yet included his idiosyncrasies and all-too-human flaws.

More recently, a profile turned up on another actor, Warren Beatty, in a West Coast newspaper. It opened with a fawning account of the filmmaker, chronicling at length how the reporter had hung out in buddy-buddy fashion with Beatty and what a swell time they had. It was an embarrassing piece of puffery that weak editorial judgment had let slip into print.

Both Biskind and the second reporter were experienced, respected journalists. Why had Biskind been able to maintain his distance while the second reporter seemed to lose all objectivity?

With Beatty, it appeared to be a classic case of a media-savvy star charming and seducing an interviewer, hoping for a softer piece, and the star-struck reporter falling for it. Such hero-worship is no sin; but it's unprofessional when we allow it to damage, rather than inspire, our work — something that's happened to many of us at one time or another, including yours truly.

To some extent, nonfiction writers are a gullible and needy lot; working on "the outside," often reporting on the successes of others when we wish we could claim more of our own, we sometimes feel like "wallflowers at the orgy," as a veteran journalist once termed it. That can lead to mean-spirited envy, the hatchet job — or its opposite, the worshipful puff piece.

The powerful and publicity-minded often spot our need to have them like us, because our own lives might not shine as brightly. It can happen in any field — sports, business, medicine, education, politics, anywhere there are successful women and men worth interviewing. That's why they so often flatter us, praise our work, buy us expensive lunches or gifts, even suggest we ought to work for them (*after* the article appears, of course). And some of us lap it up.

The danger is not in having this weakness, or related flaws, because we all have them; the trouble comes with not being willing or able to recognize, acknowledge and overcome them. Denying or simply ignoring our soft spots makes them easily exploited by others and can seriously impede our ability as reporters.

It's important to capture a person's positive qualities in an article, but it's also a reporter's duty — uncomfortable as it sometimes might be — to ask tough questions and to look for the negatives that round out, sometimes even define, a subject. You don't have to do a hatchet job to give a story balance and depth; you just have to be a reporter first and fan second. If you write your piece worried that your subject might not like it, you probably belong in publicity, not journalism.

What to Do About It

Often, you can avoid a gushy tone simply by replacing sweet adjectives with concrete example. For instance, instead of telling us that a corporate executive is "surprisingly nice" or "amazingly considerate," mention that she was prompt for the interview or asked permission to smoke. If your subject was *inconsiderate* — or terse, manipulative, foulmouthed, whatever — be sure to let us know that, too. Arguments on a film set? Insensitivity by a doctor toward a patient? Sexist remarks in the locker room? Criminal past? Mustard on the tie? Watch for the details, good and bad, that reveal the person. If they're pertinent, put them in your piece. They will help to make it more credible — and compelling.

CONFLICT OF INTEREST

One piece of advice beginning nonfiction writers hear frequently is to write about things they are familiar with and have some expertise in. However, a writer can be *too close* to some subjects to write about them with objectivity.

As a general rule, don't write about any person, organization or institution from which you derive income, or anyone with whom you have a close personal relationship, unless you state it in your article.

If you grow begonias, it's perfectly fine to write about begonias in general; the more expert you are, the more value it adds to your article. But it's *not* OK to write about the nursery that employs you, or the owner, unless you let the reader know. It's not OK to write about a begonia-growing contest that pays you to be a judge or consultant, unless you state as much in your article. Even to write about a rival or competitor without informing the reader is wrong. To get such an assignment without letting the editor know about those relationships is a blatant conflict of interest that could cause you serious professional damage in the long run.

A *TV Guide* editor once put it to me this way: "You have to give us some vinegar with the sugar." Others will tell you they want a portrait with "warts and all." As an editor, I've sent countless pieces back to contributors with the words: "Too soft. Needs an edge. Toughen it up." And I've had my own work come back with similar instructions. It's something that can be applied, not just to profiles, but any article where objectivity, thoroughness and serious reporting are called for.

Here are some questions you might ask as you go over your rough draft:

- Have I been too kind to this subject?
- Have I asked hard enough questions, or did I let her off the hook?
- Am I leaving out pertinent but unpleasant details to avoid hurting someone's feelings?
- Am I too close to this subject to write with reasonable objectivity?
- Did my subject deliberately charm me, hoping I'd go easy on her? Did I fall for it?
- Am I presenting a reporter's well-rounded portrait — or writing more like a P.R. person?
- What unflattering facts have I left out and why?

In certain publications and departments, soft pieces are appropriate. But if we make a habit of churning out fluff, we can't expect to be taken seriously as nonfiction writers — or get the choice assignments that go to those with the skills and instincts of a good reporter.

FINDING SOURCES AND INFORMATION

A newspaper intern once asked me frantically how he could get certain information on a high-profile Hollywood lawsuit. I suggested he contact the plaintiff's lawyer, since they're usually the most willing to talk.

"But how can I find out who the plaintiff's lawyer is?" the intern wondered.

"Have you checked the press clippings?" I asked.

The intern headed for the newspaper's library and came back with the lawyer's name.

"But how do I find him?" the intern asked.

My reply: "Have you tried the phone book?"

Sometimes, figuring out whom to talk to and how to find them is merely a matter of common sense.

"Who Would Know?"

"Who would know?" is a good starting question as you put together a list of preliminary sources. If you're investigating ecological disaster, an environmental organization should know. If a movie is involved, the studio's publicity department ought to know. If milk products in general are your topic, a dairy association might know. If your focus is a specific product, the public relations arm of the manufacturer should prove helpful. If you're after a particular person, ask yourself where she might work or what groups she might belong to — a union, the PTA, a particular club. If suicide is the subject, a suicide prevention hot line probably knows — or can point you to other sources.

Here are a number of resources that can be useful in locating sources and/or needed information:

The telephone book. Not only will you often find telephone numbers for names already in hand, but the Yellow Pages can provide ready lists of businesses, associations and experts related to specific goods and services. Recently, on deadline, I needed to know the approximate weight of an average single-engine light plane. The Federal Aviation Agency came to mind, but it was closed for the day. So I hit the Yellow Pages, called a company that sells and services such aircraft, was put through to the chief mechanic, and got my information.

Press clippings. Most nonfiction writers compile a file of "clips" on their subject before starting their own research and scour them not just for information, but names that might become their own sources. You can do it on your own, and supplement your files by checking clips at your local library. Use these primarily as a reference for further research, however, not for tacking together the notorious "clip" job (regurgitating printed information).

Warning: Beware of inaccurate information in print. Not long ago, writing about a life-or-death river rescue, I found the river spelled three different ways in four articles, and varying versions of how many people were saved. Double-check everything.

Data-base services. On-line computer information services are the new wave of research, indispensible for full-time reporters doing in-depth investigations and useful as well for lighter features. They vary in specialization, but for a fee, they can give you computer access to library files, resource centers, public records, magazine and newspaper articles and more. Nexus, CompuServ, Prodigy, Genie, Delphi, American On-Line, and hundreds of other on-line services are reshaping and redefining research as we move toward the twenty-first century.

Like printed mistakes, a danger of the data-base revolution is that factual errors become embedded in the system and are repeated endlessly as they get picked up in other articles. Again, check all facts.

"Take a hard look at the data," warns Los Angeles City librarian Dan Strehl, "where it came from and how it was validated."

Publicists and P.R. people. Although some reporters consider publicists and P.R. people the enemy, they don't have to be. Like journalists, they vary in skill, integrity and intelligence. While they are paid to represent and protect the interests of clients or employers, they will often provide useful background information, and they can help you with fact-checking in relation to their clients. Do not place much trust in press releases, however, except for general leads; they are often slanted toward clients and notoriously inaccurate. Use them with caution.

The best P.R. people, even while uncomfortable with your angle or the nature of your questions, will go off the record to help you broaden your scope or viewpoint and write a better story. Part of their job is to dissuade you from portraying their clients in a negative light, but they are also paid to act as a conduit between client and media. Make friends with the helpful ones; they can be a valuable part of your network of sources.

Business, professional and specialist directories. If there is a problem or activity that affects large numbers of people — rape, farming, education, shoe manufacturing, you name it — there is probably an association for it, with experts and information. How do you find these thousands of associations? Try the *Encyclopedia of Associations*, available at just about any public library. When I needed some critical feedback on a soft-drink commercial involving sightless singer Ray Charles, I looked up "blind" in the *Encyclopedia of Associations* and found nearly a dozen nonprofit organizations willing to help.

Other excellent resource books include *The National Directory of Addresses and Phone Numbers*; *The Research Centers Directory*; *State and Regional Associations of America*; regional foundation directories such as *The Guide to California Foundations*; the *Directory of Experts, Authorities and Spokespersons*; *Directory of U.S. Labor Organizations*; *Foundation Directory*; *The Directory of Medical Specialists*; and so on. And there's the umbrella-like *The Directory of Directories*, an annotated list of more than 5,000 directories published in North America, and *The Dictionary of Directories*, with a wide range of information sources.

Biographical dictionaries. *Who's Who in America* is probably the best known, but there are others, including *Current Biography*, *Celebrity Register* and *Directory of American Scholars*.

Indexes. A number of indexes at the public library list and catalog publications by title, date, article subject, author and so on. The most familiar is *Reader's Guide to Periodical Literature*, but others, such as *Magazine Index*, *Business Periodicals Index* and *CBS News Index*, encompass a wide range of information.

Public libraries. A librarian is a reporter's best friend. Reference librarians can answer virtually any question, and some major branches have special telephone access lines, such as Los Angeles County's Community Access Library Line (CALL), which will either answer your question or refer you to an appropriate source.

The librarian will help you to make sense of the huge public library research system, and to find virtually any of the myriad directories and other resource guides. You'll even find out-of-date telephone books at some branches, which can be useful in locating sources who no longer list their telephone number.

Specialized libraries and archives. You'll find them at various universities, newspapers, institutes, museums and so forth, including several regional branches of the National Archives. Three books can help you find the right national resources: *American Library Directory*, *Directory of Archives and Manuscript Repositories in the United States* and *Directory of Federal Libraries*. Check your local library for regional directories.

Learning centers. The public affairs office of any major university should be able to connect you with an expert in a particular field. Sometimes, a professor or researcher has a book or paper out on your topic, or is happy to just be involved and quoted as an authority. Two publications can also help you find experts from academia: the *National Faculty Directory* and *Directory of American Scholars*.

The federal government. Uncle Sam is the biggest publisher in the country — tens of thousands of titles each year. Many libraries carry the *Monthly Catalog of U.S. Government Publications*. For a shortened version, *Selected List of U.S. Government Publications*, write to the Superintendent of Documents (General Printing Office, Washington DC 20242). The biggest problem in getting information, of course, is bureaucracy; be patient, or look for a federal bookstore in a major city.

In addition, the National Referral Center of the Library of Congress can refer researchers to more than 13,000 associations across the United States.

Other reporters. At times it pays to call a writer and ask if she is willing to give you the telephone number of a source mentioned or quoted in an article. Some reporters will be miffed that a competing writer is taking this shortcut; others will be helpful, particularly if you are sincere and friendly and you explain that you've exhausted other avenues and are pressed by a deadline. Offer to be there as a source for them in the future and, if they help, follow up with at least a note or telephone call of thanks.

Here are two excellent books to help you sort out the complicated but bountiful world of research and investigation: *Knowing Where to Look: The Ultimate Guide to Research* (Writer's Digest Books), by Lois Horowitz, and *The Reporter's Handbook: An Investigator's Guide to Documents and Techniques* (Investigative Reporters and Editors, Inc., University of Missouri).

♦ ♦ ♦

Lining up sources is one thing, interviewing quite another. It's a craft unto itself, which is why it warrants its own chapter.

So, on to Step Ten!

Step Ten

Getting Them to Talk

I was once assigned to interview an actor-writer-producer-director infamous for his monumental ego, violent temper and irrepressible need for power and control. This multiple hyphenate lived with his wife and children on an expansive estate of lavish gardens, tennis courts and sparkling swimming pool, guarded by electronic surveillance equipment and Dobermans who bared their teeth at visitors.

The *auteur* and I sat opposite each other in a quiet room of his plush, two-story guest house. I turned on my tape recorder. He turned on his tape recorder, no doubt to let me know I had better quote him exactly. Although I was a bit taller, he somehow managed to give the impression of peering down at me.

"Before you ask any questions," he said, speaking without a smile, and in a tone one might address a child, "I want to get a few things straight."

He then rattled off several denials. He denied that he wore women's clothes, a rumor he claimed his enemies were spreading in a conspiracy to destroy his career. He denied being a "sexual pervert." He denied that, in a rage, he had once thrown a chair at a studio executive. He denied a couple of other things that I had never heard before and could never have printed anyway, since they were actionable — unless, of course, he spoke of them himself, on the record, which he was doing.

As he continued to lecture me, the spindles of my tape recorder spun silently; I remained quiet, even deferential.

My story appeared on a Sunday. Naturally, I quoted his denials high in my copy.

On Monday morning, I got a call from his publicist, who had set up the interview and who had just been fired.

"What do you do with a client," he asked, "who starts off an interview denying he wears women's clothes?"

I relate this anecdote because it illustrates something important about interviews: Each is as different as people are different. You rarely know what to expect, what style or approach to take, or what you'll get until you're in the middle of it.

THE CRAFT OF INTERVIEWING

Interviewing is the area students most often tell me they wish we'd covered more thoroughly; they find the process mysterious, challenging, even intimidating, as I did when I first started doing it.

The problem with trying to "teach" interviewing is that it is much like writing, in the sense that you must do a lot of it to become good. More-experienced writers can offer valuable criticism and advice, but ultimately, you must find your own way, developing skills and confidence through the actual practice of the craft.

Only more so with interviewing.

Writing, after all, is a solitary act. You alone are the one in control, and you can rewrite what you've done, as many times as you wish, getting expert feedback along the way, if you so choose.

Interviewing requires you to sit down with a stranger and try to get him to talk frankly and openly, sometimes about issues or details he doesn't want to talk about. Somehow, you must make the most artificial conversation seem "natural." All kinds of things beyond your control can go wrong, distracting and disrupting the interview. There's no teacher or editor at your elbow to point out problems as you go; you're on your own, often with but one chance to get it right.

Some writers and writing teachers like to set down "rules" for conducting interviews, such as what kind of question to open with, how to structure the interview and so on. These guidelines can help you prepare and can provide you with a safety net of techniques and strategies once you are underway. But beware hard-and-fast rules that tell you how an interview "must" be conducted. Every interviewer will develop his own style, adapting it to all kinds of situations with all kinds of subjects for all kinds of assignments.

There's another good reason for staying flexible: The best interview is the one that takes on a life all its own, offering wonderful surprises.

Selecting Your Sources

"Eighty-five percent of the people out there want to talk," says Joseph H. Galloway, senior writer, *U.S. News & World Report.* "Nobody listens anymore—everybody wants to talk. Give someone a sympathetic ear, and they'll tell you just about everything you want to know." But you can't interview *everybody* on a particular subject; at some point, you must narrow your list.

Here are a few criteria for picking and choosing:

Level of expertise. What are their credentials and experience? Are they well suited to speak on your angle? How truly knowledgeable are they on this particular topic? Job titles, position and other professional credentials can be important and can give some weight to your story, but don't restrict yourself. If you're doing an investigation of local toxic dumping, you'll probably want to interview environmental experts, but don't overlook the parent who lives near a dump site, or the local doctor baffled by rising cancer rates in the area.

Try to think of the offbeat source, not just the predictable one. If you write about big-city traffic nightmares, you may wish to talk to the traffic commissioner, but you might also consider a cabbie, a bicycle messenger, or the victim of a hit-and-run driver.

What they have to offer. This goes back to the question, "Who would know?" and suggests another, "Why would they want to talk?" Reporters who deal with controversial subject matter learn early that the best sources often fall into two categories: victims and enemies. That's because they have an ax to grind, a score to even.

When I investigated a string of plagiarism and copyright infringement cases for *The Los Angeles Times*, I invariably started with the attorneys for the plaintiffs, who armed me with affidavits and other damning documents. When I looked into Jane Fonda's business problems, I went to disgruntled former employees for ammunition.

The reason these people talk willingly, of course, is also the biggest drawback: They operate from strong bias, not from objectivity or (necessarily) a sense of truth and justice. Regard what they tell you with skepticism; check every claim thoroughly.

How articulate or "colorful" they are. Do they talk in a direct, real, quotable way, offering some substance and informing your readers? Or are they shy, stilted, stuffy, overly cautious? If you do a piece on stuffy people, of course, line up the latter type. If you write a piece on rodeo cowboys or cowgirls, find the flesh-and-blood subject with some "juice."

Through your network of contacts—friends, other writers, P.R. people, etc.—ask about specific sources. If they've been quoted elsewhere, see what they've had to say and how they said it. Try to call ahead and sound them out. As Michael Schumacher writes in *The Writer's Complete Guide to Conducting Interviews*, "A colorful knowledgeable source is always better than a drab knowledgeable source. . . ."

Whether they might add something special. What can they contribute to your piece that you don't already know or have? Can they bring a different perspective? Do they have a particular background or access to special information that will beef up your article?

Accessibility/availability. Do they have a reason to talk with you, and do you have a chance at getting to them? Be realistic when lining up sources. You may want a leading business or political figure or an entertainment or sports superstar for an article you plan, but unless you are on assignment for a major publication, your chances are slim to none.

Not long ago, a student in one of my classes wanted to interview a television star, angling on a nonprofit foundation with which the actress was associated. The student, a sweet woman in her seventies, had never sold an article and had no assignment from a publication, yet insisted on trying for the interview. Not surprisingly, she was turned down.

Except in the rarest instances, "important" people give interviews only to writers with firm assignments from solid publications.

On the other hand, you might land an interview with an appropriate source who has a book to plug, or the head of a local organization or business who would welcome the publicity.

Making the Approach

How you get to a subject will depend a lot on who you go after. Generally speaking, the higher the person's position or the greater his success or fame, the more likely you are to have to go through layers of insulation.

If you do a short feature on a singing shoe repairer, let's say, you'll probably call or stop by his shop and ask for an interview. If it's a piece on a shoe designer, you may talk to his assistant first. If it's the president of a shoe company, the firm's public relations office will probably handle your request. If it's a celebrity, a publicity or public relations firm is the likely place to call or write (as a rule, agents and managers do not handle press matters, but they can refer you to the publicist who does).

The key word when introducing yourself is professionalism. Some tips:

- Have a letter of assignment or the name and telephone number of your editor in case they wish to double-check.
- Be relaxed, confident, courteous, and know what you are going to say.
- Understand clearly the nature of your assignment and what you intend to cover, but *do not be specific about the exact questions you intend to ask or the angle of your article.* A good general rule is: Never reveal more than necessary. Inexperienced reporters often get nervous and jabber, trying to

fill silences or to ingratiate themselves with subjects. Don't; be succinct and to the point. You don't want to give away too much of your position or viewpoint, particularly if you intend to do some serious probing the subject may not like.

- Without overdoing it, be positive and upbeat, even flattering, if necessary. When appropriate, appeal to their sense of fairness, integrity or self-importance, and appear to be on their side.

Again, these are general guidelines that will work in many situations, but not all. Be prepared to roll with the punches.

Faking It

Although I've stressed the need to have a bona fide assignment to get to "big" people, that isn't necessarily the case with subjects of less prominence. Roughly the first dozen magazine pieces I wrote were on spec, and I don't recall ever being turned down for an interview. I simply presented myself with plenty of confidence, *assuming* in my approach and manner that I would get the interview.

"I'm putting together a piece for such-and-such a magazine," I might tell them, "and hoped I might interview you about such-and-such. . . ." The word *spec* never came up; sources were happy to cooperate. It's important to remember that I was not dealing with the higher levels of Hollywood, the White House, major corporations or other sources likely to question how concrete my assignment was. My interviews then were with social workers, small-business owners, college coaches, and others who were generally flattered to be asked and, in many instances, had something to gain from the exposure, even in the smaller publications for which I was writing.

At times, by working closely with cooperative editors, you can gain extra support when seeking interviews. An editor, for instance, might provide you with a letter stating something like, "We love your idea on such-and-such and would like to see 2,000 words by Dec. 1," never mentioning the word *spec*. (If you're unclear about the difference between writing on speculation and on contract, review the sidebar on page 9.)

Although I bluffed my way into interviews at times, I wouldn't advise anyone to bend the truth too much because (1) it's unprofessional, (2) it's unethical, and (3) it can come back to haunt you.

Still, a little *chutzpah* never hurt anyone, least of all in the reporting game.

MEETING RESISTANCE

Some journalists feel that when a person enters the public spotlight, achieving the status of celebrity or public figure, he loses his right to privacy.

As a reporter, I've certainly pressed hard to get certain people to talk to me; I'm sure I've been downright obnoxious at times. But I also believe the rich and famous have every right to turn us down. No law on this earth says they are required to give their time and thoughts to the media; such people are constantly beseiged for interviews, and they must make choices.

Your subjects, or their publicity representatives, must weigh several factors in deciding whether to grant an interview, such as:

- Who the reporter is.
- The publication, its reputation, readership, circulation, etc.
- The nature of the article and the slant they feel you might take.
- The timing of the article and the benefits of exposure just then, or the risk of "overexposure."
- Whether it's worth taking time from a busy schedule, expending resources and so on.

In short, whether an interview with you is in their overall interests — what they will get out of it, in exchange for giving you the lucrative commodity of their words.

If you're on assignment for a respectable publication and present yourself well, most of the time your interview requests will be granted, unless you attempt heavy-duty investigative reporting that makes certain parties nervous.

But what if they say no?

Use what leverage you have to try to change their minds. That leverage will depend on who you are, the "importance" of the publication you're writing for and other factors. If you encounter resistance, your options range from charm to veiled threats (discreetly worded, and only as a final resort). Always start with the positive.

When I've hit such barriers, I've found myself saying such things as:

"I honestly feel a piece like this demands the voice of someone of your stature and professional standing."

"Without someone of your expertise and knowledge, my coverage of this subject is really going to suffer."

"I realize this is a controversial issue, but your side deserves to be heard."

"So-and-so has made some serious charges about your role in all this. That's why I feel it's vital that you speak on the record. Anything less would be unfair to you."

If the resistance continues and you feel it's worth it, you may have to intensify the pressure and escalate the tactics.

PLAYING HARDBALL

One ace you can play, particularly with articles where controversy is involved, goes something like this:

"I certainly respect your right not to talk about this. My concern is that a 'no comment' will make it appear that you're ducking the issue, that you have something to hide. I'm afraid that if I don't get your side of things, so my coverage is fair and balanced, you'll come out looking like the bad guy."

Sometimes, getting to a reluctant subject is a matter of circumventing obstacles, such as a publicist who is officious or who relays your interview request inaccurately or with negative bias. I once fought for weeks to get an interview with a particular TV producer; when I finally reached her—by noisily accusing the network of having something to hide—I learned that the network publicist had completely misrepresented my assignment and my intent.

To get around that kind of interference, you may have to:

- Raise your voice and make strong accusations.
- Go over the flack's head to a higher authority.
- Look for a more sympathetic person who can relay your request personally for you.
- Send a telegram, fax, etc.
- Be creative or off-the-wall (flowers, candy, balloons).
- Show up in person at the subject's place of business (which walks a fine line regarding his right to privacy).

If your subject still won't talk, it's time to ask yourself a few questions:

- How badly do I need this particular interview for my article?
- How crucial is it to the integrity and completeness of the piece?
- How pushy, even antagonistic, am I willing to be, and is it worth the trouble?
- Am I in a position—do I have the clout—to make demands?

Interviews are essentially a tradeoff: The subjects scratch your back, you scratch theirs; you get your story, they get their name in print. Relentlessly pursuing an elected official or a crucial source for an investigative piece of public importance is one thing; demanding that a reluctant subject talk to you so you can line your wallet from the sale of a lightweight feature is quite another.

If you're a good reporter, you'll press hard for your interviews (after all, they can only say no). But you should also know when to respect their right to privacy and leave them alone.

WHEN TO LET GO

If and when it becomes clear that you've lost the interview, find another source and move on. If it's a "core" interview, a crucial part of the assignment you agreed on, let your editor know you'll make a substitute. There will be times when losing a key interview means you must abandon an assignment altogether. Take it in stride; it happens.

Suggestion: Always call back one last time, just before filing your story. Sometimes, that last call is the one that gets you the interview, if only a "phoner."

The day before I was to leave Manila, and after three weeks of trying, I finally gained access to the Philippine government's chief censor. I got the crucial interview by mustering all my charm with the censor's assistant.

"Please tell your boss," I begged, batting my baby blues, "that if I don't get this interview, all my time here will be wasted, and I'll be in big trouble with my editor."

The chief censor, part of dictator Ferdinand Marcos's ruthless machine of repression, proved to be a matronly woman, American educated, with a warm personality and rich sense of humor. I asked her why she had resisted my requests for an interview for so long.

"Oh, I don't know," she said, shrugging. "I just didn't feel I had anything important to say."

SETTING GROUND RULES

Some interviews will be set up quickly and simply; others will be granted only after certain ground rules are agreed upon, including:

How the interview will be conducted. This can be in person, by telephone, by mail or by fax machine, with writer and subject exchanging questions and answers in writing. But face-to-face interviews are generally preferable, and necessary for personal profiles, when eye contact and incidental details are so important. Sometimes, however, the only way you can reach a source is by telephone, for reasons of geographical distance, scheduling, etc. Certain types of articles — such as roundups, with many sources — don't lend themselves to meeting everyone in person. And some subjects, intimidated by eyeball-to-eyeball meetings with reporters, actually open up more on the telephone.

If possible, avoid written questions and answers; they will be carefully prepared, edited and sanitized, with no spontaneity or life to them. They wrest control from the reporter and put it in the hands of the source.

Alone or with a second party. If possible, try to sit down one-on-one with the subject; having a publicist or attorney in the room can prove distracting and inhibiting. If you have the clout, arrange to have the publicist leave after introductions; ask politely, *before* the meeting.

If you interview someone who is underage, however, as I did Tatum O'Neal when she was only eleven, have another adult present to avoid any later suggestions of coercion or impropriety.

Where. The backdrop can be a crucial factor if you do an in-person interview, particularly if it's a personal profile. Don't sell this negotiating point short. (More on choosing your interview setting later.)

Time. Agree ahead of time on how long you will have. Be sure your source is aware of those parameters and has cleared the time for you.

When I was freelancing for *The New York Times*, I generally requested — and usually got — two meetings of at least two hours each for profiles. *TV Guide* liked its writers to spend time with a star on the set of his TV show, and in another location that revealed something of his personal side, such as out riding horses, playing golf, or just at home with family or pets. Anecdote and telling detail were so important to *TV Guide* that I usually asked to hang out on the set for a full day, in addition to two sit-down interviews. *Dynasty* was the only set that was ever closed to me, and it was one of the weakest pieces I ever turned in, while entire days spent on the sets of M*A*S*H, *Newhart*, *The White Shadow* and other shows provided a wealth of incident and color.

What will be discussed. At times, publicists try to protect their clients by putting certain subject matter off limits, sometimes to find out what you're after, what angle you have in mind. You must negotiate limitations, should any be raised, then decide if you can live with the restrictions, or if you should walk away from the interview. Don't make promises you don't intend to keep, but don't let them unnecessarily restrict you, either.

When I interviewed stage and film actor Matt Salinger about his career, he made it clear he didn't want to answer questions about his famous father, J.D. Salinger, the publicity-shy author of *Catcher in the Rye*. So I framed certain questions in relation to Matt's work, such as: "Did you become an actor deliberately to get away from writing, and out of your father's shadow?" "Do you find it difficult forging your own identity with such a famous father?" "As an aspiring producer, do you harbor any dreams of bringing *Catcher in the Rye* to the screen, as your father has so long resisted?"

While cautious, Matt was responsive enough that I was able to get some of J.D. Salinger into my piece.

In the case of Jane Fonda, her publicist flatly forbade questions about business; we were only to discuss Fonda's TV miniseries, *The Dollmaker*. Reluctantly, I accepted the terms. However, in discussing unions and worker's rights, which were part of the TV story line, Fonda herself crossed the boundaries, opening up the discussion to wide-ranging business and political issues. I felt free to follow, and was able to ask nearly every question I wanted. She didn't hesitate to answer, and at the close of our interview, I thanked her for being so generous.

"Oh, that's all right," she said with a grin. "I don't like puff pieces!"

Copy approval. As I write this, I've just learned that the inflight magazine of a major airline has a new policy: Profile writers will be required to submit their manuscripts to their subjects for approval, to avoid offending anyone. Some writers of integrity are turning down profile assignments with this magazine but, sadly, others with less backbone are accepting the conditions, making them little more than glorified publicists.

Subjects have no business telling you how you may write your story, portray them in it, or which of their quotes you may use. Only in rare situations would a self-respecting journalist grant copy approval to a source, such as with material that is particularly personal or potentially painful, or if the interviews spanned an unusually long time, allowing for inaccuracy or inconsistency.

When someone requests copy approval, it's often out of naiveté, since reputable reporters don't grant it. Be polite and diplomatic in explaining your position, and you'll usually find they'll talk with you anyway.

Checking facts and quotes. This is quite different from copy approval. Generally, I have readily agreed to check facts; not only does it ensure accuracy, but it gives me another chance, as mentioned previously, for a brief, follow-up interview, when I can slip in more questions if they're needed.

Checking quotes becomes more tricky, because often, when a source hears his words read back, he gets nervous and tries to recant. If you have someone on tape and the audio is clear, there's no reason to check quotes. I agree to check only those I'm unsure about (because of hurried note-taking, for example) or that I have extensively rearranged or edited for compression or readability.

On rare occasions, I have also agreed to check with sources the *context* in which certain quotes are used, if they are particularly nervous, and if I want the interview badly enough. However, *I never submit the actual copy to anyone, even for fact- or quote-checking; I read it aloud.* Once you allow your subject to see how you've put your piece together, you can open yourself to all kinds of problems.

Follow-up. If possible, arrange for at least one follow-up interview, if only by phone. I generally save this until I've written my rough draft and can see the holes. Subjects are usually happy to grant it.

Choosing Your Setting

With some interviews, you don't have a lot of choice about where it's to be done. Your subject may want to talk only in an office or other mundane setting, leaving you without many creative options. If you do have some leeway, though, make your setting work for you. A few guidelines:

Pick a setting that is appropriate for your subject. When I profiled the owner of a successful bicycle shop, I had him in the shop, repairing a flat, which is the way he got started. When I talked to a cop about a serial murder case, I met him at the roadside location where he first examined a victim's mutilated body, adding a touch of reality and horror to my story.

Look for colorful or "action" backdrops. For my mule-packer story, I rode along when a young packer transported a family and their gear deep into the mountains. Coming out with another group, we were caught in a tumultous lightning storm, with mules bucking and pitching loads. I got to see the young packer doing his job at its most challenging, which provided valuable dimension to the piece.

Choose a setting that might reveal something special about your subject. For a profile of the Rev. Jesse Jackson, I got the unexpected opportunity to do one of our interviews in center field of an empty Dodger Stadium, with 56,000 empty seats looming impressively above us. As he looked up at the stands and dug his toe into the center field grass, the middle-aged Jackson recalled his days as a college baseball star and his choice to turn down a pro contract in favor of the ministry; it was a bittersweet moment that brought out candor, humor and emotion I hadn't seen in him.

Pick a background that will make your source more comfortable. One of my toughest interviews was with taciturn actor James Broderick of "Family," for a *TV Guide* profile. After two or three days on the set with him, I didn't have much. But I learned that he was an avid jogger, who ran along the beach. I arranged to jog several miles with him, with my tape recorder running, and he relaxed and opened up.

If it helps, get your subject alone, away from the hubbub. There are times when busy settings add color to your research, but also get in the way of the interviewing process; work hard to find alternative environments.

When I was in New Mexico to cover the production of *The Milagro Beanfield War*, I arranged to ride with the film's director, Robert Redford, as he drove his turbocharged Porsche down out of the mountains at the end of a day's shooting. Not only did it give me the chance to see him involved in one of his passions, high-performance driving, it gave us a long stretch of quiet time alone, away from the distractions of the busy set.

Avoid noisy backgrounds that interfere with audio. I learned a hard lesson about clamorous backdrops after I agreed to meet actors Cicely Tyson and Paul Winfield in a hotel coffee shop. The interview went well, but when I got home and played back the tape, I could barely make out the words beneath the clatter of plates. Ordinarily, restaurants are fine for interviews; unfortunately, we were next to a noisy busboy station. Be forewarned.

PREPARING FOR THE INTERVIEW

One of my first heavyweight magazine assignments, for *Los Angeles*, was with a vice-president in charge of casting for one of the three major TV networks, an exceptionally busy executive who granted me an hour in her office. As the interview stumbled along, she grew increasingly peevish, and finally cut off one of my vague, rambling questions.

"I think you should figure out just what it is you're writing about," she said sharply. "You need to find some focus for your questions, and get them into some reasonably logical order. Because they're all over the place, and so general that I find them almost impossible to answer."

I could feel my youthful face burning, and she must have witnessed some startling shades of red.

"I'm sorry," she said, softening a bit. "I didn't mean to be so harsh. But before you go into an interview, you've got to do some homework."

I had learned what almost every nonfiction writer does at one point or another: Going into an interview unprepared is a quick way to disaster.

There are several ways to avoid such debacles:

- Background your subject thoroughly.
- Know what you need from the interview.
- Plan and prioritize your questions.
- Think through a "framework" for the interview.
- Try to go in fresh and rested.

No interview will ever fit your plan to a "T," and there will be times when you abandon your strategy altogether, going with the flow. But going in with no plan at all is like driving cross-country without a map.

Do Your Research

Before sitting down for an interview, try to answer as many questions as you can on your own. Save your precious interview time to ask questions only your subject can answer. That means perhaps asking questions of ancillary sources and doing substantial reading beforehand.

How much is substantial? *The more in-depth, wide-ranging and serious your assignment, the more background you need going into your interviews.*

If you are assigned a profile on a shoe-store owner for your local newspaper, there may be nothing previously written on him. Perhaps he has a business bio, or something published in a local fraternal or business organization, but if not, you may have to ask the source directly basic questions such as when he was born, where he was educated, what year he opened the business and so on. Still, you'll probably want to know beforehand whether selling shoes is a growth industry, something about changing styles, how many shoe stores operate in the United States, whether the chains are killing the independent shoe retailer and so on.

The more you know about the general subject, the more you are liable to ask intelligent, meaningful questions and uncover areas that will give unexpected dimension to your article.

If you're interviewing a prominent shoe designer, there is certainly some biographical information available on that person, perhaps from a P.R. representative, or a book of biographical data. You'll want to know about shoe design in general, and about this designer in particular, before your interview.

If it's a famous athlete who endorses shoes, you'll want to find out which teams he has played for, what his winning record is, championships and other accomplishments, income from endorsements, previous products endorsed (especially rival shoes) and other pertinent information. You might even do a photo search on the athlete, to verify if he actually wears the brand he promotes.

As you do your backgrounding, you'll not only gather material that will be used in the article itself, but you'll find your discoveries triggering questions you never would have thought to ask.

Know What You Need

Investigative reporter Don Ray advises, "Try to know the answers before you ask the questions." By that he means, go into your interviews armed with so much background, your source must deal straight with you—or get caught at passing off something less than the whole truth. Even if you don't do the kind of investigative work that demands such formidable research, knowing what you need ahead of time, at least in a general way, will help you get it.

To be sure you're clear about the *purpose* of the interview, ask yourself these questions:

- What areas is this source liable to be most knowledgeable about?
- Within those areas, what specific information do I hope to uncover?
- How does that information fit into my article as I see it?
- What areas is my source likely to be reticent about discussing?
- Have I prepared myself with enough background in those areas to ask probing questions, or to spot evasion?
- If I can come out of this interview learning only three things (or five, ten, twenty), what should they be?

You can't know *everything* about a subject, of course, which is what makes the interviewing process so interesting and valuable. Don't let ignorance stop you; let it be your guide.

Before I interviewed author Judith Krantz, I'd read each of her books, many reviews, and a number of her better-known nonfiction pieces. I knew how much money she'd made off book royalties and sales, studied as much background about her earlier years and her family as I could find, and learned a good deal about her husband, a film producer. I felt confident and adequately prepared.

When I met her in her plush Beverly Hills home, however, I found I was in way over my head. Early on, she made an offhand reference to her "Adolfos," and I had no idea what an Adolfo was (he's a dress designer). So I did the wise thing: I admitted my ignorance.

"Forgive me, but I'm a little out of my element here," I said. "What's an Adolfo?"

She took the cue, and led me graciously on a room-by-room tour of the house, chatting happily about everything from "our Man Ray" (an original Man Ray painting) to her endless throw pillows and a collection of English snuffboxes; she even showed me how she had planted apple trees in the garden to obscure distant palm trees and give the feeling of southern France.

By asking an honest question, I opened up a world of incident and detail that revealed a lot about Krantz's life and character, particularly her need for nesting and security.

Be as prepared as you can be for each interview, then let your curiosity and questions fill in the rest.

PLANNING AND PRIORITIZING QUESTIONS

The secret to getting people to talk, comedienne and talk show host Joan Rivers wrote in *McCall's*, "is that almost everyone likes to talk about themselves. They don't want to hear about *you*; they want to tell you about *them*.

"So rule number one is to just keep asking questions."

Many times, appropriate questions come to you in the course of a candid, free-flowing interview, suggested by what's being said (or *not* said). As Rivers puts it, "Your next question — your lifeline — will be found in their previous answer."

But most interviewers plan at least some of their questions.

Art Spikol believes in making a list of questions, then forgetting it until the end of the interview, when you refer to it quickly to see if you've covered what you need. "Don't use a list of questions, because all that will do is get you answers," he wrote in one of his *Writer's Digest* columns. "You want the interview to have a life of its own; one thought should lead naturally to the next, and you should feel free to take little detours around the subject."

My own method is to list every question I want to ask, then number them, prioritized according to need, in a notebook that goes with me into the interview.

Never, however, do I allow my sources to see my questions; it can make them curious or uneasy, and break the fragile "reality" of the interview.

I don't ask questions in the order I've prioritized them; I start out with softer, more comfortable warm-up and "get-acquainted" questions, see where the interview takes me, and pop in planned questions when it feels right. However, I sometimes hold off questions that might antagonize my subject until late in the interview, or until the very end. It's wise to work up to your toughest questions, so that you have most questions answered before you get a "no comment" or some other type of rebuff, including an angry subject declaring, "This interview is over!"

As each of my questions is answered in the course of an interview, I discreetly cross out that question in my notebook, while maintaining as much eye contact with my source as possible. When all my questions are crossed off, I know that I've covered the basics.

This approach works for me. I know one writer who refuses to rely on a written list of questions, going into interviews armed only with a tape recorder, his background on the subject and his curiosity.

Each writer will find what's most comfortable and effective for him, developing different strategies for different situations.

Framing Your Questions

How you word your questions will have a big impact on what you get back.

In *The Writer's Complete Guide to Conducting Interviews*, Michael Schumacher breaks questions down into open-ended and closed questions.

Open-ended questions, which often begin with "how" and "why," encourage lengthy responses, such as analysis, description, opinion, anecdote. Examples: "How exactly does the chain of authority work in producing a weekly TV series?" "Why did you leave the creative decisions to others?" "How does this kind of programming affect how children view women?" "Why weren't you on the set the day that particular show was shot?"

Closed questions tend to elicit succinct, specific responses, such as "Where were you the day the show was taped?" or "Who exactly was in charge?"

You'll use both in an interview, mixing them up according to the personality and comfort level of your source, the pacing of the interview, time constraints, and what you feel you need on a given point.

You'll also want to vary the weight or substance of your questions, from the most general or complicated question, such as, "Do you feel television is destroying literacy in our children?" or "Describe how your new sewage system works and how it will save our waterways from pollution," to the most mundane question, such as, "What shade of lipstick are you wearing?" or "What do you read when you're in the bathroom?" The reason: *Sometimes, it's the trivial question that reveals the most about a person or provides the odd detail and human touch your article needs.*

In planning ahead, beware of certain types of questions:

Questions that are overly vague.

Vague: "What was the extent of your involvement in the project?"

Pointed: "What exactly was your role in the project, and how much of your time did it require?"

Questions that lead to a "yes" or "no."

Yes or no: "Are you happy with your marriage?"

Explanatory: "What are the greatest challenges you've found in married life? The greatest rewards?"

Questions that are too long or complex.

Long and complex: "I noticed that when you first came up in professional tennis, you tended to rush the net a lot more. Was that because you were younger and quicker, or has there been a change in your strategy for other reasons, and how do you feel it's affected your success?"

Shorter and simpler: "Why did you stop rushing the net so much in recent years, and how has it affected your play?"

Try to frame your questions so that you:

- Get specific answers.
- Amplify or clarify previous statements.
- Move the conversation into deeper territory.

If your source is unusually tight and terse, see if an open-ended question loosens him up. For conversations that lag, meander or become too vague, keep on hand closed or "time-and-place" questions that bring your source back to earth, speaking from a place of fact and firsthand experience, rather than opinion, theory, speculation, analysis and the like.

Examples:

"Describe what your match with Michael Chang was like, from the moment you stepped on the court."

"Tell me where you got your wedding dress and exactly how you picked it out."

"Go back to the night you decided to come out to your parents. What were their reactions when they learned you were gay?"

If your source falters because of shyness or awkwardness, help him by leading him to something even more concrete, such as:

"Where was the match played? What was the weather like that day?"

"Were you alone in the bridal shop, or with someone? Why did you choose that person to go with you?"

"What room were you in when you told them? What exactly were you feeling?"

"STRUCTURING" THE INTERVIEW

Almost all interviews have parameters. The shorter the time frame and wider the scope of questioning, the more you'll need to plan and structure the interview.

When you've listed and prioritized your questions, run a hypothetical interview in your mind, asking yourself:

- Will I be able to cover everything in the time I've been allowed?
- How does the schedule affect the time I can take to get acquainted or warm up?
- Do I need to plan for areas that may require deeper probing or more complicated responses?
- Am I listing questions that are not necessary, that might take me off

on tangents, or that I can answer through ancillary research?

Once more, interviewing is akin to writing, with a beginning, middle and end: You schmooze a little, putting your subject at ease; move into the middle part of the interview, covering the bulk of your questions; and head into the home stretch, nailing the important or clarifying questions, and wrapping it all up. Along the way, you improvise and make adjustments, relishing those unexpected moments and revelations that make an interview special.

It's your job to control and direct the interview, without it seeming to be controlled or directed.

THE INTERVIEW ITSELF

Three skills go a long way toward allowing an interview to evolve productively: *listen*; *don't interrupt unnecessarily*; and *show genuine interest in what your source says*.

Beyond that advice, I'll try to anticipate some of your questions, based on those I hear in the classroom.

Tape or Notes?

Without a doubt, in an ideal world, you'd use tape every time, because it records everything. I almost always use it if I'm writing a profile of some depth, or if I'm dealing with controversial or sensitive subject matter, where a source might dispute what's been said.

Even when I tape, however, I also take notes, for a few reasons. It's good to have backup in case your recorder or tape is defective, or gets lost or stolen. A notebook allows you to scan your list of questions, check them off, and add new ones as the conversation suggests them. It also lets you note incidental detail about the subject, the environment you're in, random thoughts.

Start your tape running either well before the main part of the interview begins, right after shaking hands, or discreetly at some point *after* you've warmed up. Keep it to the side, where it's least noticeable, and act as if it's not there.

For all the advantages of taping, however, I lean more on note-taking when I do quick interviews on the telephone for short items, stories on short deadlines, or roundup pieces where dozens of interviews might be involved. The reason: I don't want to spend endless hours transcribing my tapes — and I don't allow others to transcribe my tapes for me, because they may make errors or miss meaningful inflections and pauses.

I find that jotting notes in a notebook, when done judiciously, rarely harms an interview. But don't suddenly start scribbling madly when sources launch into revealing conversation; that's the quickest way to get them to clam up. When they start rolling, it's usually best to relax and maintain eye contact. Use shorthand or develop your own system, so that you can jot down notes almost casually, without distracting the subject. You won't be able to write down everything; learn to listen for the valuable quote, and edit and paraphrase the rest as you go. If the subject gets ahead of you and you're in danger of losing a valuable quote, don't try to keep up; forget the last statement and jot down the important one. You can always go back later and clarify what you've missed.

My advice to the novice interviewer would be: Use a tape recorder every time out, as a backup, until you develop a skill for taking notes and become accustomed to the interviewing process as a whole.

One more thing: Always take along extra batteries.

Electronics stores sell inexpensive devices that allow you to tape telephone interviews, but you're required by law to notify the subject that you're doing so.

How Should I Open?

It depends a lot on who you talk to and how long you have. If it's a busy person and a short interview, you can't waste much time. On the other hand, you can't hit him with the hardest question right off, either.

Sometimes, it's a simple, "Thanks for making some time for me." Other times, you're forced to go with something like, "I guess our time is pretty tight. Shall we get started?" And sometimes, you can be more personal, commenting on a book you see out on a table, thanking him for his excellent directions to the meeting place, making an observation about his latest work. Just don't be so cordial that you become obsequious.

Getting the Subject's Trust

Sometimes, despite the opening small talk, a subject will remain on edge. Check your body language; can you alter it to put him at ease? You may want to move closer, even touch him innocently on the arm or hand, or sit off at an angle, rather than face-to-face. While eye contact is usually helpful, perhaps you're eyeballing him too directly, without letting up. Are you smiling, speaking in a gentle voice, laughing when it's appropriate?

If your subject remains uneasy, there is another trick of the trade: Reveal something personal about yourself that relates to the conversation, something you wouldn't ordinarily tell a stranger. It might be an acknowledgment about your troubled marriage, sexual orientation, past problems with drugs or alcohol, guilt over making an error in an article—some confession that suggests openness and vulnerability.

Conversation or Confrontation?

As a rule, I try to generate friendly, intelligent conversation, becoming confrontational only if the situation demands, and I think most nonfiction writers operate pretty much the same way. I once had an interview over dinner with a lovely actress who had just starred in a movie in which she played a rape victim—raped repeatedly by a "supernatural force." I saw the film essentially as a slick exploitation movie that degraded women, and as we ate and talked, the actress gradually caught the drift of my questions.

"Is this the angle you're going after in your story?" she asked, her smile fading.

"It's certainly an issue to be discussed," I said.

"I have a feeling it's the *point* of your story."

She'd nailed me; the honeymoon was over.

Playing to both her intelligence and political sensibilities, I asked, "Do you think the image of women in movies, particularly as they're so often portrayed by men, is an issue a journalist should overlook?"

She dropped her eyes, and I pressed on. She defended the film for awhile, but after some prodding, finally admitted that with a limited number of lead roles for women, she sometimes took less-than-ideal parts, hinting that this was one of them. The shift in our conversation didn't make for a pleasant dinner, but it provided a more honest interview.

There will be times when an interview becomes stormy near the outset, and you must find a way to steer it back into calm waters, or risk losing it. For a newspaper item on the changing image of *Rolling Stone* and its attempts to attract more affluent, mainstream readers, I talked over the telephone to an executive at the magazine. I wondered if his marketing campaign might be selling out, even ridiculing, the counterculture audience that made the publication successful in the first place. He became outraged and demanded to talk to my editor.

"I'll be happy to put you through to my editor, if that's what you really want," I said. "But all I'm doing is asking thoughtful, probing questions. Isn't that one of the things *Rolling Stone* prides itself on?"

He calmed down, and we continued in more respectful tones. By appealing to his sense of pride in the magazine, and his sense of fairness, I diffused a volatile situation and salvaged the interview.

Not every nonfiction writer is cut out for confrontational interviewing.

You must think about how tough a reporter you're willing to be — or *become* — or what other kinds of assignments might be more suitable.

Broaching Uncomfortable or Challenging Questions

There are several ways to help a tougher question go down more smoothly, among them:

Soften a hard question with a compliment or praise. With the Rev. Jesse Jackson, my approach went like this: "You've obviously had an incredible impact on American politics and society, and you're looked up to as something of a hero by millions. Yet some people, blacks included, see you as rather pompous, even arrogant. . . ."

Indicate empathy. Find a way to get inside your subject's skin, and show you're on his side, or at least that you're trying to see things through his eyes. When I interviewed a gang member who had gunned down another teenager, I prefaced my questions about his brutal behavior by asking him about the oppression of urban poverty and feeling trapped in a violent neighborhood.

(I also bought him lunch, which didn't hurt.)

Adopt a playful tone. Some interviews are a cat-and-mouse game as you try to chase your subject into corners. When I interviewed actor Denzel Washington, he was on guard from the beginning, tired of reporters trying to get him to talk about racial issues. I adopted his playful, sparring style, using humor as much as possible to keep the atmosphere relaxed and the conversation active.

Distance yourself. Make your stand behind a reporter's objectivity: "I don't necessarily agree with them, but your critics claim that you. . . ." Or: "As a reporter, I'd be remiss in my duty if I didn't ask you about. . . ."

Keep it general. If you can't force yourself to ask a subject an extremely personal or sensitive question, steer the conversation into the general area, and see where it leads. If he is alcoholic, for instance, and you feel it's pertinent to your article, move the conversation toward health, then addictive behavior, then to a question like, "Have you ever had to deal with chemical dependency in a friend or loved one?" still keeping it at arm's length. You may find that the subject opens up on his own as the questions get closer to home; and if he doesn't like the line of questioning, he can divert it or cut it off.

Find a side door. Sometimes, it helps to edge toward the sensitive question from a related subject area. When I was interviewing a paraplegic and his bride-to-be, I had to get to the touchy matter of sexuality. As he discussed his future goals, I asked, "Are you planning on having children, or is that not in the picture?" He replied that sexually, he functioned fully, and had a satisfying romantic life; he smiled, pulled his fiancée close, and gave her a squeeze.

Be straightforward. When you finally stop hemming and hawing and ask a difficult question matter-of-factly, you may be surprised how well your subject handles it. When actor Eric Roberts emerged as a film star, I noticed during our interview traces of a stutter I hadn't heard on screen; I'd also seen no mention of it in profiles I'd read. I said simply, "Every once in a while, I notice a stutter, but you seem to have it under control." He talked frankly about how serious his speech impediment had been when he was a boy and how he had worked to overcome it, which added a poignant touch to my story. After it appeared, he sent me a note that said, "Thanks for telling it like it was."

Work out a compromise or acceptable approach. At times a subject area is so charged or delicate, it's necessary to broach it either during the interview or beforehand, when ground rules are being set, to see if there's a way of discussing it that's agreeable to the subject. For instance, a source might be willing to discuss a topic in a general way, or if names aren't used.

You can apply this same strategy to situations when your subject wants to go off the record with material. As previously noted, there is a difference between "not-for-publication" and "not-for-attribution." Try to convince your subject that direct attribution is not as dangerous as he thinks; if that fails, see if he'll let you use the information in some other way, such as attribution to "an anonymous source," if your editor allows it.

If at all possible, avoid off-the-record remarks, because they can place hot information in your hands and tie your hands at the same time.

By the way, if a conversation starts on the record and a source makes a remark, then tries later to put it off the record, technically, it's too late. If it's to be off the record, a source should let you know in advance, not afterward.

Let Them Talk

This is the most basic advice for any interview, but it especially applies if you suspect a subject is unwilling to discuss a particular area. Once, I called film director Peter Bogdanovich, hoping he'd talk about his ex-wife, Polly Platt, who claimed she helped him write his early scripts without getting credit. He refused to discuss that part of his life. I said nothing. "Really, I have nothing to say, it's a closed issue," he insisted. Again, I let the uncomfortable silence hang there. He started talking and told me all I needed.

Don't talk unless it's necessary; learn to let pauses and silences work for you.

Above all, don't butt in when your subject is on a roll, revealing useful information.

Getting Anecdotes

What may be the most vital element of nonfiction writing is often the most difficult to wring from a subject. Countless times, in desperation as an interview ends, reporters try to get a source to "recall" a funny or revealing story; it almost never works. Good anecdotes generally come in the ebb and flow of rich conversation, but some specific strategies can help.

In his highly recommended book, *The Craft of Interviewing*, John Brady suggests, "One key word will incite anecdotes: when. 'When did you realize you would need open-heart surgery?' Like a slow pan in a movie, 'when' takes the subject to a scene, a setting, and thence to a story."

Brady also recommends using the reporter's four other W's to instigate storytelling:

"Where were you when you heard John F. Kennedy had been shot?"

"Who told you your house was on fire?"

"What are some of the most unusual questions children ask about sex?"

"Why did you run away from home on Christmas Eve?"

I would add the H-word:

"How exactly did you happen to be photographed sharing a joint with Charles Manson?"

Pacing the Interview and Keeping It on Track

As the interview progresses, be aware of three factors: your subject's responses, your priority questions and your time. If your subject gets off on a tangent, but it's anecdotal, interesting and potentially useful, let it go until it seems to go nowhere and eats up too much valuable time. Then gently direct it back to where you want it, in any number of ways:

"That's really interesting, but getting back to what we were talking about a moment ago. . . ."

"You know, you mentioned something a few minutes ago that I wanted to clarify. . . ."

"You've had some fascinating experiences! Tell me, did you ever. . . ."
And point him in the direction you need him to go.

Pacing has a lot to do with the quality of the answers you get. If you feel a question has been answered adequately and you need no clarification, find a way to move to the next question or subject area. Sometimes, that's as simple as glancing at your watch and saying, "Before my time runs out, I'd better ask you about. . . ." Or, as the clock winds down, ask politely if it's possible to have a little extra time. Often, you'll get it.

If push comes to shove, note the time, and tick off the questions you still need to cover. As I approached the end of my hour with Jane Fonda, I said, "We only have a few minutes left, and I've still got several important questions."

"Fire away," she said, and answered each of my remaining questions in succinct, articulate fashion.

◆ ◆ ◆

There will also be times when you must do spot interviews on the run or under adverse conditions, and the rules quickly change. I've had to interview bloody plane crash victims being wheeled on gurneys into emergency rooms, kayakers as we paddled through a pod of killer whales, backpackers as we trekked through grizzly bear country, and, once, a pop star as we fled hundreds of hysterical, pubescent girls as they chased him down a London alley.

During experiences like those, you have two things to rely on: your notebook or tape recorder, and your ability to focus your thoughts and questions. "Structure" evaporates, and the interviewing process becomes more intense and unpredictable — and more fun — than you ever imagined it could.

INTERVIEWS THAT FAIL

When *The New York Times* assigned me to interview Ed Asner, the actor was starring in the TV series *Lou Grant*, a popular character he had developed as a costar on *The Mary Tyler Moore Show*. At that point, he had not done many interviews, was not yet involved in politics, and warned me amiably, "I'm a tough interview. You can try, but I just don't have much to say."

I followed him around for a week as his new show got off to a rocky start, and did several sit-down interviews with him that were almost painful for both of us. Finally, I gave up, and wrote my profile as best I could. I turned it in, and the editors turned it down.

"The guy is dull as toast," an editor said. "Is this all you could get out of him?"

It was, and the article never appeared. Asner wasn't dull as toast. He was an intelligent and very nice man who happened to be on the taciturn side at that point in his life, and who had run into an inexperienced reporter.

I was stung by the failure, and recalled that I had read a *TV Guide* profile of Asner years earlier that I had enjoyed. I looked it up. It *was* an entertaining piece, but there was almost nothing of Asner in it, not his quotes, anyway. The writer, apparently faced with the same problem I encountered, had fashioned a first-person nostalgia piece, recalling fondly what the character of Lou Grant and *The Mary Tyler Moore Show* had meant to him through the years. It was a brilliant job of turning a sow's ear into a silk purse.

Sometimes you just have to walk away from an interview, if the subject is uncooperative or just plain uncomfortable. Don't take botched or unproductive interviews personally; they are a fact of the nonfiction writing life. On the other hand, don't automatically give up because you don't have reams of scintillating quotes. Try these approaches first:

Discuss the situation with your editor to see if you can find creative solutions. I know now that I should have turned the Ed Asner encounter into a behind-the-scenes look at a new television show in ratings trouble, using my supplementary interviews and wealth of incident and color I picked up on the set to salvage the assignment.

Supplement your quotes with those already printed in other publications. An hour with Harrison Ford, who is notoriously uncomfortable with interviews, rendered little. I reinforced my piece by scanning every article on him I could find, lifting bits of information, an anecdote or two and even a couple of quotes. (That's perfectly acceptable; only the way information is written can be copyrighted, not the information itself. It's wise, though, to check the printed information for accuracy.)

Go to alternate sources. Again, to flesh out Ford, I talked to his *Star Wars* costars, Carrie Fisher and Mark Hammill, who talked volubly about him. And when I ran into a detective who gave terse responses to questions about a complex sting operation, I sought out his more talkative partner for what I needed.

Try writing a different kind of article entirely, perhaps in the first person. When a rock star stood up Brenda Day for a scheduled interview, she abandoned the profile and wrote a funny, perceptive piece about . . . being stood up. The situation challenged her to be more imaginative and to write in a much different voice, and the piece was among the best she's done.

◆ ◆ ◆

Now that you know how to get the goods, it's time to explore the skills and techniques of wordcraft — the focus of Step Eleven.

Step Eleven

Writing It Well

L ate one night, during the writing of this book, I had an intense discussion with an undergraduate college student who dreamed of being a widely read writer.

I argued that good writers are not born, but evolve, over time, as they develop discipline, voice and craft. The young man, who had yet to actually write anything, countered passionately that writing should be "spontaneous" and "free," uncompromised by revision or recognizable technique. As our conversation headed toward the third hour, I realized he was determined to convince me — or, perhaps, *himself* — that effective writing does not require hard work. Finally, almost in desperation, he cited a famous novelist as proof that fine writing is effortless.

"Ernest Hemingway was a great writer," the young man said, "and look at his writing. It's so *simple!*"

At first, I thought he was joking; then I realized he was not.

"You could not have chosen as an example," I said, "anyone who worked *harder* at achieving that effect."

"Are you sure?" the student asked. He looked confused, demoralized — as if I was knocking down his carefully constructed illusions about instant mastery and quick success. "Because his writing, the sentences are so, it looks so . . . easy."

Before Hemingway was a fiction writer, I explained, he was a reporter who filed hundreds of articles, developing solid writing skills. Hemingway had a rule: Write the story, then go back and trim out half, honing every line until it was "clean and true." It was Hemingway who said: "We are all apprentices in a craft where no one ever becomes a master."

"I didn't know that," the young man muttered unhappily. He swallowed hard. "I guess writing's not as easy as I thought."

"Creative writing may be easy," I suggested. "It *should* be free and spontaneous, and it's a good place to start. Professional writing requires a little more work."

In his valuable book, *The Random House Guide to Good Writing*, Mitchell Ivers cites the above words from Ernest Hemingway, along with these: "Prose is architecture, not interior decoration."

I believe it's crucial that beginning writers find their natural writing voice and rhythms by engaging in daily writing unrestricted and uninhibited by criticism, rules, form, and the pressure to write "professionally." At some point, however, if they want to publish and be paid for their work, they must apply themsleves to *craft* — and distinguish their writing from that of the talented but unpublishable amateur. That's what this and the following chapter are all about.

DEVELOPING "STYLE"

Style — that special but elusive quality that gives our writing distinction.

Style — the one element most beginning writers work hardest to achieve.

Style — the last thing a writer should worry about, or try to "develop."

What exactly is "style"? It's simply the natural way you write, after you have discovered who you are. It is *you*, reflected in the words you choose and the way you put them together, suited to particular subject matter and markets.

"Style is an idiom which *arises spontaneously* from one's personality but which is *deliberately maintained*," wrote Quentin Crisp and Donald Carroll in *Doing It With Style* (italics are theirs). "Or to put it another way: To be a stylist is to be yourself, but on purpose." The two authors point out that each of us is unique; there is not another person quite like us in the universe. No one has lived, experienced, seen life exactly like each of us has. "Misguidedly, and tediously," they write, "most people try to compensate for this unnerving state of affairs, either consciously or unconsciously, by becoming more like others. The stylist exploits it by becoming more like himself."

Often, when an editor says, "It needs more style," or asks, "Can't you make it a bit more stylish?", what she really means is that it needs more energy, humor, pace, imagery, livelier phrasing — something that will punch up text that is flat, dull, uninspired. Or she might mean: "Can you find a style that's better suited for this material?" But style itself is not something an editor can order up, like a billboard paragraph or a set of bullets or a tighter lead. It cannot be taught or created as an act of will. When you try consciously to put style into your writing, you'll manufacture writing that feels false, pretentious, contrived.

When we start out, most of us probably copy, consciously or unconsciously, the style of writers we especially admire; the most famous and accomplished writers will readily admit this. It's nothing to be ashamed of; in fact, patterning our work after a favorite writer is a good way to get started, a useful method of perceiving and practicing the elements of strong writing. Eventually, though, we must let go of a forced or copycat style, and ease into a way of writing that taps and expresses our own, unique personality.

Perhaps understanding what good style is is to understand some things it is not:

• Good style is not self-consciously "grand," or "sparing," or "literary," or otherwise designed to make people admire or envy us.

• It is not being deliberately wild, zany or experimental to prove what free spirits we are.

• It is not sticking in puns, clever phrasing or other gimmicks for their own sake.

• It is not forcing irony or wit into our work to the detriment of substance and structure, or simple credibility.

• It is not sprinkling exclamation points throughout lackluster prose to try to make it look energetic.

• It is not writing long and convoluted sentences, or ridiculously short ones, just to challenge the reader or prove how "different," "unique" or "cool" we are.

• It is not cramming our writing full of literary allusion or esoterica to show how widely read we are or what a great vocabulary we have (leave that to the likes of Gore Vidal and George Will, who are and do).

A "good style" might include any of the elements mentioned above — even all of them — but not if it calls undue attention to itself and works against your natural voice. Effective style is not the literary equivalent of a drunk at a party with a lampshade on his head, a stripper jiggling for the crowd, a precocious child whining for attention.

"Don't distract a reader with your style," Rita Mae Brown advises in her offbeat writing manual, *Starting From Scratch*. "That's you showing off. A great style is one that appears effortless and one that is individual."

Rather than begging to be noticed, good style *grabs and holds* our attention as we read, because it feels like the real thing, and we trust it.

Becoming a "Stylist"

Some writers, whose work is more easily recognizable, are known as "stylists": Tom Wolfe, Annie Dillard, Fran Liebowitz, Jim Murray, M.F.K.

Fisher, Art Buchwald, Jimmy Breslin, Mike Royko, Hunter S. Thompson, Susan Sontag. It is often their style of writing, as much as what they write about, that captivates us (or turns us off, depending on taste). But in a sense, we are all stylists, if we know who we are and write enough to become comfortable expressing it; it's just that some write with a more conspicuous—perhaps more entertaining—style than others (one reason "stylists" so often get the plum personal columns).

Colin Campbell, I suppose, is a "stylist." In his Diary column in the *Atlanta Journal & Constitution*, he sometimes writes with a kind of rollicking, rolling effect, having lots of fun, even using the frowned-upon exclamation point and redundant parentheses to exaggerated effect. In the following excerpt, he writes about the many kitschy tourist attractions in Tennessee, and in particular a place called Rock City, almost like an excited child scribbling a post card home:

> My favorite wonders included Fat Man's Squeeze (a narrow defile through mountainous boulders), the swaying Swing-A-Long-Bridge (which I'm sorry to say was closed that day), a herd of white fallow deer identified as "reindeer" in honor of the holidays and, last but never least, a once-natural limestone cavern that had been walled with glittering quartz and hung with thousands upon thousands of pieces of *actual rock coral from somewhere in the tropics!*
>
> This is *more* than nature!

Campbell is obviously writing with a very personal stamp. But so is James Wolcott, though with a much different tone and pace, in this *Vanity Fair* excerpt:

> From his fiction he earned feeble amounts. And his married life was a forced march into misery. His Welsh wife, Lynne, was a bitter lush. A snarl in the next room, a staggering embarrassment, a public reprimand.

That is style—economical, hard, tough, yet vivid.

My friend Carol Easton would not think of herself as a "stylist" in the narrower sense; she prefers a more traditional approach, eschewing "fancy" writing. She cites Lillian Hellman's *Pentimento* as one of her favorite books because, she says, "You can see it all so clearly, right down to the bottom. I've never cared for writing that shows off." Yet Carol's writing reveals her own character as much as more exhibitionistic writing. In her biography, *Jacqueline du Pre*, which chronicles the life and premature death of the famed English cellist, Carol ends with this description of one of Du Pre's own recordings, played for her as she lay dying:

> Jacqueline loved her recording of the Schumann concerto; her interpretation, dark and melancholic, expressed the inexpressible. The concerto's three linked movements are pure, distilled emotion: Zola called it "the voluptuousness of despair." The first movement is full of longing, the second tender and poetic. Near the end, there is a transition, and then the orchestra and cello begin together, softly nostalgic, as though Schumann could see his life receding. The ending is a powerful, bombastic, final farewell that makes us weep — and comforts us.
>
> The music remains.

Because writing is calm and understated does not mean it is without style.

Think of style as *sincerity*.

"Style is freedom," Crisp and Carroll wrote. "It is freedom from the need to be competitive, from the need to be fashionable, from the need for 'success,' from the need for approval. But it is also more than simply freedom *from*.

"On another level it is a continuing celebration of one's singularity."

Forget about trying to "get," "find" or "develop" a writing style. Forget style altogether, and simply become the best writer you can. As you write, and grow as a writer, your style will show itself to you. Then, as you gain experience as a professional nonfiction writer, you will find yourself writing in varied styles that are appropriate for different markets, article types and subject matter, but are no less a reflection of your character.

FINDING YOUR VOICE

When I was a young man, an even younger friend read a piece of fiction I'd written and said to me, "It's a good story. You write well. You just have to find your voice."

He had published his first novel at the age of twenty-one and was on his third at age twenty-four. I wanted to know his secret. He had just revealed it, but, at the time, I didn't understand what he was telling me.

Voice is one of the most difficult concepts in nonfiction writing to grasp. The term is used in various ways by different writers, editors and writing instructors, which doesn't help. Often, they use "voice" to refer to *viewpoint* and/or *attitude*, sometimes *tone*, sometimes *rhythm*.

"In your natural way of producing words," writes Peter Elbow in *Writing*

FIVE FIGURES OF SPEECH
THAT CAN ADD SPICE TO LIFELESS COPY

Jack Hart, staff development director and writing coach at *The Oregonian*, cites four figures of speech that can help writers avoid the "dreary repetition of stock phrases" that leads to hack prose: the pure metaphor, the simile, the allusion and the personification. To these we might add the play on words—puns, and the more general "turn of phrase." For the most part, these stylistic devices involve the imaginative process of viewing one thing in terms of something else.

"Truly original writers learn to view reality through kaleidoscopes of overlapping images," Hart wrote in his *Editor & Publisher* "Writer's Workshop" column.

Let's take a look at some examples:

The pure metaphor describes one thing in terms of another. Metaphor can be brief, merely a passing reference, as in this example from Wallace Stegner's *Where the Bluebird Sings to the Lemonade Springs*: "The West has had a way of warping well-carpentered habits, and raising the grain on exposed dreams."

It doesn't have to be so literary, however. Mike Ferrara, writing in *Family Fun*, suggested that "for a growing family, a minivan is the automotive equivalent of a Swiss Army knife—it's the van with 101 uses."

A metaphor can be extended, as Laura B. Randolph did for her lead in an *Ebony* profile of a rising star:

> Six years ago Wesley Snipes was installing telephones in New York. Today, he has his own direct line to the power operators in Hollywood. With touch-tone speed, he's gone from unknown to unforgettable, from obscurity to celebrity.

A writer can keep the metaphor alive, weaving it throughout the piece, or even extend it fully into an entire article—as Kemper Shrout did for *Thrasher*, comparing a skateboard to a seductive woman. It opened like this:

> It's the first time a boy is intimate. The boy is fascinated by her. Like all boys, he notices her looks first. She is long and slender. Her tail has a tempting shape; it curves seductively. Her

continued

nose is upturned, charming. As lovely as she is, she is no Be-
atrice; she is a Jezebel. She is another skater's board, so she's
been ridden many times before. That doesn't stop her from luring
the boy; she maintains no morals. She whispers wantonly, "Stand
on me. . . . Ride me."

Fortunately, this was the lead to a *short* article — four long paragraphs in all. Sustaining such a self-conscious and overheated metaphor
is tough, although *Thrasher's* teenage male readers probably weren't
studying it for literary merit.

The simile makes a direct and explicit comparison. In *The New
Yorker*, critic Kenneth Tynan likened the experience of interviewing
reclusive talk show host Johnny Carson to "addressing an elaborately
wired security system."

Also in *The New Yorker*, Alastair Reid wrote of a put-upon cabbie
who sighed "as only taxi-drivers can sigh — a long escaping hiss of
world-weary air, like a deflating tire."

**The allusion makes a point or adds meaning by referring to some-
thing familiar, frequently from pop culture.** One example: My comparison elsewhere in this chapter of a strong, assured writing voice to
John Wayne's big-screen image.

Other possibilities: "a nude scene that would make Madonna
blush," "a romantic glance worthy of Julio Iglesias," "a shoe collection
Imelda Marcos would envy."

**Personification invests an inanimate object with lifelike human
or animal qualities.** An engine whines in protest, a tree droops wearily,
a train lets out a plaintive moan.

**The play on words/turn of phrase, offering a twist on a cliché or
familiar phrase.** Puns are the most common form of wordplay, applying
a word or words in a different way, or emphasizing a different meaning,
as when a reporter used "pregnant pause" to describe an actress' hiatus
from work to have a baby.

A classic example of clever turn of phrase is Dorothy Parker's famous line: "She ran the gamut of emotions from A to B."

These rely on phrasing that is already familiar, even clichéd, giving
it a new twist, as Pat H. Broeske did in a *New York Times* piece about
Hollywood's tendency to alter classic books for box-office appeal: "In

continued

the film industry, reading and writing are not nearly as important as arithmetic."

While the purpose of cute wordplay is usually to punch up or lighten copy, it can also be used to serious effect. In a first-person piece for *Essence/Men* on the tendency of males to repress their feelings, Ray Smith noted that while unabashedly heterosexual, he was also "a man who wants the ability to express emotions and feelings as openly as the next woman."

Wordplay shouldn't merely startle or amuse us, but also help to make a pertinent point.

◆ ◆ ◆

Some writers seem able to toss off metaphors, puns and other clever figures of speech with utter aplomb; most of us must work harder at it. Here are some tips for those who want to add some metaphorical sparkle to their prose:

• Write down a clever phrase when it comes to you, particularly during the research phase; don't assume you'll remember it. When I visited the commercially cluttered city of Honolulu, it reminded me of "the Home Shopping Network with humidity"; I jotted it down and used it later in a travel piece.

• If it's not inhibiting or distracting, search for it as you work; get up and pace the room, look out the window or go for a walk, in search of the right metaphor, simile or allusion.

• Let the material suggest it to you. Think context, and see what your imagination comes up with. Articles on the plethora of vampire movies and books, for example, always yield plenty of puns ("as the count rises . . ."); just beware of the tired, obvious and overworked.

• Find it in the revision stage. "Rewriting is partly a process of making better word choices," advises editor Irv Letofsky. "Look at areas of copy that are routine, a little flat. Find a more clever, funny or colorful way to say it."

• Imagine yourself at a party, or other social situation; put yourself in the role of the wit. See if that helps you find a more lively voice, and rewrite from there.

Without Teachers, "there is a sound, a texture, a rhythm — a voice — which is the main source of power in your writing."

Viewpoint, attitude, tone, rhythm, even style, are integral to what I think of as voice. But voice, as I use the term for this book, is something more difficult to discuss, to grasp. It is a quality most editors know instinctively when they hear it in an article, yet have trouble explaining to writers who haven't found it.

Voice, for our immediate purposes, is the confidence and authority with which you write, beginning with your opening and sustaining through every line. It gives your writing a special strength, forcefulness and believability that sets it apart from the weaker, wooden, uncompelling stuff. It reflects your care and commitment to the subject at hand, and the self-assurance with which you tell your story or argue your position.

It is often a quiet, unnoticed strength, rather than flashy stylistic technique or a demand by the writer that you listen — the difference, say, between John Wayne walking purposefully down a dusty main street and quietly pushing open the saloon doors, and Sylvester Stallone beating his chest and making bombastic threats. While Stallone often appears desperate in his movies, Wayne always seemed calm and in control. Those same qualities are part and parcel of an effective writing voice — in a way, voice reflects the confident control you have over your material.

If style is *how* you write — the way you execute and dress up your writing, how it looks on the surface — voice is an unseen force that drives your narrative and comes from deeper within. Like style, it comes with time, experience, grasp of technique — but, most important, simple self-confidence. The deeper you know and understand yourself, and the more writing you do, the more powerful your writing voice is likely to be.

KNOWING WHAT IT MEANS TO YOU

Viewpoint gives power and direction to voice. Unless you know how you feel about what you write, what it *means* to you, your writing voice is likely to tremble and crack.

Without viewpoint, an article or book is little more than a dry, mechanical "report." Granted, there is a market for such writing, particularly in the technical and hard news fields. But feature writers are paid to *write* — not just gather, analyze and organize facts — which includes investing their material with something special, that which only they can bring to it. That includes viewpoint.

In my proposal for this book, for example, I wrote with a clear viewpoint: that discipline, productivity and craftsmanship, coupled with genuine interest in the subject matter, are the bedrock of successful nonfiction writing.

I've done my best to maintain that viewpoint, and I believe it's helped sustain my voice. Writing articles is no different.

Sometimes, you'll hear a particularly strong voice and viewpoint in a first-person article, as in this opening of a Gail Sheehy piece in *Vanity Fair*:

> Six weeks before Gary Hart killed off his presidential candidacy, I had a story in the works describing the war that raged within this double man. It was a war to the death. After studying Hart on and off for three years, I had become convinced that this time around it was not a question of if Gary Hart would destroy himself but a question of when.

And later, this:

> The key to the downfall of Gary Hart is not adultery. It is character. And that is an issue that will not go away.

This is obviously a writer with strong command, not just of language, but of viewpoint, attitude, tone, all the elements. And what it all adds up to is a powerful voice that does not equivocate.

Because first-person writing can be so direct and expressive, taking the writer straight to the heart of her opinions, writers sometimes assume that's the best way to express "viewpoint." But one can write in the third person, never uttering the word *I*, and infuse one's work with viewpoint. It can be understated, without such an obvious bias. For example, this is how *Los Angeles Times* writer Elizabeth Mehren opened a story datelined Northampton, Massachusetts:

> They were in love, they were planning to be married, and they wanted the world to know about it.
>
> But Karen Bellavance and Beth Grace never dreamed that by placing their engagement announcement in the local newspaper this fall, they were setting some sort of precedent.

Mehren's approach is direct, restrained, almost matter-of-fact; yet her voice conveys respect, understanding and empathy for the lesbian couple she writes about.

Another writer might have opted for a more overt approach, or a more sensational tone.

TONE AND THE MARKETPLACE

Tone is another one of those words that is used in different ways by different people. Some use "voice" and "tone" synonymously; they are certainly closely linked.

For our purposes, think of tone as *how you use your voice*: angrily, placatingly, zealously, coolly, outrageously, ponderously, sarcastically, disparagingly, respectfully, wryly and so on.

Look at how a light, whimsical tone makes a zoological topic more entertaining, as reported by *Newsweek*'s Peter Annin:

> Deep in the murky swamps of Louisiana lurks a ravenous beast that is wreaking havoc on the terrain. No, it's not the alligator, it's not the Creature from the Black Lagoon, and it's not even David Duke. It's a massive fifteen-pound ratlike critter called the nutria, whose reproductive powers are almost as mighty as its gargantuan appetite. This hungry herbivore has become so prolific in Louisiana that it is wiping out vital wetland vegetation . . .

Tone is no less important in writing than it is in real life, in a conversation with a friend or stranger; it can help you communicate, or it can work against you.

When I wrote in *The Los Angeles Times* about a friend who died of AIDS-related illnesses, my anger was deep, because state government had agreed to provide him the home health care he needed only if he was willing to give up the preventive medicines that were keeping him alive — in effect, forcing him to commit suicide. As I wrote, though, I opted for a more cool, controlled tone:

> In a matter of days, Brad developed pneumonia. He went blind after a week or so, lost the use of his legs not long after, then suffered in pain for a couple of days until his morphine was adjusted to a higher level, which eventually rendered him disoriented. He was dead within weeks.
>
> The government had one less case to deal with.

By letting my anger seethe rather than scream, I felt I could communicate Brad's story more effectively. I also felt it would allow me to tell my story *in this market*, a general-interest newspaper. For another market, my tone might have been quite different.

Finding the right tone for your material and market can mean the difference between attracting or turning off readers. Writing in *Virtue* about marital trauma in a Christian marriage, counselors Sally and Jim Conway chose a calm, supportive but authoritative tone, as if they were sitting and talking directly with the worried spouse:

> Take time to catch your breath. In the first few days, quietly think

through your situation, ask God for wisdom and peace, and carefully consider the outcome of any action. Attempt to talk with your mate. Don't demand to know details, but offer to work on solutions.

If a similar piece appeared in, say, *Ms.* or *Redbook*, the tone would likely be quite different.

An excellent example of writing for the market is the following piece on fishing with a bamboo rod, written by Ed Hartzell for *Flyfishing*. He adopts the voice, tone and style of an avid outdoorsman and storyteller:

> The fish hit just where Mike said it would, and I let out my steelhead whoop. One jump, two, and a final one before a good run downstream. He came in reluctantly. Not a large fish, just a Rogue River half-pounder, but my first one from that famous water. "Now you have got your feet wet on the Rogue," Mike laughed. The rain got worse in the next hour, so we picked up our gear and headed up the bank.

Tone can be especially important for the writer who makes a living delivering opinions — the essayist, the commentator, the critic. No one is less "readable" than a weak writer who is also a self-important know-it-all.

Tom Shales, TV critic for *The Washington Post* and a *strong* writer, is particularly adept at delivering his commentary in a way that lets the reader know exactly how he feels, without browbeating. He writes in a wide range of styles, and his voice is invariably clear and strong, even when it's at its most placid and conversational, as in this excerpt:

> One series of commercials, at least, is fairly honest about what's being pitched. These are the ads featuring Dave Thomas, owner of Wendy's. Typically the commercials show Dave rejecting some dainty French sissy food and opting instead for a big juicy burger. Big juicy burgers make you fat. Dave is a big fat guy. He seems comfortable with that, however, and it's nice to see some nutritional realities get some tacit acknowledgement.

As low-key as that excerpt is, it's got attitude, and reflects solid craftsmanship. Read it aloud, and listen to the rhythms; note the beginning-middle-end structure that supports the paragraph: Shales sets up his subject, develops his theme, concludes with his final point.

Viewpoint/attitude/tone + craft = voice

THEME AND UNITY

Writing in a strong voice demands something else closely linked to viewpoint: knowing your theme.

In *Make Your Words Work*, Gary Provost writes that "theme was always one of those literary terms that made me afraid to be a writer."

For many years, I felt the same. Theme seemed like such a big, vague, "important" concept; and I just didn't get it. Then a friend suggested I think of theme the way I'd look at an argument I just had with someone close to me, to find out what it was really about. Let's say we fought over which TV show to watch—the surface issue—when it was really about something else. Resistance to a controlling personality, maybe, or standing up for one's rights.

Theme is what your article means on a deeper level and in a larger sense. If the subject of your article or book is what the reader "learns" about, the theme is what the reader meditates upon.

Again, the idea of a writer's commitment to discipline, productivity and craftsmanship—a sense of pride and professionalism in one's work—underscores everything in this book. If I didn't understand that, if I didn't write from that "place," I wouldn't be able to put it together as I have. That theme is the unbreakable thread that I hope pulls this book together, gives it unity.

Some other examples:

• When Carol Easton chronicled the tragically short life of Jacqueline du Pre, she also meditated upon a more profound subject: how the grace and beauty of art can help us transcend life's frustration and limitations, and give it meaning, even when it's brief.

• An article I read not long ago in *The Los Angeles Times Magazine* examined the tremendous immigration influx that is having such an impact on the city. Beneath all its facts, figures, anecdotes and quotations, however, was the idea that we must all learn to tolerate and respect each other, or put our very survival at risk.

• When Pat H. Broeske profiled John Travolta for *The Los Angeles Times*, her piece, on the surface, was about his declining career; the theme, however, was about the cruelty of the Hollywood star-making system and the fleeting nature of fame.

• My *Los Angeles Times* profile of a pioneering oculist who designs flawless prosthetic eyes was actually about the satisfaction one gets from helping damaged people feel whole again.

Even if your piece is as slight and simple, say, as a how-to article on weaving hair cornrows, it's probably about something more: the personal rewards of good grooming, perhaps, or of ethnic beauty and pride.

Only *you* can decide what is behind your words. That doesn't mean you state it overtly, in so many words. Let your theme *guide* you, almost in a subconscious way, helping you make certain choices and keep your story on track.

"Theme, like slant, is a junk detector," Gary Provost writes in *Make Your Words Work*. "It tells you what to leave in, and what to leave out. Leave in the stuff that relates to your theme. Take out everything else."

ORGANIZATION AND STRUCTURE

We've all heard the basic rule about structure: Beginning, middle, end. First act, second act, third act. Introduce it, develop it, conclude it. Boy meets girl, boy loses girl, boy and girl get back together. It's the foundation for virtually all successful writing.

But within that broad structure are other structural elements, such as logical development, linking of ideas, transitions, pacing and so on. For many writers, this process of "putting it all together" comes naturally; they seem to have an instinct for it. As they write, the pieces of their article fall easily, logically, into place. Others, however, write article after article that editors send back with notes like, "Sorry, but I find this a real mess," or "It's all over the place."

The Outline Debate

Are outlines the answer?

Opinion is divided on this. Some writers feel that outlines limit spontaneity and lead to dull writing; that they destroy any chance of a writer finding her natural rhythms and voice. Others feel that outlines are essential for constructing tight, seamless — and quickly written — articles that certain markets demand.

As an editor, I've often suggested that during revision writers try outlines for their unwieldy manuscripts; sometimes it helps, sometimes it makes matters worse. As a writing teacher, however, I find myself suggesting outlines less and less, because I've come to feel that the beginning writer needs to develop writing *instincts* before developing writing *forms*. I'll spend more time on outlining in Step Twelve — the rewriting and polishing chapter — because it's during revisions that outlines may be the most useful.

For now, I suggest a seven-step process that stops short of outlining but may help the writer who lacks a sense of structure:

GRAMMAR AND USAGE (BRIEFLY)

When *Harlot's Ghost* came out, Norman Mailer opened his novel with this sentence:

> On a late winter evening in 1983, while driving through fog along the Maine coast, recollections of old campfires began to drift into the March mist, and I thought of the Algonquin tribe who dwelt near Bangor a thousand years ago.

To my mind, Mailer is a fine, fine writer, not just of novels but also nonfiction; *Armies of the Night* remains one of the important books in my life. But Mailer apparently is not a strict grammarian. His opening sentence, as written, indicates that *recollections* were driving the car, when he obviously meant that a person was driving the car; Mailer's publisher, Random House, acknowledged that editors should have caught the "dangling modifier" before publication, but Mailer later defended it the way it was written, saying, "I like the rhythm as it stands."

In a way, I feel better knowing that Mailer occasionally makes mistakes or bends the rules, because so do I. Sometimes, I make the simple, human gaffe. Other times, I deliberately violate a grammatical rule if I feel it improves the writing. This can get you into terrible trouble, of course; there are readers out there who watch for grammatical miscues like a starving cat stalking fat mice.

A woman in Seattle found two sentences ending in the preposition *at* in a *Writer's Digest* article of mine (on effective writing, no less). She wrote a letter to the editor calling it "a grammatical abomination for which there is no forgiveness," concluding with this directive: *If you fancy ending your sentences with that redundant little two-letter word, do it in the privacy of your home and not in a magazine for the nation's writers.*

I confess to weakness in this area, especially in the classroom. I'm the kind of writer who can jot down a perfectly good sentence — most of the time — but can't diagram one. The kind of writer who knows instinctively to avoid the dread dangling modifier — but frequently forgets the term.

To students, I make remarks like, "That doesn't sound right. It doesn't work. They call that ... what *do* they call that...?" And a

continued

student more educated than I will offer, "dangling participle" or "incorrect pronoun reference" or whatever it is I've spotted that I'm too ignorant to articulate.

So, for this book, I'll simply offer this advisory: Don't flail yourself like a penitent if you commit the occasional "grammatical abomination"; if no one else forgives you, I will.

On the other hand, most writers who lack a thorough grounding and understanding of proper English grammar and usage, and consistently make grammatical mistakes, tend to be blissfully unaware of it. That might or might not be you; to check, study Strunk and White's *The Elements of Style* and particularly Mitchell Iver's *The Random House Guide to Good Writing*, if only for brush-up. Together, they will tell you pretty much everything you need to know in a clear, practical way.

Additionally, you may want to consider computer "grammar checkers" such as PowerEdit, Grammatik V, RightWriter and Correct Grammar, which are all IBM-compatible and may have Windows, Macintosh, Unix and DOS versions for wider computer application. Research these carefully before buying — computer magazines review them regularly — because they vary in complexity and capability. Generally, those most recently written will prove more effective. Beware of becoming dependent on grammar checkers to the detriment of your intrinsic writing skills, which also holds true for computer spell-checkers, thesauruses and the like.

1. Develop a system of indexing and filing, organizing your research material *before* you start writing, so that you know where everything is and can get at it quickly and easily. Or, if your notes are not all that voluminous, simply number the pages, then make a list of broad information categories, so that you know where to look. But don't go into the writing without first organizing your material.
2. Stop thinking of your article as an article. Think only about the first step — your opening.
3. Start writing. Get at least your lead down on paper. If it feels right, keep going through your billboard paragraph, if you decide to write one. If it still feels good, and you know where you're going, keep writing. If you sense you're just writing to write, and it's slowly getting away from you, stop.
4. Start thinking of your material as individual building blocks. Don't view it as a huge mass of research, or as a big, overwhelming article.

Think of it as a construction process, block by block. What is your next logical block?

5. Write freely and spontaneously until that block feels complete, relying on your organized files along the way. Keep writing block after block, building your article a section at a time, until it's finished.

6. Make a three-by-five-inch card for each block. Arrange them in the same order you've laid them out in your article, on a bulletin board, table, the floor. Look them over, top to bottom. Do they seem to fit logically? Do you like the flow? If not, rearrange your cards until the sequencing feels right to you; create new cards for points you may have overlooked but want to cover.

7. Rewrite using your new set of blocks.

Between steps four and five, you may want to pause and rearrange your research files to suit your new block approach, but don't do anything that slows you down too much, or gets you locked into a plan or other mode that feels inhibiting or constricting.

Try to get it all down on paper in as continuous and spontaneous a process as possible, letting logic be your guide.

Format as Structure

Certain formats and set structural approaches can help frame your material. Some of these, such as the list article—in which your main points are simply numbered and listed—will impose a rigid form on your material that you may find too limiting. Some writers, however, manage to be creative within such frameworks. Mary Ellen Strote, for instance, used a calendar/diary format for "The Making of a Cowgirl," a *Westways* account of Strote's participation in a weekend cattle roundup. To organize and break up her piece, she used subheads like "Friday Evening," "Saturday Morning" and so on as she told her tale chronologically. She included a sidebar with information on various dude ranch and outdoor organizations—sidebars being another device that can help to structure your material.

When I wrote my aforementioned *L.A. Reader* piece about a serial killer's teenage victim, I had to find a solid framework for material covering nearly a year and involving the lives of several characters. The use of *parallel narratives*—moving back and forth between the victim's and the killer's story as they converged—provided the structural support I needed.

Either one of those two pieces could have also been written:

- *Scene-by-scene*, with writer relating the story in a series of brief, vivid scenes that become the building blocks, set off graphically, without formal transitions, almost like a movie with quick cuts.
- *Place-to-place*, in which physical space would determine the progression of the article. My serial killer piece could have moved from the victim's school, to the freeway where he hitchhiked, to the killer's van as the victim got a ride, to where the body was dumped, to the morgue and so on.
- *Person-to-person*, with the writer moving to various characters (teacher, victim, killer, cop, parents, etc.), telling each of their stories.
- *Circling*, in which the writer winds her way inevitably back to the beginning. Strote, for example, might have gone full circle by riding out and returning on horseback. In my piece, we might have started and ended in the classroom, with the victim's teacher talking.
- *Varying focus*, in which the writer looks at a place, person, issue, etc. as if through an adjustable lens. Again, Strote might have started with a wide shot of the ranch, focused in on the corral, moved into the bunkhouse, right to a particular person. Or vice versa.

These are just a few devices that can provide a framework for your story. As with billboard paragraphs, different writers will use different terms for structuring techniques. Don't concern yourself with labels; find what feels good for you and use it.

More important, invent your own structures as you go along, because, as a *Writer's Digest* editor once put it, "there are as many ways to write a story as there are stories."

TRANSIT AUTHORITY

Transitions are what get you and your reader from one paragraph or one section to the next in a *logical* progression. There are obvious transitional phrases — *meanwhile, in the meantime, on the other hand, therefore,* et al. — that are useful at times, but not if they become proliforous, awkward or shortcuts to effective writing. Consider:

Wilson insists a writer should write every day to develop a sense of discipline and craft.

In addition, he feels a routine is necessary to establish continuity and guarantee productivity.

However, I refuse to become a workaholic and give up my life to my profession.

Therefore, I plan to write five days a week tops, and take a break on weekends.

DON'T BE A "REPEAT" OFFENDER—
UNLESS IT MAKES A NICE SOUND

In general, clean writing means copy that has been cleaned up of repetitive words and phrases, because repetitive writing generally makes for cluttered and messy copy.

Now, let's try that sentence again, properly cleaned up and without the repetition:

In general, clean writing means copy in which distinct words and phrases are used only once, or repeated as seldom as possible, to keep an article free of clutter and redundancy.

Part of the rewrite process is going back over your copy again and again, looking for repetition the way a devoted gardener searches for weeds. In time, you'll develop built-in radar for such excess during your initial draft, instinctively pruning, then planting new words.

There are times, however, when a writer may want to deliberately repeat certain words and phrases for stylistic effect or visceral impact.

"Sentences that are built alike," writes Gary Provost, in *Make Your Words Work*, "land on the ear the same way and they gain a cumulative credibility."

The following example is from a *Redbook* self-help piece by Judith Viorst:

Pete was, to mince no words, a four-star pain in the ass, and although Jane was smitten, she had grown sick and tired of being emotionally mistreated. Sick and tired of waiting by the telephone. Sick and tired of being hurt and humiliated. Sick and tired of his making her feel that she was unworthy of decent, loving treatment.

Notice how Viorst uses the phrase "sick and tired" to set up three successive sentences, and emphasize how frustrated and angry Jane must feel. Notice also how strong Viorst's writing voice is, and how technique gives it strength.

In the following excerpt, from a *Washington Post Magazine* piece about chronic fainters, Jon Cohen uses repetition to convince readers just how often the malady strikes, and how disruptive it is to one's life:

I fainted when I took the blood test for my marriage license.
I fainted when I had my ear pierced. I fainted three separate

continued

times while volunteering on the pediatric ward of a hospital. I fainted when I saw my brother lying in a hospital bed. I fainted four separate times while dentists—one of whom was named Dr. *Payne*—probed my mouth. I fainted when a waiter in Spain graciously attempted to clean another surfing wound . . . I could go on, but I'm getting queasy.

Note how Cohen came up with a tag (kicker, final thought) for the paragraph that (1) made use of the building rhythms of his sentences and "paid them off," (2) did it humorously, and (3) further underscored his point.

When several sentences in a row sound the same by accident, the effect is usually to bore or obstruct the reader. But used carefully and purposefully, repetition can make your writing more pleasing to the ear and give it added power.

Like any writing device, it can also grow self-conscious; use it sparingly.

Now this:

Wilson insists a writer should write every day to develop a sense of discipline and craft, and a productive routine. But I refuse to become a workaholic, giving up my life to my profession. My plan? To write five days a week, taking weekends off.

Which do you find less stilted, more readable?

Whenever possible, eliminate a transitional phrase by writing creatively—looking for a better choice—while maintaining the writing flow. Even a little word like *but* can get the job done.

The best transitions won't be "planned"; they tend to come naturally out of the writing process itself.

Smooth Transit

Shifting time, setting, line of thought, etc. must be logical, but it doesn't have to be complicated. An investigative piece in *The Pittsburgh Press*, by Andrew Schneider and Mary Pat Flaherty, jumped readers thousands of miles this way:

That same day, an ocean away in Hawaii, federal drug agents arrive at the Maui home of . . .

That's a pretty obvious jump, but it gets us there.

A sure voice and straightforward storytelling will produce the most effec-tive transitions, as this example proves, from a *Chicago* profile by Ben Jorav-sky of sixty-six-year-old developer Jerry Wexler:

> My final conversation with him is classic Wexler: He's calling from the telephone in his bathroom. It's four o'clock in the afternoon and he's toweling off after a shower.
>
> "Susan and I were just roller blading at Navy Pier," he says. "I only fell down once."

Without relying on a formal transition, the writer takes us forward in time, right into a new location, and straight back to his subject speaking.

Here's a nice transition, moving us smoothly from past into present, from *The San Francisco Examiner*; it's from a travel piece on southern France by Martina Winn, a former student of mine:

> Medieval pilgrims came to Conques seeking absolution for their sins, or cures for their afflictions. My husband and I came seeking the sacred past of Conques, worn into the stones of the church by centu-ries of belief.

A less-skilled writer might have written something like this:

> Once, medieval pilgrims came to Conques seeking absolution for their sins, or cures for their afflictions. However, my husband and I came more recently, seeking the sacred past of Conques. In a sense, it was worn into the stones of the church by centuries of belief.

Both are correct; but only the first is smooth, polished, professional writing.

When It Gets Too Smooth

Early in my reporting career, a copyeditor at *The Los Angeles Times*, David Kishiyama, took me aside and gave me advice that went more or less like this:

"You're constructing your articles *too* carefully. They're so perfectly put together, so seamless, they're apt to lull the reader to sleep. Don't worry so much about formal transitions and perfect structure. Surprise readers, shake them up once in a while."

Kish suggested that sometimes, it's better to leave transitions out and jump from section to section abruptly, changing scenes and time frames, shifting the pace, keeping readers off guard. He told me to let the copy desk take care of transitions with subheads, "dingbats," and other graphic section breakers.

It was the first time anyone had told me I was writing *too* carefully — a valuable lesson for a writer who had grown up with an English teacher for a mother, one who constantly stressed flawless grammar and construction. The advice Kish gave me that day not only caused me to look at nonfiction writing in a different way, it liberated me to loosen up, to be more creative. I began to think of articles as having an invisible "transitional system" based not on planned structure but on logical progression and flow.

Jane Harrigan, in *The Complete Book of Feature Writing*, edited by Leonard Witt, puts it this way: "Instead (of relying on transitions), think of each idea in your story as an island. Your task is to write bridges between the islands to keep readers from drowning.

"The only building material strong enough for these bridges is logic."

Sometimes, those bridges are built on *this* side, rather than *that* side, of the water. We tend to think of transitional phrasing as something that should start off a new section, but you can also write *to* the next island, building a transitional tone into the last line of the section you're about to leave.

The following opening of a commentary I wrote for *The Los Angeles Times* is a clear-cut "island" that concludes with wording that suggests a natural break:

> Not long ago, *Newsweek* columnist George F. Will laid into Jack Kerouac, the author most noted for chronicling the Beat Generation.
>
> Will, the Mr. Peepers of the political right, argued that the rebellion of Kerouac's period, and the "sandbox radicalism" of the 1960s that followed, was essentially the acting out of immature malcontents who have long since sold out to conformity, materialism, and other aspects of mainstream American life.
>
> "Respectability is the cruel fate of yesterday's radicals, especially in the 1980s," Will concluded gleefully.
>
> I can understand why Will would smirk at Kerouac. With his neat bow tie and prim, unsmiling demeanor, Will seems the most dour and emotionally constipated of our political commentators.
>
> Kerouac — crazy, freewheeling, creative, troubled, unafraid to reveal his darkness along with his joy — must have threatened the hell out of young George.
>
> I empathize: My own upbringing was at the altar of the safe and predictable.

But in 1969, I got a jolt. I read *On the Road*. It was a breakthrough for its time, and a catalyst that helped change my life.

◆ ◆ ◆

That opening was my first, big structural block; the final paragraph, and particularly the last line, followed by a graphic "dingbat," gave me the freedom to change time, place, setting, tone, etc. without having to wave a red flag when I got to the next island.

By building a bridge within the natural flow of the writing, I prepared the reader for the coming shift.

◆ ◆ ◆

In writing this book, I relied heavily on graphic section breakers and structural devices such as subheads, bullets and sidebars; I indicated most of them in my manuscript sent to the publisher. I do the same in articles, unless the copy desk at a particular publication considers this an intrusion into its territory (it doesn't hurt to ask).

That last point brings us back to the subject of *knowing the market*, and how that knowledge is related to craft: By being aware of the visual style and layout techniques of the magazine or newspaper section you write for, and by thinking like an editor and an art director/copyeditor, you can suggest these transitional and structural devices within your copy.

WRITING WITH RHYTHM

Did I say that voice was the most difficult writing concept to grasp? I might be wrong. It may be rhythm — something you must develop an ear for, more than an eye. Writing rhythm has to do with the structure, the ebb and flow, the "feel" and "sound" of a sentence. Does it move with ease and grace? Or is it awkward, stilted, haphazardly written? And how can we tell?

One way is to read your work aloud, have someone read it to you, even record it and play it back. What does your ear tell you? Do sentences seem to go on forever, packed with too much information or too many phrases? Are they written in a convoluted or artificial manner that we would never use in ordinary conversation? Are they so blunt they seem awkwardly abrupt within the context of our overall style and tone?

Sometimes, the minor, seemingly insignificant alteration can improve a sentence. In Step Seven, for instance, I wrote this line:

Guideposts can be as varied as you want them to be, as long as they serve their purpose.

In rewriting, I changed it to:

> As long as they serve their purpose, guideposts can be as varied as you want them to be.

The two versions say the same thing in exactly the same number of words. Yet the second version is better. I can't explain why; it just is. It *sounds* better. It's more *effective*. To me.

Just as you listen to music, you can develop an ear for good writing rhythm, in your own writing and in that of published writers whose work you enjoy and admire.

Varying Sentence Lengths and Rhythms

Writing with rhythm doesn't necessarily mean writing "fancily," or "beautifully," or "impressively." Sometimes, it means writing *simply*, varying the lengths of sentences for variety and pacing. However, even the simplest style must have sentence structures and rhythms that (1) feel comfortable or "right," (2) suit your material, and (3) serve your purpose.

When I got a traffic ticket and accepted the option of attending traffic school to clear my record, I turned my experience into a freelance piece for *The Los Angeles Times*. Here are three paragraphs from that piece that demonstrate minimal, yet deliberate, rhythm:

> Five branches in my neighborhood promised professional comedians for instructors. I picked Lettuce Amuse U Traffic School.
>
> A woman answered the phone and put me on hold. The line went dead.
>
> I was not amused.

The sentences are truncated, the rhythm minimal, staccatolike. But it suits the deadpan style, and each succeeding paragraph is shorter, written that way to build a rhythm that helps set up the final line, or the payoff.

"Listen" to how *Los Angeles Times* writer Irene Lacher uses varied sentence lengths and rhythms to pace the following lead:

> Molly Barnes was in good company. All around her were striking David Hockneys and imposing Morris Louises, but the most astounding work-in-progress at the museum that evening was Larry Rivers.
>
> Not the painting. The man.

Here's an example of a more elaborate, rolling rhythm, from a *Los Angeles Times* restaurant review by Michelle Huneven:

TEN SERIOUS TIPS FOR WRITING HUMOR

Humor writing is one of the trickiest and most challenging types of nonfiction to handle deftly, the high-wire act of nonfiction writing. To pull it off, one must write in a voice that is absolutely sure and steady, or a writer's "funny riff" can quickly become wincingly, embarrassingly sophomoric or lame. With humor, readers are poised and ready to dismiss the writer, even *disdain* the writer, at the first false note.

Here are ten tips that can help get you—and your reader—across writing's high wire:

Don't try to write funny. Instead of writing humor, write *humorously*. Put another way: Don't try so hard; stop showing off.

When I wrote a piece on cats for *The Los Angeles Times* op-ed page, I wanted to write in an amusing style, but I also had learned the hard way (translation: rejections) not to go for "jokes." So I opened by simply relating these observations, relying on tone to convey the humor:

> I noticed Walter Cronkite recently on the cover of a national magazine. He was holding his cat. Like Walter, the cat was chubby and gray. It looked directly into the camera with large yellow eyes that seemed to say, "I'll put up with this for maybe 10 seconds, buster, so you'd better snap off a good one pretty quick."

Don't use a sledgehammer when a feather—or at least a ball peen— is more appropriate. There's a time for subtlety and understatement (*most* of the time).

Don't try to make every line funny. Use only your best material, then let up. The tendency of some less experienced humor writers is to belabor each funny point, as if the joke is so good, they just can't let go of it. Often, they'll write a nice payoff—then keep going, piling on more, unable to resist milking one more laugh, burying their best lines and destroying the humor with overkill.

Instead of trying to write funny line after funny line, relate your observations in an amusing way, with an occasional line that stands out as funnier than others, but that feels *natural*.

Attitude is everything. Know what your attitude is toward the par-
continued

ticular material you're working on. Bemused? Outraged? Chagrined? Cynical? Pompous? Sanctimonious? World weary? For an example of maximum attitude — in this case, *disdain* — take a look at this excerpt from a Judy Tenuta piece in *Esquire* complaining about "wimpy" men:

> What ever happened to the kind of love leech that lived in his car and dropped by once a month to throw up and use you for your shower? Now all these pigs want is *commitment*. It makes me sick. These Alan Alda, family-focused, dead-men-do-eat-quiche hogs all say, "Oh, now that it's the Nineties, we're sensitive. We just want to sit around with a bunch of men and cry." Well, go to a Yankees game!

Establish your attitude in the first line and sustain it right through to the end. Every line of your copy must convince; even when you're being outrageous, you must write *as if you yourself believe it.*

Write with point of view and "edge." Most humor writing I encounter in the classroom is "soft." A writer thinks his or her clever wordplay is sufficient to interest an editor. Editors look for funny writing, but they also look for humor that has something to say. That doesn't mean you have to beat your chest over an issue, or that your prose must drip with acid. It simply means it should *have a point.*

When Tom Shales poked fun at Michael Jackson "mania" in his *Washington Post* column, Shales created farfetched fantasy to comment on our obsession with pop culture icons; yet he wrote in an understated manner:

> The people of the United States woke up this morning and discovered they had lost all interest in Michael Jackson.
>
> No one wanted to hear him sing, no one wanted to see him do the moon walk, and no one wanted to watch him turn into a werewolf. Panic swept the record industry and two or three companies folded immediately. In department stores throughout the land, gloves were being bought in pairs once again.

In his typical low-key style, Shales underscores the ridiculous excess of "Michaelmania" and media hype. Read through your most recent humor piece, and ask, "What's the point?" Do you have one?

continued

Use concrete detail and specific reference. The "show, don't tell" dictum that applies to nonfiction in general also applies to humor writing; when possible, replace generalities with concrete detail, keeping references specific.

Dave Barry relies on wild exaggeration to generate laughs, but he also keeps his outrageous humor rooted in reality. In a *Washington Post Magazine* piece, he gave a Dave Barry-style account of a weekend boating trip with the guys:

> One of the men, Larry, was fishing, and he hooked a barracuda right where we had been swimming. This was unsettling. The books all say that barracuda rarely eat people, but very few barracuda can read, and they have far more teeth than would be necessary for a strictly sea food diet. Their mouths look like the entire $39.95 set of Ginsu knives, including the Handy Arm Slicer.

There's humor in the familiar and specific, such as brand names. Or, as Barry might put it: a "$39.95 set of Ginsu knives, including the Handy Arm Slicer" is funny; "a set of carving knives" isn't so funny.

Find your focus; stay on track. This is fundamental writing advice that some aspiring humor writers feel they can ignore; they believe that anything they put down will work, no matter how far it strays off course. After all, if it's "funny," people will keep reading no matter how many tangents, right? Wrong.

Just tell the story you want to tell, using pertinent details and incidents that feel like a *natural part of the story*. Resist throwing in irrelevant jokes and asides; hone to the backbone of the piece.

When in doubt, trim whole sections. Often, the problem with flawed humor is simply that you are so in love with your humor, or so familiar with it, you are unable to spot the weak stretches.

Here's a useful exercise: Take a piece of writing you feel you've already worked to death and cut it in half (that's right, in *half*). If it's a 2,000-word piece, for instance, trim it to an even thousand, not a word more.

By forcing yourself to find the essence of your material, and make the most careful word choices, you'll start to hear a clear, strong — and

continued

funny — voice emerge from the clutter and confusion.

Along those same lines:

Make every word count! This is another truism applicable to all writing that applies even more stringently to humor, where economy of style is crucial. With the fragile artifice of humor, readers are ready to stop reading at the first sign of ragged rhythm, awkward syntax or verbiage.

Take another look at the various writing examples I've cited in this section; you won't find much excess. Now look over your own manuscript for extraneous words and phrases.

Consider format as a way of enhancing the humor. Sometimes, using format devices such as bullets or lists is not only a good way to compress, focus and structure your material, but may be funny in itself.

Writing some years ago for *Rolling Stone*, P.J. O'Rourke parodied the social advice "list article" by writing a step-by-step guide to proper manners . . . for using cocaine. A sample:

> 5. Who pays?
>
> There's considerable debate about this. Some say the guest should pay for cocaine as a way of saying thank you to the host. Others say the host should pay for cocaine as part of the entertainment. Most people, however, say society should pay for cocaine by having to watch maniacally self-indulgent movies, fragmented TV sitcom plots and fractured and pathetic live performances by brain-boiled comedians and pop musicians wound up tighter than a Hong Kong wristwatch.

O'Rourke had a neat list of twelve more "Common Problems of Etiquette Explained," and it was funny stuff. Don't limit yourself to standard article form; be imaginative.

Read your work aloud; get trustworthy feedback from others. Developing an "inner ear" for cadence, pacing and timing is especially important with humor. Read your manuscript aloud, listening to it as if listening to a standup comic, for whom both tight writing and almost flawless rhythm are essential.

There's a reason even the most successful comics try out their acts in small clubs before taking them to the big time; it's easy to believe in your own laughs and fall in love with your own jokes.

continued

> To develop your ear for effective humor, you may need to share your writing with others. Objectivity is particularly difficult when writing humor; there are few things more painful than chortling over your prose — then having to admit that maybe it's not so funny after all.
>
> Getting feedback from teachers or trusted writing friends may be a necessary process before you develop that humility and objectivity that tell you what works and what doesn't.

In a town where capellini alla checca has become as endemic as the hamburger, Dan Tana's remains a bastion of well-simmered meat sauces, fettucine alfredo, and steaks the size of paperback bestsellers.

Read that sentence aloud, and listen to the almost musical flow. It's not fancy or showy; just careful word choice and construction, with rhythm that builds to an effective crescendo.

Some claim that one is born with writing rhythm, that it can't be learned or taught. I have only to look back at dozens of articles I wrote when I started out to know that's not true; I had yet to develop even a marginal sense of rhythm. Here's the opening of the first freelance magazine article I sold, published twenty-five years ago in *American County Government:*

A solid, three-story white house stands proudly on the corner of a lower middle-class San Diego neighborhood. The house is larger than the other homes in the area and perhaps better kept, but like other homes, it shelters a family.

Despite the fact that there are no bars on the windows and no high fence surrounding it, the house is, in essence, a jail. Nineteen convicted criminals are serving "time" here instead of in jail.

My writing in those two graphs is flat, littered with redundancy, with construction that leads nowhere in particular, and breaks off abruptly. Let's rewrite and polish for better word choices and a more purposeful rhythm:

It stands proudly on the corner of a lower middle-class San Diego neighborhood, a three-story white house that shelters a most unusual family.

Neatly maintained, it has no fences, no bars across its windows. Yet this innocent-looking structure is essentially a jail, home to nineteen convicted criminals who are part of the growing "halfway house" movement — and part of a growing national controversy.

The revised version may not be stylish or memorable writing, but it has considerably more clarity, rhythm and thematic quality than the original.

As you write, don't just watch the words as they appear on paper or your computer screen; listen to the sound they make.

WRITING AS "PROCESS"

Other writers and writing instructors can add to or expand on the techniques we've just covered. Among the books I'd especially recommend are several already mentioned: Iver's *The Random House Guide to Good Writing*, Provost's *Make Your Words Work*, Zinsser's *On Writing Well* and Blundell's *The Art and Craft of Feature Writing*, the last a particularly valuable guide because of its insight regarding the use of storytelling techniques in nonfiction writing.

In books like these, as well as in classes and workshops, you'll sometimes encounter contradictory advice. Don't let conflicting approaches confuse or paralyze you; they are simply reminders of how many ways there are to write well, and how each of us must ultimately sort it all out and find our own way.

One thing virtually all writing mentors agree on, however: Writing well is not just a cerebral or technical activity, but a *process*; interrelated steps, intuitive movement forward, creation. While building blocks and careful construction have their place, writing well is not a feat of engineering from a meticulous blueprint. Think of it more like surfing or ballet, where skills and balance are important, but mean little without the natural flow.

That's why it's so important to establish a writing routine, ongoing and uninterrupted, so that such qualities as rhythm, voice and style have the chance to develop and become second nature.

It's during the rewriting phase that our writing becomes more deliberate and purposeful, when most writers take their work to "the next level" — polished, publishable, marketable. Not by accident, it's also the next phase in this book . . . Step Twelve.

Becoming Your Own Editor

S ometimes, as I watch Michael Jordan make his dazzling moves so smoothly on the basketball court, I wish I had the natural talent to write lovely, perfect prose as effortlessly. Then I wake up to reality and remember that Jordan didn't get where he is without a *lot* of effort. In fact, as a high-school sophomore, Jordan was cut from the varsity team. He had the talent, but not the skills. So he went back to work, putting his game through endless drills, practicing fundamental movements hundreds, even thousands, of times, developing first into a basketball crafts-man and eventually into the most artistic basketball player on the planet.

What's my point?

That writing is not so different.

In a sense, Jordan became his own coach, able to recognize his weak-nesses as an athlete and push himself to overcome them; the process of repetition and refinement freed him to be his most expressive.

Likewise, as writers, we need to *become our own editors*, developing the objectivity to recognize our weaknesses and the discipline to reshape, whit-tle and hone our material until it expresses what we want to say as effec-tively as possible.

Some writers worry that disciplined revision will destroy their personal vision or "artistry," yet it's the way any accomplished sculptor works with raw clay, trimming and shaping and smoothing it into a polished piece.

Freelance nonfiction writers, in particular, need to develop the editor within, because we operate with so little feedback, in what I call the "free-lance vacuum." Without an "inner editor" to guide us, we can spend years suffering endless rejections or paltry sales and never understand why.

The more a writer can turn in polished copy that requires minimal revision, the more in demand that writer will be. Chronic meddlers aside, most newspa-per and magazine editors live and breathe to find writers like that.

REWRITING AS OPPORTUNITY

Your job in the rewrite stage is to make your prose as clear, tight, accurate and evocative as you can. Depending on what you accomplished during your first draft, that can mean a lot of work or relatively little; it requires not only looking at your manuscript as a whole, but polishing line for line.

In my early drafts of this chapter, I reworked the opening section perhaps a dozen times. I trimmed words, added new ones, trimmed some of those, moved words and sentences around, altered ryhthms, thought harder about word choices and exact meanings, et al.

Finally, it felt OK to me, and I moved on — for a while.

In the final polishing phase, I did more tampering, cutting several graphs from the Michael Jordan section and adding a thought that came to me as I brushed my teeth: *The process of repetition and refinement freed him to be his most expressive.* It was a notion I'd expressed in another part of the book, but it seemed to fit better here. Initially, I wrote *repetition and practice*, but I'd already used the word *practicing*, and I liked the alliterative sound of *repetition and refinement*. And so on.

To some, this kind of fussing might seem obsessive; to many professional writers, though, it's just familiar revision and polishing, *what we do to make the writing better.* Some of us may do it more than others, and some of us more (or less) effectively. But every writer I've encountered improves his original copy substantially through revision — at least the ones who make a living at it. That's because all writing can be improved. How you accomplish that is no great mystery, and the ability to do it is no rare gift of talent.

Flawed writing is just unfinished work, a set of problems to be solved and better choices to be made — an opportunity to improve your work.

During this chapter, we'll look at ways to take advantage of those golden opportunities.

Method and Mind-Set

When it comes to revisions, we can divide most nonfiction writers according to three general approaches:

Those who give their copy a superficial once-over, then turn it in. These writers operate out of self-delusion, certain that their writing is so brilliant it must remain untouched; or deep insecurity, unconsciously sabotaging their chances of success by turning in second-rate work. Their assignments invariably come in late, or at the last minute, looking dashed off. Editors must consistently rewrite and polish the work of these lazy writers and check their facts extra carefully. They sustain marginal livelihoods by using their clips — polished by previous editors — to fool new and unsuspecting editors, but eventually they're found out. Their careers are lifelong exercises in excessive market-hopping and frustration.

Those who concentrate hard and make fixes during only one rewrite, or a limited number of rewrites. These writers write strongly the first time around, with great self-assurance; they fear that by going through their copy too many times, they will become hypnotized by the cadences and the words, losing their objective eye, and no longer seeing the problems; or that they'll lose trust in their original voice and muck things up. These writers are blessed with self-confidence and instinct for wordcraft, but they must be careful they don't get lazy, convincing themselves the job is done when it's not. They like to get their copy in quickly, then progress to the next money-making assignment ASAP.

Those who read through their copy endlessly, polishing their material meticulously. These writers feel compelled to go over their manuscripts countless times, from beginning to end, making sure every word, phrase and clause is exactly where they want it, that the whole thing "sounds" just right; too often, they value craft over creativity and content. They must fight the "manuscript hypnosis" and blindness that come with so much meticulous rewriting and be careful not to get so analytical that they rewrite the life out of their copy. At deadline, you must pry the manuscript from their hands; they can be insufferable perfectionists.

For better or worse, I fall into the latter category. I've listened to those writers—professionals and academics alike—who advise against overly picky rewriting; I've tried, unsuccessfully, to revise in a more relaxed and less compulsive manner. In the end, I decided there is no one way to rewrite, except to do it well.

No matter how we make revisions, doing it well requires a special state of mind that allows for maximum humility and objectivity about our work.

Developing Your Inner Editor

To rewrite, you must get out of your writer's skin and into an editor's. But not just *any* editor. Too often, the editors who give us assignments become surrogates for the parents who once gave us orders to clean up our rooms, eat our peas, or "behave properly." Subconsciously, we may feel we must write just the way they want us to, or we'll be punished or unloved. But most editors—the good ones, anyway—want you to write the article *your* way. They want a piece that's well crafted, but that also stands out from all the others, with a special quality only you can give it.

That's why it's so important for us to become our own editors, freeing ourselves from guilt, pressure and the need to please, the things that inhibit

COMMON COPYEDITING/PROOFREADING SYMBOLS

⋀ Make correction indicated in margin

Delete; take ~~words or letters~~ out

Close up (no space) li ͜ke this

Delete charact ͡er and close up

Spell out (abbrev)

Insert a let ͭer

spac ͛emark

Transpose (way) (this)

(stet) Ignore ~~editing~~ marks; let it stand

⊙ period

⌐ comma

/Lower ¢ase

upper case

⌐ Move this to the left

⌐ Move this to the right

Straight underline indicates italics

Wavy underline indicates boldface

run in with previous line

¶ Start a new paragraph

To indicate end of article:

# # #

or

-30-

us from taking creative risks and writing with a strong voice.

At the rewrite stage, listen to your own deep, natural, instinctual editor, the one who knows a clean line from a ragged one, a well-paced story from a sluggish one, a terrific conclusion from one that is merely serviceable — the things you instinctively see and know *as a reader*.

Isn't it strange how clearly we see writing problems when we read the work of others, but get blurred vision as soon as we turn our eyes to our own manuscripts? (That's one reason the students in my classes spend so much time critiquing and editing the work of other students — it helps them learn to spot weaknesses and problems in their own writing.)

Here are some suggestions for welcoming and nurturing your inner editor, and seeing your copy more clearly:

Role play. Read your rough draft as if you are its editor. Be perceptive, brutally honest — a tough taskmaster.

Pretend it's someone else's writing. Look at your manuscript as if a stranger wrote it. My normal routine when I get up in the morning is to read a newspaper or magazine with my coffee. When I rewrite, I substitute my manuscript for the paper or magazine, trying to read it with the same detachment.

Try simple, pure concentration. As you wake, focus on the rewrite task at hand, nothing else. Go directly to the manuscript, with minimal detours and diversions; if necessary, stay in your robe. Pick up the manuscript, focus, and start reading.

Put it away for awhile. If time allows, put your rough draft aside and work on something else. Come back to it after a period of days or weeks with a fresh eye.

Give yourself a break. Do something strictly for relaxation. Shop, meditate, get a massage, go to a movie, take a hike, or spend the day at the beach. Some people like to immerse themselves in housework or gardening for a while, or just pet the cat. Take a breather.

Come to it rested. Rewriting when you're tired is tough. Try to start fresh, after waking. If you can, break up your long rewriting stretches with short naps.

Read a good writer. Read a short piece of writing by a favorite writer. It will remind you of what good writing is and how it sounds, and it will inspire you to a higher standard. It's a good daily practice, anyway, and can be especially helpful during revisions.

Develop rituals. Hemingway, I once read, sharpened a dozen pencils and laid them out in a row, all at a certain angle, before he began revisions; when the last pencil was in place, he knew it was time to begin. Personally,

FOLLOW THIS SIXTY-EIGHT-QUESTION CHECKLIST AND GET YOUR REWRITE "RIGHT"

Here are sixty-eight questions to ask yourself before sending your article out. (That's right, sixty-eight.) If any answer is no, you have more work to do.

THEME AND CONTENT

Do I fully understand the assignment and what's expected of me?

Do I know what *type* of article I've been assigned?

Do I understand the scope I'm expected to cover?

Have I written the article the editor anticipates?

Have I covered the main points thoroughly?

Is my word length in accordance with the assignment?

Am I able to state my angle in a concise phrase or sentence?

Am I able to capture the essence of my article in a headline or title that suits the target publication?

Have I written a good "billboard paragraph" high in my story that sums up and helps focus my piece, if my material and style call for it?

Have I maintained that focus throughout the article?

Are my theme and message clear?

Have I written an article that will give readers insight or valuable information, make them think, inspire them to action?

Have I gotten to the "why" of the subject, not just the who, what, where, when, how?

Have I supported my more general statements with examples?

Have I done enough research, collected enough facts, figures and anecdotes—*details*—to write a convincing, compelling article?

Have I used those details wisely and judiciously, rather than packing in so many I bore the reader?

Is my article believable as a whole, with balance, supportive research and a credible tone?

If I paid cash at the newsstand to read this particular article, would I feel satisfied with its content?

Would it answer all my questions?

WRITING QUALITY AND READABILITY

Does my lead grab and involve the reader?

Does it get to the point fairly quickly?

continued

Is it appropriate for and relevant to this particular subject?

Is it clear and concise, rather than belabored or trying for too much?

Does it establish the tone I want?

Am I sure I haven't buried a better lead deep in the story?

Have I saved my best bit for a kicker, when it could be an effective way to get the story going?

Does my kicker sum up what my piece is about and leave the reader with a distinct impression, rather than just trailing off or ending abruptly?

Have I used the best element possible — quote, anecdote, summary statement, etc. — with which to end?

Will it leave the reader feeling satisfied?

Is my writing colorful, vivid, energetic, rather than flat, sluggish, uninspired?

Is it relaxed and conversational, rather than stilted and overly formal?

Are the quotations in my piece compelling, rather than dull?

Have I used my strongest, most meaningful quotes, and paraphrased or eliminated those that are weak or rambling?

Have I broken up quotations, sprinkling bits and pieces throughout my article the way a good cook spices up a meal?

Have I structured and tightened anecdotes for maximum payoff?

Do my anecdotes feel like the real thing, rather than contrived or lacking in credibility?

Have I given my article the cliché test and eliminated every trite phrase?

Have I replaced each multiple-word phrase ("made a decision") with one word ("decided") whenever possible?

Have I inspected each word, searched for a better choice?

Am I using word power, instead of relying on a limited, lackluster vocabulary?

Have I microscoped each sentence to see if it can be improved?

As I read my article aloud, is there an effective or appealing rhythm to my sentences?

Have I varied their structure and length for purposeful effect, both within the sentence and within the surrounding blocks of text?

continued

Have I rewritten or eliminated all sentences that are long, confusing, overly complex?

Have I trimmed every sentence, every word, that isn't absolutely necessary?

Have I deleted "very" and other needless terms?

Is my description vivid and specific, rather than bland or vague?

Is my pacing fast or varied enough for impact and readability?

Have I broken up paragraphs for maximum effect?

Does every word, phrase and sentence in this article serve the story and the reader, rather than my need to "show off" or prove what a good writer I am?

STRUCTURE AND ORGANIZATION

Does my article feel unified and "of a piece," rather than unwieldy and marred by tangents?

Does it move forward logically from point to point, with a clear beginning, middle and end?

Have I developed and sustained my main theme throughout?

Are my transitions smooth?

Have I turned blocks of information into sidebars when appropriate?

Have I spread out chunks of material that would be better condensed in one related section?

Have I been careful not to repeat myself needlessly?

Should I try an outline to better organize my material?

Have I "overorganized" to the point that it seems too formal and lifeless?

PROOFREADING AND MINOR FIXING

Have I gone over every line, checking spelling, punctuation and grammar?

Have I gotten rid of repetitive phrases and duplicated words where synonyms can be used?

Have I double-checked the meanings of words I'm unsure about?

Have I attributed all quotes, and to the proper sources?

Are my quotation marks all in their correct places?

Have I used the proper verb tense?

Have I used the active voice, whenever possible and appropriate?

continued

> Have I done a serious typo search?
> Have I double-checked facts, *assuming nothing?*
>
> ◆ ◆ ◆
>
> As you gain experience rewriting, add your own questions to this checklist, and use it as a refresher.

I have a "magic chair" for rewriting, as well as a "magic clipboard"; I revise only with a red or blue felt-tip pen, depending on my mood. OK, it sounds silly — but it works!

Consider your environment. If you need silence, find a silent place; if you need people around, go where people are. Or try rewriting in an unfamiliar place, such as a cafe or park; see if the change gives you a fresher perspective.

Set your clock. Some writers allow themselves a certain time period to goof off before working, and set a time when the rewrite process starts. Set your alarm clock; when it rings, you know it's time to begin rewriting with clarity and objectivity.

Review your research. Go through your notes and transcripts. They may suggest facts, quotations, anecdotes, or other elements to be added, expanded, deleted. You'll also return to your manuscript with the confidence that comes from knowing your material thoroughly.

Read it aloud. This is always a good way to listen for your writing patterns and rhythms. Be aware of sections that are long, boring, self-conscious and so on.

Get professional feedback. If you feel stymied, confused, worn out, and blind to your manuscript's problems, seek experience and advice. Classes, consultation and professional writing friends are all good sources; relatives and nonwriting friends are generally not. Avoid advice from those with an ax to grind or a reason to do nothing but give you praise.

PROTECTING THE ORIGINAL VOICE

With rewriting, we face the conflict between trusting our original voice and crafting an article we can sell. It's a point that troubles many writers who want to nurture and get on paper a "pure vision," and not tamper with it too much afterward.

"Don't change words, because in this practice you are deepening your ability to trust in your own voice," Natalie Goldberg admonishes in *Writing*

Down the Bones, her Zen-inspired guidebook for "freeing the writer within." She warns writers to beware rigid form and format, as well as the tyranny of didactic editors and instructors. Peter Elbow echoes that caution in *Writing Without Teachers*, which encourages aspiring writers to find their voice by regular free-writing periods unabridged by self-editing, attention to grammar, or other restraints. " 'Trying to write well' for most people means constantly stopping, pondering, and searching for better words," Elbow advises. "If this is true of you, then stop 'trying to write well.' Otherwise, you will never write well."

I pretty much agree — for first drafts, and especially for beginning writers. That's the time not to be critical of ourselves, not to stop, ponder and search, not to worry about writing well. That's the time to get it all down on paper, almost like telling a story to a friend. But there comes a time when nonfiction writers must make the language clear and precise, pay careful attention to form, smooth away the rough edges.

Those of us who make our livings writing for specific markets and specific editors, often on strict deadlines, will always work under certain demands of form and craft, with changes pressed upon us — changes with which we may not always be comfortable. For me, meticulous rewriting is a way to enhance and protect my voice, while making it more appealing to the marketplace. The tighter, cleaner and sharper my work, the less others are likely to mess with it.

Even Goldberg concedes the need for editing and revision, advising writers to "not be sentimental about your writing when you reread it. Look at it with a clear, piercing mind."

Peter Elbow goes even further. In his more recent — and more realistic — book, *Writing With Power*, he confesses that he spends far more time in revision than in original writing. "Revising requires wisdom, judgment, and maturity," he writes. "There is no way to get these qualities except through practice and experience."

TIGHTER AND CLEARER

"Tighten it up!" may be the most common order you hear from an editor after you've filed a story.

You'll be surprised how many other problems disappear when you prune your prose with resolve. It affects clarity, focus, pacing, et al. — yet it's a skill many writers take lightly or not at all. That's because deleting our precious words and phrases, sometimes entire blocks of copy, hurts. Often, the need to trim will have nothing to do with the quality of our writing, but simply space limitations; it's not uncommon, even with a short article,

GIVE YOUR WRITING THE PERSONALITY TEST

Every article, like every human being, has its own personality. If its personality is ho-hum, dull, by-the-numbers, it will probably be rejected.

Some techniques, such as using the active rather than the passive voice, help add brightness and vitality to your writing. But it goes much deeper than that.

Go over your piece again. Does it reflect your abiding interest in the subject? Does it convey a sense of confidence, energy, enthusiasm? You can't fool an editor by injecting false enthusiasm into your writing with exclamation points, breathless or gushing prose or other phony devices. The life-force of an article must be in every word, every line, every detail you choose. They reflect what you feel about the piece, even though you may write in the third person and never add a personal comment.

Think of your article as a stranger, someone with whom you've just had a chance encounter. Was this person memorable for some reason, or one of those many people we pass by who leave little or no impression on us?

Think about why certain people seem indelible: They might be energetic, funny, colorful, crazy, frank, argumentative, challenging, courageous, admirably straightforward. Perhaps they are warm, perceptive, insightful, inspiring, elegant, poignant, a pleasure to look at. Or horrifying, disturbing, infuriating. And so on.

Now think of why some people are easily forgettable: bland, shallow, superficial, lifeless. Not much character or personality. Few qualities that make us want to spend much time with them.

Identify the characteristics in your writing that give it life. Even the most basic news item must be informative.Even the most simple how-to piece must be helpful, must teach something. More complex pieces — profiles, historicals, exposés, roundups, travel articles, etc. — require much more. The life-force of your article can only come from your personal, heartfelt interest in the subject, your particular "take" on it, and the craft with which you invest that in your work.

Test your own writing for signs of life. Make a list of the qualities in your article that will make an editor want to share it with his readers. If you find that list on the short side, think about why your article lacks personality, and what you can do about it.

to be ordered suddenly to cut hundreds of words. When you must trim, it helps to realize that *you're being forced to make more scrupulous choices, and often you end up with better writing.*

The more your readers must work their way through verbiage for less reward—too many words with too little payoff—the fewer readers you will have.

First Step: Slash and Burn

When you weed the garden, start with big patches. For a *Writer's Digest* piece on rewriting, I put it this way:

> The piece isn't right. Accept it. Put your pride and ego aside. Detach from it. Now attack it.
>
> You're Indiana Jones, cutting through dense foliage to the temple treasure. Hack away at leaden leads, verbose sentences, endless paragraphs, dull quotes.
>
> Move fast. Slash and burn. You're not writing now, but tossing out garbage. You're a valiant rewriting commando, using a red pen to cut through columns of enemy type. Forget about all the work that went into building those precious sentences and paragraphs. They are just clumps of words. There are countless more where those came from—*better ones.*
>
> Keep going. Wield a brutal pen—excise whole sections if necessary. All the way to the end.

How do you recognize a "whole section" that's expendable? Here are some clues:

- It slows the article down without saying much.
- It repeats a point you've already made.
- It isn't relevant to what's immediately around it, or to your overall angle or theme.
- You've included it because you discovered it during research and don't want to "waste" it.
- You used it for padding to meet your assigned word length.
- You promised a source that you'd mention it (never make those kinds of promises).
- It's one of your favorite passages in the piece, such great writing that it can't be cut, no matter what.
- You think it makes you look good, plugs a favorite cause or some other self-aggrandizing reason.

The same warning signs apply to every quotation, anecdote, and other bit of copy in your manuscript.

If it doesn't belong, get rid of it.

Pruning With Precision

Trimming line for line, word for word, is probably the most difficult rewriting stage of all. In a sense, it's looking at writing that's pretty good, *lines that work*, and finding fault with them.

You may not have to tamper with every line; but as you become more adept at revising, you'll be surprised by how many welcome opportunities you find for improvement. For example:

> You get paid not only to write, but also to rewrite. At least that's the working principle of writers who are proven professionals.

That's reasonably good writing — grammatically correct, and more or less to the point. But it's not the line a professional would turn in. Try this instead:

> You don't get paid to write, but to rewrite. That's the credo of the professional writer.

The rewritten version says the same thing — better — in fewer words.

Learn to prune ruthlessly. Read every sentence carefully, with relentless concentration and stealth. You're a soldier going house to house, room to room, closet to closet, your senses alert, looking for the enemy. Trim out every unnecessary word you find. Another example:

> He was talented enough, but he just didn't have the skills.

In my initial draft, that was the original line in the first paragraph of this chapter. In revisions, I made a quick fix:

> He was talented, he just didn't have the skills.

And another:

> He had the talent, but not the skills.

Is that kind of fine-tuning worth the time and trouble? Am I being too picky? After all, there's only a difference of a couple of words, and a few syllables, between the original and the final version.

First of all, I like the final version better. It feels "right" to me.

But let's get back to that issue of how many words and syllables were deleted in revision — two words and five syllables, to be exact. Which means

---

TRIMMING WIDOWS

Sometimes, at the galley proof stage, an editor will request that you trim a certain number of inches from your copy.

One way to comply with minimal damage to your article is to first find and trim widows.

The term *widow* refers to one or two lonely words that hang at the end of a paragraph after your article is typeset, when the last sentence fails to fill out the line.

Let's say you are ordered to trim five inches from your article. Find out how many lines equals an inch (generally four or five). Let's suppose you must cut twenty lines to get rid of five inches of copy. Before cutting whole lines, look for widows hanging at the end of paragraphs. Go through the paragraph. If you can delete a word or two within the graph equal in length to the widow, that will pull the widow in, eliminating an entire line by only losing a word or two. That's because a widow of only one or two words, by taking up an entire line, equals an entire line.

Find widows, and you can avoid making too many sizable trims.

---

two fewer words and five fewer syllables my reader must work through to get to the end of the sentence. Let's say I make a dozen changes like that on the average page. Two words times a dozen equals twenty-four words; five syllables times a dozen equals sixty syllables. Multiply those by 500 manuscript pages, and I've deleted 12,000 words and 30,000 syllables — 12,000 *useless* words and 30,000 *useless* syllables. That doesn't even take into account excising entire blocks of copy.

Obviously, as I rewrite, I don't think this analytically; I rewrite instinctively for sound and rhythm and flow and feel, what my ear tells me.

There will be times when superfluous words or syllables are useful and valuable, contributing to the quality of the rhythm and feel of the writing. Sometimes, "extra" words fall naturally on the paper for that reason as you write. If they improve the writing, leave them in. You will find them in this book, and in virtually all published writing.

The secret is sensing which to leave in (fewer) and which to take out (more), while rewriting with the finest editorial microscope.

Here are examples of pruning opportunities to look for:

- **Unnecessary modifiers or qualifiers:**
  To reach the very highest levels of your profession. (*Very* is rarely needed.)

WHEN THE "VERY" RULE VARIES

Beware writing gurus who lay down absolute rules, such as: Never use the word *very*.

Use it judiciously — very judiciously.

Most of the time, it is extraneous. But don't eliminate it from your vocabulary. Sometimes, it just "feels right" in your copy. And sometimes, you can use it for special effect, as Patricia Leigh Brown did in a *New York Times* piece about a woman who purchased an antique log cabin:

> The old adage says, "Never shop when depressed."
> But Judyth van Amringe was depressed. Very depressed.
> Business was slow. At the flea markets she frequents early on Sunday mornings, when the rest of the world is dreaming, the pickings were slim, very slim.

Good writing is writing that conveys information clearly and communicates with the reader, even when it defies formulas and rules. Sometimes, that's *why* it's good writing.

"I could kill you!" she screamed, clearly unhappy. (Delete *clearly unhappy.*)
A gorgeous knockout, really tough trip, truly ugly argument. (*Gorgeous*, *really* and *truly* are unnecessary.)

- **Long form phrasing:**

Trends within the industry (Industry trends)
Glance of someone's eyes (Someone's glance)

- **Redundancy:**

An article that just ran recently . . . (An article that just ran)
Markets to sell to . . . (Markets)
Plagued by countless car alarms . . . (Plagued by car alarms)

- **Weak verb use:**

These publications are constantly changing editors. (These publications constantly change editors.)

- **Simple verbiage.**

The first journalist to ever personally interview . . . (Delete *personally.*)
When interviewing, ask questions of your subjects . . . (Who else would you ask questions of?)
Both of them were . . . (Both were)

Then there's the unkindest cut of all: getting rid of our favorite bits of wordplay—those big, important words or fancy phrases we hang on to because they prove what clever writers we are. Those should be the *first* to go.

Writing Sentences for Clarity

Careful pruning not only eliminates clutter, it adds to the clarity of each sentence.

Here are some other opportune areas:

• Overly long sentences, or convoluted sentence structure combining clauses.

He took the writing class, not to learn to become a better writer, but to develop a sense of discipline, which every writer needs, along with regular assignments, if he hopes to become a professional.

Break it up with a period, semicolon or colon, rewriting for clarity:

He took the writing class, not to learn to become a better writer, but to develop two things a writer needs to be a pro: a sense of discipline and regular assignments.

• Sentences in which clauses delay getting to the subject.

Writing her article, and daydreaming about being at the beach, Cathy lost her focus.

Better: *As Cathy wrote her article, she daydreamed about being at the beach and lost her focus.*

• Delayed quotes.

Joe, seeing what the problem was, but not wanting to make trouble, said, "Let's just leave."

Better: *Joe saw what the problem was. "Let's just leave," he said, wanting to avoid trouble.*

• Weak verb phrases that can be replaced by a single verb.

We made the decision to go.

Better: *We decided to go.*

• Passive voice, or object-verb-subject.

The silence was shattered by a gunshot.

Active voice (subject-verb-object): *A gunshot shattered the silence.*

• Unnecessary use of the verb *to be.*

He was sprinting straight for the goal line.

Better: *He sprinted straight for the goal line.*

• Too many numerical figures packed into one sentence.

Studies indicate that 80 percent of those attending the three-month program lost an average of twenty-two pounds in the first six weeks.

Break up the sentence, separating the figures; two figures per sentence — three, tops — is a good rule of thumb.

- Abstract terms, rather than concrete.

The number of vaccinated children in the county was unusually low, indicating a potential epidemic of several diseases in the near future.

Concrete: *Only 40 percent of the county's children were vaccinated, indicating potential epidemics of chicken pox, measles and other diseases by 1995.*

A good general rule for sentence clarity: If you must write long sentences, try to precede and follow them with short sentences. This also varies and improves *pace.*

PACING YOUR STORY

When you rewrite, you'll probably find copy that moves too slowly, rather than too quickly. A number of suggestions previously discussed have an impact on pace. Here are some other opportune areas for adding energy to sluggish prose:

- Long, belabored openings that get an article started slowly.
- Paragraphs that run on and on without a break.
- Long stretches of any one kind — description, quotations, statistics, analysis, opinion — that might be broken up or balanced and varied with other elements.
- Long quotes that could be paraphrased to better effect. Any quote that runs on for more than a few short paragraphs should be unusually colorful, meaningful or revealing. A few short sentences is probably a better gauge.
- Too many long sentences, not enough short ones.
- Excessive sentences that begin with prepositions or qualifiers, such as *but, and, first of all, even then.*
- Too many words that describe general feelings and thoughts (felt, loved, must have known) rather than specific physical action (kissed, fainted, tossed his cookies).
- Absence of people and action. Get people on the page, doing things, and it will give life and energy to your manuscript. When possible, use storytelling techniques to bring narrative power to your copy.
- Stilted, formal style, rather than conversational flow.

Two specific techniques — constructing sentences for speed and condensing expositional or descriptive copy into "broad strokes" — are also invaluable for picking up your pace.

Speed Construction

By speed construction, I mean sentences with hard-driving force and rhythm; extremely tight writing, including incomplete sentences; using specific devices such as *clustering* (packing sentences and paragraphs with lots of details) or *dashes* — like this — for compression; and loading sentences with strong action verbs.

When I wrote for *TV Guide*, profiles were generally limited to 1,500 words. That meant tight writing, punchy copy and quick pace. For a profile of Steve Kampmann of *Newhart*, a passionate golfer, I opened with this:

> There are many people who have excellent reasons for getting up at the crack of dawn. Those who deliver milk. Early morning disc jockeys. Truck-stop waitresses. But what rational defense can there be for rising with the sun to swing an iron stick at a tiny ball and curse when it doesn't go where you want it to?

Notice three elements in that paragraph: strong verbs, incomplete sentences, and a concluding sentence characterized by a "rolling" rhythm.

When I needed to increase the feeling of anxiety in my *Los Angeles Times* humor piece on car alarms, I piled on details (clustering) and relied on strong action verbs:

> The alarm took over my life. It woke me from countless sleeps, leaving me haggard. It sent me racing from parties in strange neighborhoods, frantically squeezing my monitor to stop the maddening sound. I fled stores, restaurants, trysts to shut it off. It taunted me to try to find peace and quiet; just when I thought I had, it started screaming at me again.

Here's another example of clustering from my Kerouac commentary, which was limited by space restrictions to 1,200 words:

> Back home, armed with more Kerouac, I left for Mexico with another pal, surfboards wedged into my battered VW van. During five glorious months, I got inside my first "tube," was attacked by sharks, thrown unjustly into jail, dug wells with Mexican laborers, slept with pigs, got drunk on home-made tequila, danced to mariachi music at village weddings, hallucinated — legally — on peyote buttons, and never misbehaved.

I could easily have taken many paragraphs — pages even — to cover the same material. The result, though, would have been lethally slow.

"Broad Strokes"

One of the best ways to cut to the chase and get your story moving again is to use a *broad stroke* — condense a long stretch of description into a single (or no more than a few) succinct sentence or phrase.

In an early draft of my last Jane Fonda profile, written in the mid-1980s, I wanted to compare her with the actress-activist I had interviewed a decade earlier. I went on at great length about how different she was, not only physically but as a person, taking eight paragraphs to say it. But when I reread my rough draft, I realized that it slowed the article down at a point when the copy needed to move. I knew I had to trim severely.

When I filed my polished version, I used a single, broad stroke to bridge time and to pick up the pace:

> This was a different Jane Fonda in 1984: confident, in command, but warm and good-humored, with a deep, calm maturity at forty-six.

A more personal kind of profile, for a different publication, might have warranted more space and detail for that phase of the article; but my focus was Fonda's business and political life, and I wanted to get on with it.

Often, a striking metaphor or other figure of speech can serve as your broad stroke, cutting through endless description. *Dallas Morning News* sports columnist David Casstevens described a boxing gym where heavy bags dangled from the ceiling "like giant sausages." And in *The New York Times*, Alessandra Stanley captured the essence of a school principal in short order:

> Mr. Leder, an engaging and energetic man who sweeps across the school's floors like an opera house impresario . . .

(For more on figures of speech, see sidebar, page 190.)

Writing with broad strokes is particularly useful for condensing historical exposition, geographical movement and physical description. In his *Boston Globe Magazine* piece on coach Dale Brown and the LSU basketball team, John Powers covered a lot of ground with this broad stroke:

> He wanted a hungry team with a hard edge to it, so Brown went to big cities like New York and Dallas and Louisville.

And, later, this one:

> Brown's spiel, in city and bayou, was the same: We'll be your family.

(Notice the use of colons in some of these examples; they can help structure and pace a sentence, helping it to "pull up" abruptly and cut to the point.)

The most effective broad strokes are simple and direct, compressing months and years into a few words when space limitations require it, or because it serves the narrative.

A former student of mine, Julian "Bud" Lesser, writing in *American Cinematographer*, summed up the end of a historical collaboration between producer Leland Stanford and photographer Eadweard Muybridge like this:

> Injured pride unravelled the bonds.

Five words; that's economy.

CHOOSING YOUR WORDS CAREFULLY

When you microscope each word in every sentence, don't just ask, "Is it necessary?" or "Can I eliminate it?" but also, "Can I find a better word?"

Let's use the second sentence of Chapter Eight as an example. This was an early version:

> The winning essays were to be printed in an "anthology" — actually a cheap booklet of shamefully shoddy quality — that would then be offered to the parents of the "lucky" students at a couple bucks apiece.

After several revisions, something about it still bothered me. Finally, I spotted the problem in the last sentence and made this change:

> The winning essays were to be printed in an "anthology" — actually a cheap booklet of shamefully shoddy quality — that would then be foisted on the parents of the "lucky" students at a couple bucks apiece.

Offered to *foisted*.
What a difference a word makes!

Meaning and Purpose

Too many times, when trying to find better words, students end up with words that are inappropriate or slightly off the mark. It helps to realize that effective word choice is fairly simple:

1. Each word, as Gary Provost puts it, *has a job*.
2. Choose the word that does the job best.

The broader your vocabulary and more exact your understanding of meanings, of course, the better your choices will be. Three practices can help in that area:

- Speak with more precise meaning in regular conversation, eliminating lazy word choices even when you're not writing.
- Read a lot, and be conscious of how words are used, looking up unfamiliar words or usage.
- Make a concentrated effort to build your vocabularly. A freelancing friend claims that studying *Word Power* religiously gave his career a significant boost; others swear by crossword puzzles or thesauruses.

Then, as you finecomb your copy, ask questions like these:

- Is this word dated? Can I find one that's more contemporary?
- Is it weak? Can I find one that's more powerful?
- Is it clichéd? Is there one that's fresher?
- Is its meaning clear or muddled as I've used it?
- Is it bland? Can I make it vivid?
- Would a different word affect the tone (irony, poignancy, etc.) in a way that would enhance the article?
- Am I confusing similar words (nauseous for nauseated, principal for principle, etc.)?

And so on.

Let's look at another example, a lead from a rough draft of mine, opening a *TV Guide* profile:

> Tim Reid grimaces as he hefts the iron; sweat runs down his straining face. All around him, others pump with the same painful determination, grunting, groaning, cursing. The place sounds like a medieval torture chamber, but it's just one of those $500-a-year fitness gyms where members try to transform themselves into the kind of fantasy bodies that fill the pages of muscle magazines.

Now, the revised version:

> Tim Reid grunts, groans, curses. All around him, cries of pain mingle with the clang of iron. It sounds like a medieval torture chamber, but it's just one of those $500-a-year bodybuilding emporiums where members try to transform themselves into Conans and Conanettes.

The difference came primarily from key word changes; those choices affected the tone, pacing, energy and length of the paragraph.

Being so exact is a less-cerebral activity than you might imagine. Personally, I rarely go to a thesaurus; I believe most of the words I need are already within me. Nor do I find myself thinking hard to find the right word, because, in that way, I often come up with one that feels contrived or out of place.

Finding the precise word is often a matter of having a good feel for your material, its sound and meaning, form and content, all working together — symphonically, if you will. Once again, read your copy as if it's music, to see where the rhythm and sound lead you — to which trims, and to which new words.

STRUCTURE AND ORGANIZATION

It's one thing to scrutinize a single line or paragraph for weaknesses; it's quite another to read through an entire article to see if it holds together. After reading through hundreds or thousands of words, we often feel lost, no longer able to tell if the structure is solid.

That in itself is a strong sign it's not.

An article's structure doesn't have to be obvious, with neon signs flashing on and off saying, "That was the beginning, here comes the middle!" or "That was part two, get ready for the big finale!" But if it doesn't have a semblance of form, moving logically from beginning, through the middle, to the end, you've got problems. Some symptoms to watch for:

- It feels unwieldy, disorganized.
- It lacks a sense of direction, a logical movement forward.
- It strays.
- It lacks *focus*.
- It seems too slow in some areas, and too thin and hurried in others.
- Related chunks of material are spread all over the place, instead of grouped together.
- Blocks of information that could be in sidebars throw it off track and slow it down.

If you get a sense of any of these as you read your rough draft, it probably needs reassembly.

Take another look at the seven-step "block-building" process detailed in Step Eleven, and consider trying it, if you haven't already.

Or you may want to develop an outline, the road map that can get you back on track to your destination.

Giving Your Article a Backbone

Outlines can take many forms, from the simple to the complex. They can be as basic and skeletal as a list of numbered steps, or a more detailed blueprint.

When *Writer's Digest* asked me to put together a how-to article on practical tips for improving articles, I spent an hour or two at a neighborhood cafe with a cup of coffee, contemplating ways to improve flawed writing. I came up with nine I felt were particularly valuable, listed them, wrote a line or two describing each, switched them around until I was happy with the order, went home and started writing. That simple list was all the "outline" I ever needed.

For more lengthy and complex articles or series, particularly the investigative type, I've spent a day or even several days constructing a logical, manageable structure for wide-ranging material — interview transcripts, documents, myriad notes and other data — that would otherwise overwhelm me.

My *Los Angeles Times* piece on Jane Fonda, for example, involved dozens of interviews, clippings, legal documents, and files stacked nearly a foot high. After I wrote my opening of several hundred words, I stopped, organized and indexed my material, then spent two days going through it and making a step-by-step outline. It looked like this:

I. Fonda's wealth, success/"Big Chill" factor (as now written)
   A. Dilemma of former counterculture activist running multimedia business empire. (summary/billboard)
      1. Mention "The Dollmaker" up high; air date.
   B. Deliberate effort to reach mainstream, win hearts of middle America.
      1. Confessional quote about antiwar activity, Hanoi trip, etc. (Fonda transcript, page 6)
   C. The Fonda "transformation"
      1. Bullets of best examples — fitness empire, Super Bowl, Warhol, the new home (see list, File 3).
II. Anti-Fonda reaction
   A. From the Right, etc.
      1. Peter Collier quote (File 4), Erica Jong (see clippings, *Ladies' Home Journal* profile)
   B. From the left, or conservatives won over
      2. Gallup poll (File 1), "more power to her" quotation (Smyth, File 4)
      Etc.

Even in using the outline above, I abandoned it now and then as I wrote, following my own instincts. If I strayed, I went to the outline for guidance back.

As my writing becomes more personal, and less involved with extensive research, I find myself working more often without an outline, either before or during revisions. After years of steady writing, I find I'm better able to combine the two basic writing steps—writing and revising—into one, followed by more meticulous fine-tuning and polishing.

As noted in Step Eleven, there's a sharp difference of opinion about rigidly structured articles. Art Spikol, for one, is deeply suspicious of them.

"Outlines limit spontaneity," he wrote in *Writer's Digest*. "Follow an outline and yes, you'll get everything said—but at the expense of not allowing your reflexes to work. . . . Give yourself a chance to respond to your own rhythms."

Now listen to Connie Emerson in *The Writer's Guide to Conquering the Magazine Market*: "Spontaneity, as far as my experience (and that of other writers I've talked with) is concerned, hasn't sold many articles. In fact, doing what comes naturally is what keeps many writers—especially nonfiction writers—from selling.

"Instead of producing spontaneous creations, you want to put your material into analytically on-target, rejection-proof form."

That depends a lot on the type of article you write, and on the target market. A business or investigative article, for example, might demand a more careful format than a personal-experience or humor piece. *Vanity Fair* or *Rolling Stone* might value qualities such as style, viewpoint and vivid description as much or more than concise analysis or flawlessly organized copy, qualities that may be at a premium with other publications.

I know one thing: Outlines can lead to dull, programmed writing, even creative paralysis, in the hands of the less-experienced writer, particularly in initial drafts.

I also know that there are times when an outline has saved me from being overwhelmed, particularly with more substantive and complex articles.

Be aware of the potential value of outlining—and of the dangers.

REFINDING YOUR FOCUS

When I wrote the article for *Western's World* about a two-week kayaking trip through the islands of Alaska's Prince William Sound, my theme was how the wild outdoors can teach us leadership skills that can carry over to our working life. My subject matter was a group of professional men and women taking this kayaking trip with the National Outdoor Leadership

School. That's what I wrote about, and I guess I did it well enough, because *WW* published it, along with several of my color slides. But the article always troubled me. It seemed too loose in structure, directionless, lacking a strong narrative; line for line, the voice felt weak, erratic.

Rereading that article recently, I spotted the problem: I'd tried to tell the story of the entire group, which was too much for me to handle. Picking out one or two individuals would have helped me find focus. A perfect choice would have been a dentist from Michigan, who'd signed up for the rigorous course so he could return home and share more outdoor activities with his son. His story would have brought more heart and humanity to the piece, along with much-needed focus.

If you sense that your article might be out of focus, back up and ask: What is my subject? Then ask: Am I sure?

It's not uncommon to mistake theme or *broad subject matter* for the subject of your article — the person, place, event or phenomenon that you're actually writing about. It may be that you're trying to explore the entire jungle — dense, sprawling, easy to get lost in — when you need to narrow your focus. Let's say your subject matter is the Amazon rain forest. Pretend you're looking at your article through a cosmic microscope. Screw down your lens: What is it about the rain forest you want to examine? What fascinates you? Could it be an endangered plant or flower that's beautiful or valuable to science? Can you tell the story of the disappearing rain forest through one individual who's working to save it?

When I look back over my articles that I feel had the most focus, people are usually at the center. Mando Ramos, the boxer, gave me the focus for examining generational alcoholism; O. Robert Levy for writing about prosthetic eyes and helping people in need; Joanne Winkler for writing about the tragedy of drunk driving; Luke Messenger for writing about the fragile survival of old-time mountain packers; Polly Platt about women struggling to find their rightful place in the film business; Tim Reid about the determination to succeed and survive in the face of racism and inequity.

Finding your focus before you write your story can help you organize your research; finding it during your rewrite can help you better organize your material for a more unified article.

A review of Step Two (finding the angle) and Step Seven (billboard paragraphs) may also help.

STARTING OVER

It won't happen often, but there will be times when you realize you must go back to square one. Don't be intimidated or disheartened by rewriting from the top. It's a chance to save your piece, and with the magic of computers, massive rewriting is not the cut-and-paste drudgery it once was.

Starting over begins with that first line—the first glimpse of the trail that soon disappears into the overgrown jungle.

Close your eyes; listen to your inner voice. What first few words do you hear? What images do you see? Jot them down. Find a new lead that gives you focus, establishes your voice, and sets the tone for your revision. Write from there.

I know how painful massive revision can be—I've had to do it many times. But let me tell you a story, something that happened when I was an editor with *The Los Angeles Times*. I wrote about it in one of my *Writer's Digest* columns:

> A freelance writer with only one or two published articles sent us a query and we asked to see an article on spec. Her first draft was vague, rambling, short on details—but promising. We asked for a rewrite. She turned it in on time, with substantial improvements. But it still needed more work. I asked her to try to "take command" of it, to keep it in the third person but somehow infuse it with a point of view or tone that would give it a narrative thrust, a stronger voice; also, still more details. Though clearly frustrated and exhausted, she didn't gripe; instead, realizing she was new to the craft, she was willing to pay some dues. We told her to take her time.
>
> Many weeks went by. The third time around, she turned in a fact-filled, intriguing and nicely structured article, with the strong voice of a natural writer. Somewhere, in her many rewrites and polishes, she "got it." She also went out of her way to provide us with some terrific rare photographs. We gave her article a two-page spread up front and sent her a check for $800.

Here is her lead from the article we printed:

> The director lay face up on the floor of 404-B S. Alvarado St. He was a famous movie man—but he wasn't playing dead. By the time his valet found him that morning—Feb. 22, 1922—he'd taken the big sleep. His escort to eternity had blasted him into the history books with a .38.

The writer was Brenda Day, my former student from a UCLA Extension class. The article was about the scandalous, unsolved murder of Hollywood film director William Desmond Taylor in 1922, and new evidence that had recently been uncovered in the case. This is Brenda, looking back at her experience:

> This was the most difficult piece I've ever written. I felt like I was in over my head from the beginning—I'd only sold two articles and here I was writing a feature for *The Los Angeles Times* Sunday Calendar section. I worked on it, on and off, for six months, turned in three completely different drafts and rewrote interminably. "Brenda, you have such dramatic material," John Wilson told me. "Where's the drama?"
>
> So I took the most dramatic element of the story—the moment of the murder—made it my lead and did my damndest to write like a pulp novelist.
>
> This article took six months to write, but taught me two shortcuts that have helped me crank out articles quickly ever since: (1) get a good lead and the article will write itself and (2) ask yourself what's most dramatic about your subject; or, better yet, pick a dramatic subject.

Almost every freelance writer has gone through an experience similar to Brenda's, having to start over almost from scratch. It's painful, inevitable—and beneficial.

It's how you *grow* as a writer.

Making the Extra Commitment

Rewriting demands something extra from a writer, a deeper commitment, a keener eye, relentless self-criticism, almost a force of will that allows you to see deficiencies you didn't see before. If you can make that extra effort, time after time, you're on your way to becoming your own editor.

Getting feedback—escaping the freelance vacuum—can help. In the end, though, it's up to you: how hard you're willing to work, how much you want to crack those markets that are waiting to pay writers with polished skills.

It helps to realize that you can never make your manuscript perfect, that there comes a time to send it on its way.

It also helps to never be satisfied.

◆ ◆ ◆

It's time now to look at manuscript preparation and some specifics of the submission process—Step Thirteen.

Step Thirteen

Turning It In

W hen Jonathan Kirsch was a senior editor with *California*, and one of the most respected magazine writers in the business, I had the honor of teaching a workshop with him through UCLA Extension. I concentrated on marketing tips, while Kirsch focused on the writing itself. At one point, as I discussed the importance of the professional presentation of query and manuscript submissions, Kirsch volunteered some advice.

"It probably sounds crazy," he told our audience, "but when a submission comes in, I even look at the stamps the writer selected to put on the envelope."

Laughter rippled through the room, including mine.

"I know, I know," he went on. "It sounds incredibly picky. But as an editor, I look for every possible sign that tips me off, not just about the professionalism of the writer, but about character and personality as well — especially character and personality."

Kirsch's remark reflects the impact the presentation of your work has when it hits an editor's desk. An effective submission is one that stands out as better than the other 95 percent, the stuff that gets rejected almost at a glance.

When a freelance piece comes in, it usually faces preconception and prejudice. Some editors automatically distrust freelance writers they haven't worked with, assuming the worst; it's a defensive instinct developed from years of experience. One editor tells me that the great majority of articles she asks to see on spec never materialize; the writers, for whatever reason, get cold feet and fail to follow through. What does come in, she says, is rarely usable.

The freelance writing pool has a reputation, to some extent deserved, for a disproportionate number of flakes. In a profession where *anyone* — with little or no background — can pitch *any* idea to *any* publication, there's bound to be a fair number of unskilled dreamers who flood the marketplace with half-baked ideas and semiliterate submissions. It goes with the territory and hurts the rest of us who do our best to do it right.

The point Kirsch made with his remark about postage stamps was that during the submission process, you must make an extra effort to distinguish yourself from the rest of the herd, in every way possible. You can do that by presenting your manuscript with pride and care, reflecting your personal character and your high standards of professionalism.

PREPARING THE MANUSCRIPT

You want your work to stand out, to be noticed. Does that mean sending off your manuscript in a star-spangled envelope, decorated with photos of your loved ones, insignias for every organization you belong to, and stickers for every cause you support?

Probably not.

Looking professional and expressing yourself at the same time requires some taste and good judgment. While such choices as stamps, the color and quality of your stationery, and your letterhead design all help to reveal something about you as a person, you don't want to call *undue* attention to yourself or your packaging. At this stage, you have two goals: (1) to get the editor to select your manuscript from the pile and (2) to then see only your words — the content of your article — and forget the packaging.

Putting It Together, Step by Step

If you followed my advice in Step Two (sidebar, page 25), you've set up an office at home, complete with everything you need to type or computer process, print, package, and mail off your articles.

Let's start with the basics of more traditional manuscript preparation and submission, keeping in mind that electronic submissions are becoming more and more the norm, with some markets preferring and even requiring them (we'll deal with electronic submissions further down).

Some guidelines on general manuscript preparation:

• Your manuscript should be typed or computer printed, *never* hand-written.

• It should be printed on only one side of each sheet of paper. In the case of continuous-feed bond paper used with tractor-feed printers, all pages should be separated and perforated edges cleanly removed.

• Use 8½ × 11-inch *white* paper, preferably 16 to 20 lb., 25 percent cotton blend. No erasable bond (which smears).

- One-inch margins all around is standard; some writers and editors like to see 1½-inch top and right-hand margins, finding the extra white space easier on the eye.
- No script or italic fonts (underline the words to be italicized). With typewriters, pica (the larger type) is preferable to the smaller elite. With printers, ten characters per inch is standard.
- Your printer should be letter quality or dot matrix that closely approximates letter quality.

If you're still typing, use a cloth, not a carbon, ribbon — and change it the moment it starts to fade.

- Typists should use Liquid Paper or a similar quality correction fluid or erase, but *should not strike over errors*.
- Double-space your manuscripts (to allow editors to make notations), single-space your cover letter and envelope.
- The general rule is sixty characters per line, twenty-four lines per page. Don't fudge the margins to try to "sneak in" extra copy and violate your length restriction. Editors can spot it in a second; it looks awful.
- Indent all paragraphs the standard five spaces.
- Avoid awkward page breaks, such as broken quotes, hyphenated words, floating subheads (subheads at the page break, separated from following copy) and so on.
- Some writers like to type "more" at the bottom of each page until the final page, but many editors consider this outdated. As one editor said to me, "I'm smart enough to know there's more."

Now, some rules of form for your first page:

- Upper left corner: single-space your name, address, telephone number(s), social security number (for the publication's accounting and tax-reporting needs) and fax number if you have one.
- Upper right corner: word count. If you do not have access to a computer word-count function, do an approximate word count yourself. Here's how:

For short items, 500 to 750 words, count every word manually.

For a quick estimate of longer manuscripts, multiply 250 words (an average) by the number of *full* pages in your manuscript.

For a more precise count with longer manuscripts, do the following:

1. Count all the characters on two full pages of your manuscript, then divide the total by the number of lines in those two pages; this will give you the average number of words in an average line (usually

John M. Wilson   approx. 2,300 words
Street Address   (copyright optional)
City/Zip Code
Telephone Number
Social Security #

REDFORD'S LATE HARVEST

by John M. Wilson

SANTA FE, N.M. -- "You may not want to ride with me," Robert Redford says, "when you see how I drive."

Seconds later, he's gunning down a mountain road outside tiny Truchas, N.M., in a silver Porsche Targa, taking curves neatly at 60 m.p.h. Half a movie company pulls out behind him in vans and trucks, moving to valley setups while Redford scouts locations on the way.

"I used to race these things," he says, and, as he down-shifts on another sharp curve, you believe him.

If only his film were moving as smoothly.

Redford's here to shoot <u>The Milagro Beanfield War</u>, directing his second feature after winning an Oscar for his first, <u>Ordinary People</u>. And it's been a rough trip.

between nine and ten). For the sake of example, let's say ten.

2. Count all lines for three pages and divide by three to figure the average number of lines per page (usually around twenty-four to twenty-five). Let's say twenty-five.

3. Multiply average line word count by average number of lines per page to get average number of words per page.
Example: $10 \times 25 = 250$.

4. Multiply that number by the number of total *full* pages in your manuscript (add up partial pages for approximate total). Let's say you have twenty full pages.
20 pages $\times$ 250 words $= 5,000$ total words.

Writer's Market provides a slightly different formula for a more precise word count in its chapter on "The Business of Writing."

Beneath the word count, you may want to include the rights you are offering (see Step Fifteen for more specifics on publishing rights) and your copyright notice (© 1993 John M. Wilson), although some feel a copyright notice is amateurish (personally, I've never included one).

• Center the title. Begin it roughly one-third of the way down the page to allow two or three inches of white space for an editor's notes. It's common to capitalize the first letter of every word in the title, or put it in all caps and underline it; some writers boldface it for emphasis. Use common sense; it should stand out but look neat.

• Your byline appears two to three spaces beneath the title, also centered, with each initial in uppercase.

• Begin the first line of your article four lines below your byline.

To see how all this looks, see a sample first page on page 245.

On subsequent pages:

• Print a "slugline" (identifying word from your title/your name) in the upper left corner, the page number in the upper right corner; some writers prefer to put it all on the left side.

• Resume your text four lines below the slug.

On your final page:

• Indicate the end of the article with three hash marks, centered, like this:

# # #

Some writers use "-30-" or "The End" to signify the end of their articles, but both marks are a bit old-fashioned.

• Include your biocredit, if you choose. If the publication you're writing for doesn't print biocredits, you obviously won't need one. Otherwise, include one at the end of your manuscript in the appropriate style of the publication, or wait for the editor to request one.

When writing your biocredit, make it as specific as possible (e.g., "An Atlanta-based writer specializing in gardening and travel articles," rather than just "a freelance writer based in Atlanta"). If the style of the publication allows for it, you might want to write it with some wit and color as well. List only pertinent, appropriate information.

Photocopies of your manuscript are acceptable, even preferable, to originals in most cases, but they should be the cleanest, sharpest photocopies possible.

The Rest of the Package

There's more to your submission, of course, than just the manuscript; treat every element with care.

Some tips:

Cover letter. Keep it brief and to the point. Let the editor know in the first line what article is enclosed and when and how it was assigned. Do not count on her to remember you or your idea, particularly if it's been "assigned" on spec (which is not really an assignment at all, but a gesture of encouragement). Many editors, perhaps most, forget a spec assignment the moment it's made, because so few actually get written and submitted.

Mention specifically what's enclosed: title or subject of article, SASE, invoice, photos or illustrations, etc.

A few lines is all you need in a cover letter; don't attempt to promote your article, and never apologize for your material in any way (fix what's weak or wrong *before* you send it).

Mailing envelope. If your article is on the short side, only a few pages, and fits into a business-sized envelope, use the standard no. 10; but don't cram it.

If it's bulkier, use a manila envelope large enough to accommodate your manuscript; one that's 10×13 inches should do it. Use a *new* envelope, not one that's rumpled and dog-eared.

Some writers like to use a manila envelope for every submission, feeling it looks classier. The problem is, manila envelopes often end up in the slush pile of unsolicited submissions. When I use one, I add a notation in the lower left corner: *Enclosed Manuscript Assigned and Expected* (assuming your submission *is* assigned and expected).

Your name and address should be in the upper left corner (preferably preprinted with your letterhead). The editor's name, title, etc. should be typed/printed (for no. 10 envelopes) or on a mailing label (for manila envelopes) in the center of the envelope.

Photos/illustrations. When sending photos or illustrations, always use cardboard backing for protection. Number all photos and slides, and include caption sheets, with slides protected in plastic sleeves. Publications vary in their requirements for submissions of photos (original vs. duplicate slides, for example), which must be handled carefully and specifically according to each market; be sure you know exactly how a publication wants photos submitted. (For more details on combining photography with writing, see sidebar on page 249.)

SASE. Your self-addressed, stamped envelope should be large enough to accommodate the return of your manuscript and any other enclosures that may be returned, *with sufficient postage*. As with the submission of queries and clips, you may want to paper clip your stamps to the envelope rather than paste them on, so that editors can use them if they are not needed.

In the case of business-sized envelopes, a no. 9 fits neatly inside a no. 10, or you can fold your no. 10 in three sections. With manila envelopes, a 9 × 12-inch fits nicely inside a 10 × 13-inch, or fold your return manila envelope in half.

If it's a spec or unsolicited submission, always include an SASE; generally, if it's a bona fide assignment, on contract, no SASE is needed.

Invoice. Always a good idea with submissions that have been assigned (meaning you have a contract), because it expedites accounting, and some publications require it. However, if you submit on spec, an invoice is a bit presumptuous; wait to send an invoice until you've finished revisions and made a firm sale. (For a sample invoice, see Step Fifteen).

Cardboard backing. If you use a manila envelope, a piece of cardboard backing can help protect your manuscript and other enclosures. If you do use backing, use the genuine, 8½ × 11-inch backing, not sections cut from boxes, laundry inserts, and other shoddy substitutes.

Fasteners. Never staple your pages together. Use a paper clip to securely hold your manuscript, cover letter, SASE, etc.

The simpler a submission is for an editor to handle — take apart, photocopy, etc. — the better she likes it.

WHAT ABOUT PHOTOS?

Many publications prefer to handle photos themselves, separately from the writing, working either with staff or full-time, professional photographers. However, some magazines and newspapers like to see ideas from writer-photographers, and a few publications work almost exclusively with them, prefering to pay a more economical price for a package of words and pictures.

There are also some situations in which a sale depends on accompanying photos, provided by the writer, such as:

• Instances when rare, historical or exclusive photos are needed to which only the writer has access.

• Assignments that may take the writer to such a distant or inaccessible location that sending a photographer along is not feasible.

• Assignments when only you can take the photographs needed, such as coverage of an unusual event for which other photos might not be available.

In such situations, you must get photos from sources (sometimes available through libraries, P.R. firms, private corporations, etc.), find a professional photographer for a partner, or shoot photos yourself, if you have professional skills in that area.

The ability to shoot sharp, attractive photographs that meet the technical demands of specific markets can be a great advantage for a nonfiction writer. Many assignments, particularly those in the travel and outdoor categories, go only to the writer who also carries camera equipment and knows how to use it.

Having the flexibility of writing *and* shooting opens up the range of subjects a writer can pitch and cover, making that writer more in demand with certain editors, and increasing the writer's income potential.

Although a few publications accept and publish photos that border between amateur and professional—certain hunting or fishing magazines, for instance—most demand high professional standards. Top-quality magazines such as *National Geographic*, *The Smithsonian*, *Life*, *Architectural Digest*, and just about any other publication that *looks terrific* are beyond the reach of all but the best photographers.

Even with less-prestigious publications, don't pitch or agree to provide photographs with your article unless you have professional equip-

continued

ment and know what you're doing. Technical quality is particularly important with color slides. However, with a good 35mm camera and a working knowledge of lenses, filters, and the wide technical variations of film, there's no reason a writer can't also become a published photographer. Photography workshops, manuals and lots of practice are keys to success.

The risk freelance writers run when they also shoot photographs is managing to juggle both skills on assignment; at times the equipment and activity of photography can interfere with the interviewing process, for instance, and vice versa. It helps to be skilled and confident in one area before venturing into the other.

Photo specifications and needs differ from publication to publication regarding such things as film type, captioning, submission procedures, and a number of other technical details. Most publications provide guidelines for photographers upon request.

You'll find a wide range of market information regarding photos in *Writer's Market* and *Photographer's Market*; the latter provides a wealth of detail regarding the technical, business and legal aspects of shooting photos for publication, including a sample model release.

There are also a number of excellent magazines that cover the photography trade, such as *The Professional Photographer* and *The Rangefinder*, which also purchase freelance articles about the business, technical and creative sides of photography.

◆ ◆ ◆

As noted in the sidebar in Step Two, the post office will provide you with a free, up-to-date postal-rate card. *Writer's Market* also prints a handy chart that breaks down the weight of paper, envelope, etc. for easy calculation.

First-class mailing is preferable, because your package gets faster, smoother handling.

Your manuscript is ready for mailing — almost.

THE FINAL PROOFREAD

Before you slip your manuscript into its envelope, you *must* go over it like a proofreading maniac, looking for every typo, spelling error, et al.

If you use a computer spell-check, don't depend on it entirely. A computer will catch most misspellings, but does not comprehend meanings —

FINAL SUBMISSION CHECKLIST

Here are ten points to double-check before sealing up the envelope:

• My cover letter is brief and to the point, with only the essential information to introduce my manuscript.

• I've double-checked the spelling and exact title of the editor.

• I have not apologized or made excuses for the enclosures in any way.

• The first page of my manuscript bears my name, address, telephone number(s), social security number and word count.

• I've trimmed my article to the length assigned.

• I've proofread every line meticulously.

• I've packaged any supporting material, such as photos and illustrations, in a complete and professional manner.

• I've enclosed an invoice, if my article is on assignment.

• I've used a paper clip, not a staple, to hold my materials together.

• I've included an SASE with sufficient postage.

Take one last look at your overall packaging and presentation. If it looks first-rate, send it off and note the submission date in your marketing log.

---

the difference, say, between *there* and *their*, or *the* and *then*, the spelling goofs and typographical errors we all make.

To pencil in corrections, use proper copyediting and proofreading symbols, as shown on page 218.

Submitting Electronically

The way we create and send our manuscripts continues to change radically and rapidly.

As noted above, some publications and editors now refuse to work with typewritten submissions, a policy that's spreading through the marketplace, and with good reason: Computer-driven submissions save vast amounts of time, work and money at the publishing end.

Here are transmission options at a glance, subject to changing technology:

Faxing. At this writing, you should only use the telephonic fax machine at the editor's request, because of the enormous amount of junk mail—and, now, unsolicited manuscripts—pouring through the wires.

Modem. This allows you to hook your computer up to the publisher's computer system through the telephone system, sending articles like an electronically printed telephone call.

Warning: Beware power surges through the telephone lines that can damage or destroy computer circuitry; special modem surge protectors are available from top line electronics stores to supplement standard surge protectors or (better yet) UPS battery backup systems.

Computer disc. Either 3½-inch or 5¼-inch diskettes are standard, with the smaller disc safer and more sturdy for mailing.

Generally speaking, the less formatting you do in an electronic submission, the better, because of potential coding and command problems at the publisher's end.

Most editors prefer to have a hard (printed) copy of your manuscript as backup, which is a good place to indicate format variations, which editors can then implement using their software.

It's imperative that you get exact specifications from individual publications regarding disc size, modem instructions, word processor preference, IBM or MAC compatibility and so on.

Many publications provide writer guidelines for electronic submissions upon request.

Writer's Digest, and particularly its regular "Electronic Writer" column, can help you keep abreast of new developments in this area, along with various computer guidebooks and magazines.

If you're still confused about such computer matters (if so, you're not alone), you may want to get special help from a one-on-one tutor or consultant. Many full-service computer stores offer software packages that enable you to use your modem, for instance, as well as personal instruction.

AFTER YOU SEND IT OFF

You've taken the two most important steps a nonfiction writer can take — you've written the article and mailed it off to be considered. But there's still more work to do:

Log it in. Whether you use the Marketing Log printed in Step Five or some version of your own, such as a 3 × 5-inch card filing system, you must note the date of your submission and keep track of what happens to it. Don't just send it off and leave its fate to memory or to chance. Stay organized.

Reslant and move ahead. As soon as you send out your submission, don't wait around for a reply. Get started right away sending out more queries, reslanted from the same topic, or on a whole new subject. Or start writing the next article, if you've got an assignment. Keep busy.

Waiting it out. If you've written the assignment on contract, you should hear back from the editor in a matter of weeks. If it's on spec, you may have to be more patient. But if too many weeks go by—four or five would seem more than enough (even for spec submissions)—it's probably time to nudge the editor. A follow-up note reminding her about the specifics of the submission, including the submission date, is the first step; always include your telephone number and keep copies of all correspondence. If two or three more weeks pass with no response, it's probably time to try the telephone. (For more tips on using the telephone with editors, see Step Fourteen.)

If *months* pass—and it will sometimes happen—you obviously have the right to withdraw the manuscript from submission with a polite note declaring same. Sometimes, you'll find an editor has been replaced, and your manuscript has been lost in the shuffle. Illness or other extenuating circumstances may have intruded.

You'll have to learn to be as pushy or as patient as good judgment and individual situations suggest.

SETTING THE TERMS

If you're writing with a bona fide assignment, you should have some kind of contract stating the terms (word length, payment rate, kill fee, deadline, rights being purchased, etc.), or have in hand a letter of contract generated from your end for protection.

With spec submissions, however, no contract exists. If your article is accepted for publication, try to get confirmation in writing.

Writer and agent Lisa Collier Cool (*How to Write Irresistible Query Letters*) recommends a confirmation letter that can be used for confirming either an assignment or a sale, which goes something like this:

Dear [name of editor]:

I'm delighted that you have decided to [assign me to write/buy] my article [title/subject] for $[agreed payment/kill fee if applicable]. This is for [first North American serial rights, onetime use only/other terms as discussed previously]. The length will be [number of words], due on [deadline date].

Please sign and return the attached copy of this letter to indicate your agreement to the above terms. SASE is enclosed.

_____   _____
(writer's signature)   (editor's signature)

If the publication pays on acceptance, a check should be on its way to you within a week or two; if the newspaper or magazine pays on publication, however, you face a more complicated situation. Without a confirmation or contract letter, an editor can conceivably tie up your manuscript for months, then have a change of mind and send the article back, with no legal obligation to pay you. It's not unheard of for editors to hold manuscripts for a year or more this way, waiting to see if they have the right editorial mix to use an article, then return it with no more than an apology (sometimes, not even that). A confirmation letter, if you can get an editor to sign it, should alleviate that problem (if the publisher is honest, and honors the agreement). If possible, get the guarantee of full payment or at least a kill fee. If undue time passes, you might ask for an advance in the amount of the kill fee, since it would eventually be payable anyway. (Many publications won't pay advances, because it ties up working capital.)

Classier publications pay on acceptance and deal with writers on a contractual basis. Unfortunately, many others operate at a lower professional standard, squeezing as much out of writers as they can, without fair or proper remuneration. Often, when you press for decent terms and guarantees, you'll get a "take it or leave it" response.

At some point, you may have to decide if it's worth it to leave an article in the hands of a publication without any guarantees of compensation. If you have no other market for the material, it may not matter to you. But if you feel that its marketability is fading and the editor is unwilling to make a financial gesture of commitment, you may want to take it back, and try elsewhere.

◆ ◆ ◆

At this point, we're into the complicated area of dealing with editors, which means it's time to move on to Step Fourteen.

Dealing With Editors

Some years back, the editor of a Sunday newspaper section called with an idea for an article he wanted me to write. We differed somewhat on the premise, and because substantial research was involved, I went ahead only after he sent me a letter outlining what would be required of me and the slant the article would take. To reassure me, he offered me galley approval.

When the galleys — the typeset version of my story — arrived by mail, I was furious; the editors had essentially rewritten my article to suit their original take on the subject; it was not what I had intended at all.

When I called the paper to challenge certain changes, it was too late — facing a tight production schedule, they'd gone ahead and printed the revised piece, without contacting me. Ironically, they gave the article a big, attractive page-one spread, the kind writers dream about.

I got the editor on the telephone. I told him what he'd done was unfair, unethical, dishonest. I told him he was a discredit to his profession. I used a term for him that cast aspersions on his lineage.

"So," he said, barely pausing, "what are you going to write for us next?"

Amusing now, painful then.

We worked out our differences, and I did write for him again, in part because he was a decent enough guy who could admit his own mistakes, with the intelligence and the humanity to face and resolve conflict.

But there was a more important reason I continued to work for him: As someone just getting established, I was in no position to be choosy.

The hard truth is, independent writers work in a buyer's market; our fortunes depend to a great extent on the relationships we build with editors.

Editors come and go. Most of them are the allies of writers; some are not. They can help us develop bountiful careers, or dump us on a whim. As a regional editor once said to me, after I'd filed nearly a dozen articles for his magazine: "Don't take anything for granted with us. Some guy at the top will drop you in a second just because he doesn't like your choice of neckties."

And I didn't even wear neckties.

BUILDING RELATIONSHIPS WITH EDITORS

Every time you send off a query to a new market, you open the door to a possible relationship with a new "purchasing agent"—the editor in charge. If you get a go-ahead and deliver the article, you take a giant step forward.

That relationship either grows or withers depending on how you perform in the days and weeks after submitting your manuscript. You may encounter any number of opportunities for nurturing this new relationship, such as:

• Revising and improving your original article, or at least making it more suited to the editor's needs.

• Providing immediate "services" for the editor, such as getting together photos or illustrations, writing captions or sidebars, providing useful telephone numbers.

• Performing final fact-checking.

• Proofreading author galleys or page proofs.

• Pitching new ideas for other assignments.

• Being supportive and helpful in ways unconnected to your own assignment (amplification further ahead).

The more cooperative you are with an editor, the more he will want to work with you again. The more he must do at his end—rewriting, chasing photos, fact-checking, etc.—the less he'll think of you when it comes time to make an assignment.

Let's examine in more detail some of the ways you can fortify this new connection.

Making Revisions

As an editor, I once worked with a neophyte writer who'd submitted an unsolicited manuscript we found interesting. However, it needed considerable work, and he had no credits as a professional writer. I told him that if he were willing to work on spec, I'd invest some of my own time working with him.

A few weeks later, he mailed in his rewrite, which still fell a bit short. I called him and asked for a few more changes, including some minor research. He grew testy, demanding to know how much more we'd pay him for this extra work. I explained that we paid our higher rates to writers whose work needed less revision, not to those whose work required more

of our time. He said he'd think about it, and I never heard from him again —
a shame, because he was probably a rewrite away from making his first sale.

Even if your article is accepted for publication, even if it's accepted with
high praise, the editor will probably still ask for minor revisions. Welcome
this opportunity; if you get no such request, it probably means an editor is
tampering without your input.

Generally, you won't be paid extra to rewrite, unless extenuating circumstances necessitate major revisions, such as a publication's editorial shift or
an editor's error or change of mind (like asking belatedly for a whole new
slant). *The New York Times*, for instance, once held a piece of mine for
many months because of a strike, then asked for a fast update and heavy
revisions when the strike ended; the section editor doubled my fee for the
additional work. Updating under normal circumstances, however, rarely
brings the writer more pay; most editors figure it comes with your package
of services.

Often, an editor will ask for revisions that sound major, but are actually
fairly minor. Some editors have a way of overstating their case, making
their points a bit too strongly, sometimes leaving writers with the wrong
impression about how much more work is really needed. I've often hung
up after a conversation with an editor feeling like my article was a total
mess that only a major salvage operation could save, only to later have the
editor say, "Oh, don't worry about all that stuff—we just want a little
polishing."

In discussing revisions, try to get the editor to be as specific as possible.
Don't be afraid to ask, "What exactly do you have in mind?" or "What
would you suggest?" to try to get him to focus his criticism.

Insecure editors, particularly those new at their positions, will sometimes
suggest changes just for the sake of making changes, so they feel like they're
doing their job; if you sense this is the case, discreetly and diplomatically
prod them to pinpoint what they feel is wrong, and why.

You'll also deal with editors who are impatient or unusually terse (my
biggest failing as an editor, I think, for which I universally apologize). Never
take it personally; assume the editor is under unusual workload and deadline
pressure. If he becomes offensive or rude, however, try to resolve the problem (more on conflict resolution toward the end of the chapter).

Don't fuss over minor matters and become a pain in the you-know-what,
but if an editor asks for changes you strongly disagree with, don't hesitate
to discuss it; find out his reasoning, and let him know yours. Frequently,
you'll find it's more a matter of *clarification* in your copy—clearer wording,
perhaps—than wholesale alterations.

There may also be times when you feel personally uncomfortable with a request during rewriting, and you may have to argue your point forcefully, or find a way around an editor's demands. The assistant managing editor of a national magazine once called me about a profile I'd filed on a popular rock group. "It needs more nitty gritty about their private life," he said, referring to two principal singers. "Find out if she's a nymph and if he's a fag."

I'd never heard an editor use those terms, at least not in relation to anything I'd written.

"I'm surprised you'd suggest something like that," I said evenly. "It doesn't befit you or the magazine."

"Well, I didn't mean that *exactly*," he stammered. "Just . . . just make it a little more personal."

I looked through my interview transcripts and found a comment from another singer in the group about how silly it was for members of the media to pry into the sex lives of celebrities. I inserted the comment into my rewrite, in the very place the editor wanted some salacious tidbits, and never heard another word from him about it.

With such a stunt, of course, you run the risk of alienating an editor, but when your personal standards are on the line, you must know where to draw that line.

Ultimately, editors rule the roost. If you want to see your article in print, you must satisfy most of their requests; the trick is to give them what they want in a way that allows you to say what you want to say and doesn't abridge the essential integrity of the piece.

If they ask for revisions more quickly than you feel you can deliver, take a good look at your work calendar and, if you need more time, request it. (On the other hand, if they need your rewrite fast, find a way to give it to them, even if it means burning the midnight oil.) If your revisions stretch out longer than expected, give your editor a status report, and request more time. A simple note may suffice (though notes often go unread or get lost in the clutter of an editor's desk); but don't just leave him wondering what has happened to the article.

Don't think of revisions as a painful activity forced on you by editors who can't see the perfection of your work. It's a normal part of the commercial writing process, a chance to reshape and polish it; you tailor articles, not for yourself, but for specific markets and editors.

Rewriting and polishing is a developed skill, and you may lose a sale or two along the way because you just can't bring an article up to the level the editor demands.

There may also be times when you feel an editor is making you jump through hoops without really knowing or being able to articulate what he wants, and you may have to pull out of an assignment. Avoid that if at all possible, but don't allow yourself to be unfairly exploited, either.

Attending to Author Galleys

Also known as a "prepublication proof" or "page proofs," a galley is a copy of your typeset article. It's your last chance to review the editing done to your manuscript before it goes into print. Some publications automatically send you author galleys; with others, you may have to request them; and some may have a policy against letting you see them at all. If you have the chance to review your galleys, by all means, take it.

I started requesting galley approval fifteen years ago, after a copyeditor at *The Los Angeles Times* butchered one of my manuscripts, trimming sections without regard to context or logical transition; there were times when his editing was so inept it rendered stretches of copy unintelligible. (Hired through nepotism, he has long since moved on to another line of work.)

I found that going down to the paper to personally look over my page proofs gave me an opportunity not only to catch errors made by the copy desk, but to affect my own trims, and to make final adjustments in my own writing. The editor in charge not only welcomed my involvement, but eventually hired me to join the staff.

Unfortunately, not all publications allow writers to see galleys, even on request. Some editors simply don't want to get into last-minute haggling with writers who are touchy about alterations to their work.

If you are given the right, avoid making changes unless they are necessary for accuracy, or unless an editor's change in your copy is actually *harmful* to the content or to the writing itself, such as severely displaced rhythm.

I have great respect for copy desks—David Shear at *The Los Angeles Times*, the most meticulous copyeditor I've encountered, has unquestionably made me a better writer—but even copyeditors are human. Now and then, in their zeal or haste, one will "miss the point" when making changes and muck things up, inserting something you didn't mean or would never have written. Once, a respected Sunday Calendar copyeditor (*not* Shear), certain that he was right, changed a technical description in an article of mine—and got it dead wrong. I happened to be out of town, didn't see the galleys, and the error got into print.

Those are the last-minute changes—the ones that do real damage to your article—that are worth fighting for at the galley stage. You won't get everything you want when disagreements arise over editing changes, so learn which stands to make.

Get to your proofs as soon as they become available; the more time you allow yourself, the more leeway you're likely to have in negotiating fixes. If the time frame is tight, and you are working by mail, you may want to telephone your changes to the copy desk.

Strengthening the Relationship

Once you've established a connection with an editor, you can do a number of things to maintain and make it stronger. They are small "services" and gestures that may not be required of you, but that will make your work life more pleasant and pay off professionally in the future.

Here are a few:

Provide immediate support for your article. This might include pulling together photos or illustrations, even though the publication has a staff to handle that kind of thing; you may have special access to certain material, or contact with sources, that can save staff valuable time. Or it may be easier for you to set up a photo session with your subject(s), working with the photo editor. (See the sidebar on page 249 for more about providing photos.)

If you think of a possible sidebar after your article is accepted, suggest it to your editor. Drop him a note if a clever headline comes to mind. If you haven't been asked to write captions for photos, find out if you're needed in that area, or if there's anything else you can do to help expedite the piece. If someone at the publication calls regarding fact-checking, take care of it ASAP.

Don't be servile, but let your editor know you're available to do what's needed.

Ask for constructive feedback. Even after your article is set for publication, ask your editor, "What more could I have done?" or "What could I have done differently?" while the article is still fresh in his mind. Often, facing production schedules and time limitations, editors publish a piece knowing it's adequate, but not exactly what they wanted. Don't ask such questions just to be ingratiating, but to learn. Let them know you want to grow at your craft and do an even better job next time.

If in doubt about anything, ask. This may seem obvious, but beginning writers often let shyness or embarrassment keep them from asking straightforward questions, letting small problems become unnecessarily complicated. If you don't know how to mark a page proof, or where to deliver it, inquire of a copyeditor or assistant. If you've never written captions, get some instructions. If you don't know when something is due, find out. Better to ask questions than to do things wrong. The more you learn about the specifics of the publication process, the more at ease you'll be on future assignments.

Maintain communication. Send a thank-you note, funny card, or just a postcard with a word of gratitude to your editor, or to an assistant who gave you special help. When you can, add your human touch to a world that becomes increasingly impersonal because of computers and other electronic means of communication.

Pitch new ideas for other assignments. Don't flood them with junk, but come up with more on-target ideas. This is the time to study the publication even more keenly, see your editors' needs more clearly, and offer them angles they can't resist; find out if they're willing to take a list query, with summaries of several ideas, or still prefer angles to be pitched one at a time.

If possible, meet the editor in person. Try to get a breakfast or lunch meeting at a place of his choosing. A personal meeting will allow him to get a sense of you as a person, not just a voice on the telephone. Have some ideas in mind for articles, carefully thought out, in case he asks; you might make some notes and have them with you for reference.

Be helpful and supportive in ways unconnected to your own assignments. Share your contacts and sources. If you think of an idea that feels right for your editor, but that you don't want to write, drop a note suggesting it for someone else. If you come across a clipping that might be useful for a department that's staff-written, send it to your editor with a note attached. It keeps you fresh in the mind of the editor, reminds him that you have a good understanding of the market, and helps introduce you to other members of the staff.

Be patient and reasonable. Before you ask for bigger assignments, higher pay and the like, let the editor know you can deliver what he needs, on time, with consistency. That may mean one or two articles, or many, depending on your quality of work, the editor and the publication. Some markets, like *TV Guide*, have a set scale of increasing rates based on how many articles you file; for others, pay raises are a subjective decision. Some editors will try to keep you at the lowest rate possible for as long as they can.

You'll probably sense if and when it's time to start pressing for better assignments and bigger checks — usually when the editor starts contacting you with assignments, instead of the other way around.

◆ ◆ ◆

USING THE TELEPHONE

For all the talk about writing query letters in this book, over the long haul, you'll probably handle more "correspondence" by telephone. That's because, once an editor knows you and your work, it's easier for him to pick up the telephone and call, or take a call from you. As a general rule, never call without writing first; you'll learn which editors prefer calls, and which don't.

You'll use the telephone to discuss details such as overdue replies on queries you've sent and the status of assignments in progress; you'll even use it to pitch new ideas to editors with whom you have especially strong relationships.

The keys to using the telephone effectively are clarity and confidence. Vagueness and a faltering voice on the telephone can be lethal, even when you're loaded with marketable ideas.

Here are some other guidelines:

Know who you're calling. If you call a specific editor—and you should—know his exact title and function.

Know when to call. Find out from the editor or an assistant which day(s) of the week is generally best to call, and what time. If the editor has meetings in the early morning, call in the afternoon. If he puts a section to bed on Wednesday, call later in the week. And so on.

Ask if the time is right. When they pick up the telephone, let them know succinctly who you are and why you're calling—a couple of lines at most—then ask, "Is this a good time to talk?" If it is, they'll usually give you a minute or two. If not, find out the ideal time to call back.

Know the publication. If you're making your first call to a new market, be familiar with recent issues in case the editor refers to a recent article in print.

Have a reason to call. Never use the telephone to schmooze or make idle chitchat with an editor (that's what lunches are for). Know exactly why you're calling and why it's necessary to call rather than write. Let the editor initiate any casual conversation.

Be prepared. If you're checking up on a query or submission, have in front of you the date of submission, title and other essential details. If you're pitching an idea or ideas—assuming that you've established a relationship with the editor—have a list in front of you; make sure

continued

you've thought through each angle.

Keep it brief. Get to the point. Editors usually give the caller half a minute or so to grab and hold their attention. Even if they stay on the line with you out of courtesy, they might be half-listening as they take care of other business at their desk. Make your time count.

Know when to sign off. Sense when to say goodbye, and try to do it first, as a sign of respect to the editor's time. To the busy editor, every minute is precious. Don't put him in the awkward position of having to get rid of you.

There will be times when you pitch an idea to a publication knowing you may never write for it again — a one-shot deal, when relationship-building may not be so important. Most freelance writers, however, sustain careers not by writing for hundreds or even dozens of individual publications, but by building relationships with a select number of editors who give them repeat assignments.

In the end, of course, the most important building block in those relationships is the quality of your work.

UNDERSTANDING EDITORS

By and large, I believe, editors are smart, decent people who value responsible, dependable writers; most are former writers themselves, and realize that writers are the creative lifeblood of any magazine or newspaper. Many of them write on the side, satisfying their need to be creative, and feeling whole because of it.

Most of the editors I've worked with appreciate and admire spirited, independent-minded writers who have original ideas and deliver good work on time. At the same time, editors understand far more about their own publications than those who do the writing. While writers tend to operate from a place of idealism, editors are privy to the more practical side of publishing, the nuts-and-bolts inner workings and complex economic and political pressures that writers rarely have to confront. Dealing with budget and production problems, finding the right editorial mix, getting a publication out on time, surviving another edition, are the driving concerns in an editor's daily life, not placating insecure or overly sensitive writers.

On top of that, editors face an unending stream of shoddy, second-rate work from people who have no business calling themselves writers; it wearies and frustrates even the most patient editors, and more responsible writers sometimes bear the brunt, if only inadvertently. The best editors, those who are as adept at human relations as they are at laying out a page, have the backbone and decency to acknowledge when they treat a writer unfairly, and to make amends.

Such editors are easy to recognize: They enjoy their jobs and their role in the publication process, and it shows in their energy and enthusiasm.

The best ones have strong vision and leadership skills, but don't consider themselves superior to writers. They treat writers as respected colleagues; working with such editors is a pleasure.

From time to time, however, you'll run into the editor who is miserable almost every day of his working life, destroying writer morale and creating a grim environment in which to work.

Coping With Abusive Editors

These unhappy editors comprise a small minority among their colleagues. They tend to be frustrated by their role of creative midwife, and life in general; they take their unhappiness out routinely on writers and give editors as a group an undeserved bad rap.

These disgruntled editors forget what it was like to be a writer, if they were ever writers at all; many, while claiming to have a writing and reporting background, actually tried it only briefly, then slipped into editing because it proved less challenging. They seem to resent freelance writers who make a go of it, because it's what they'd be doing if they had the gumption or drive. Instead, they come to work every day wishing they were doing something else. Lacking the will to break free, they are slavishly dependent on the jobs they hate and frightened of losing their place on the career ladder, which is why independent writers threaten them so profoundly.

These are the ones who will generally mistreat you and give you grief. Obsequious with upper management, they cherish their power, lording over their subordinates. They behave like bullies, blame others for their mistakes, and seem determined to make everyone around them as miserable as they are.

We have all encountered these types, in every profession, yet it's always a shock to find such people working in the communications field, when the ability to communicate seems to be the quality they most lack.

What, if anything, can we do about them?

Here are some survival tips:

• Expect nothing from an editor except an assignment and a paycheck. An editor's job is to find publishable articles, not to be your friend or teacher; when you find one who has that extra humanity and capacity for mentoring, rejoice (this book is dedicated to one).

• Build relationships with editors consciously and sincerely — but never expect them to last.

• Cultivate more than one market, and always be on the lookout for new ones.

• Avoid gossip, politicking and backbiting. Be careful to whom you speak about the internal matters of a publication; Judases abound. Know who your real friends are; keep your own counsel.

• If you experience friction with an editor, try to deal with it directly, and get to the heart of the problem. Often, talking face-to-face resolves prickly issues; try to find a common ground. See if humor helps.

• If the editor is the uptight type who's unable to deal with feelings and handle conflict resolution, find a way to work *around* him, through assistants or other editors.

• In the end, if a situation becomes increasingly tense or unpleasant, you may have to decide how much you're willing to take and whether it's worth it. Too many other markets are out there to continue under the yoke of an editor who is incompetent, unprofessional or abusive.

• Don't obsess or dwell on negative experiences with the rotten apples of the editing profession; it will poison your outlook on writing and hurt your chances with the good apples, who predominate.

Find a way to deal with anger, resentment or other self-destructive feelings, and put them behind you. Move on to bigger and better things.

Working With Unbusinesslike Editors

After many years as an editor, a friend of mine is now trying his hand at full-time freelancing.

"Some of these editors take forever to get back to you about your ideas," he complained the other day. "They seem to have no respect for writers, or how we work. How do they expect us to do business and make a living?"

The irony is that, as an editor, this fellow was notorious for not answering his mail in a timely fashion, especially if it came from writers he didn't know.

His editorial judgment and generous heart made working for him worthwhile, and he had legions of loyal contributors, but many of them tore their hair because of the erratic and disorganized way he handled correspondence and assignments. Incoming queries and submissions were mingled in heaps about his office with old newspapers and magazines, discarded page proofs, press releases, office memos, grocery lists, fast-food wrappers. Some of those piles were actually *dusty*. He sometimes held on to articles for months without giving status reports to writers—one recalls her article being published a full *year* after it was accepted, with little or no communication about it along the way.

It might be funny, except at the other end, the writer's end, the editor's messy style caused wasted time, confusion, frustration, and probably lost income. Regretably, as an editor, this man was not alone.

We all know of publications, supposedly viable and reputable, where our queries and SASEs disappear into a black hole for months, or forever; publications that "pay on acceptance"—but somehow, it takes *months* for the check to arrive (would any self-respecting editor wait this long for his own paycheck?); editors who routinely lose photos, spill coffee on our manuscripts, forget to schedule stories in time to take advantage of their timely pegs; and countless other symptoms of poor management skills and simple discourtesy.

We've spent a lot of space in this book exploring ways writers can serve the needs of editors, ways they can improve their work, ways they can be more professional. Unfortunately, editors rarely pause to examine ways *they* might work more productively with writers, ways they can improve their *own* work, ways *they* can be more professional. Once in charge, editors seem to forget they are as human as writers, with their own flaws and foibles.

Professionalism is important for writers; it's a shame more editors don't set better examples.

So how do we "interface" with these unbusinesslike types, who are often wonderful to work with otherwise? Here are some suggestions:

Find a more efficient assistant. There are often super-efficient editorial assistants willing to help you out if you treat them with respect and gratitude. Find and cultivate these helpers.

Know the system and use the departments. Find out who does what, and work with them accordingly; deal with the editor as little as possible, except on conceptual matters. If it's suitable, get your invoice directly to accounting, your galleys directly to the copy desk, your photos directly to the appropriate assistant and so on. Check back with these people to make sure things are in order.

Try the telephone. You'll often find that the editors who are the most lax at handling correspondence take telephone calls if they come at the right time of the day or week. (See sidebar on using the telephone, page 262.)

Attempt to get a contract. If ever there was an editor for whom contracts were called for, it's the one who's sloppy or forgetful.

Always invoice them. An invoice gives an editor a piece of paper he can shuffle quickly into the right basket, then forget. (See sample invoice, page 273.)

Schedule regular follow-up. If they can't get their act together, get more organized at your end; plan dates on your work calendar for follow-up at regular intervals after your piece has been submitted or accepted. Urge the editor to make a decision or commit to a publishing date; warn him that the material will soon become dated.

Withdraw an article as a test case. If you must, take an article back, expressing your regrets; try to have another market lined up for it.

Editors sometimes forget that writers don't just write for money; we write to see our work in print, reaching an audience.

You've sold your article, performed your rewrite chores, and established a growing relationship with a new editor. You've got lots of queries out in the mail and may even have other assignments penciled in on your work calendar.

Now it's time to take care of business and look ahead to such opportunities as syndication and books—all covered in Step Fifteen.

Step Fifteen

Taking Care of Business

Aformer student of mine called not long ago with some news: She'd put enough money in the bank to last three months and had quit her Monday-to-Friday job to be a full-time freelance nonfiction writer.

"I've decided it's time to give it my best shot," she said proudly. "I figure if I don't do it now, I never will."

Three months' backup income didn't sound like much of a safety net, but I sincerely wished her well. Several weeks later, I talked to her again and asked how it was going. She sounded depressed.

"I spent the first month paralyzed with worry about how I was going to pay the bills when my money ran out," she said. "This month, I'm sending out resumés and interviewing for positions. Next month, if I'm lucky, I'll have a new job and be able to make my mortgage payment."

To her credit, she found a *better* job, one that allows her to work only four days a week, with three full days free to write. She's a fine writer, and if she can become a more *productive* writer with enough steady markets, she may yet be able to quit her job and freelance full time.

Her tale of frustration underscores a hard truth about the writing life: The biggest pressure we face is the need for *money*.

When you freelance full time, you are a self-employed businessperson. To survive, you must deliver enough product at a sufficient pace to enough customers who pay a sufficient price—and then find creative ways to spin off *by-products*. If you generate enough capital, the business stays afloat; if you don't, the business folds.

To be successful, you must do more than just sell an article now and then. You must take care of business by:

- Knowing exactly what you're selling (rights).
- Being able to collect what's owed you.

- Maintaining records and accounts.
- Planning ahead for taxes.
- Increasing your income by moving into markets beyond one-shot article sales.

Let's take a look at each of those areas in more detail.

SETTING THE TERMS

"Setting terms" in a general sense refers to all the terms of your agreement with an editor, such as payment, deadline and so on. But in a more basic sense, "terms" refers to the actual rights you sell to a publisher—for how long and in what markets the publisher owns and/or controls your article. As a nonfiction writer for newspapers and magazines, the rights you're most likely to be concerned with break down like this:

First North American Serial Rights (First NAS). When a publication purchases these rights, it acquires the right to be the first in North America to print your piece for a certain time period, usually a year, but that's sometimes negotiable. Thereafter, you have the right to offer reprint rights to other markets.

Onetime Rights. This grants the publication nonexclusive rights to publish the article in its circulation area; in other words, publications in other circulation areas may also print the same piece at any time. Newspapers frequently purchase onetime rights.

All Rights (or All World Rights). This means the publication acquires exclusive and total rights to your article, exclusive of basic copyright, for thirty-five years. Usually, publications that buy all rights pay considerably higher rates. However, such a contract also gives them control/ownership of the material in all markets, such as books, movies and TV. You give away a lot when you sign away all rights; first weigh the potential of your story in ancillary markets.

All Publishing Rights. This means you retain all dramatic rights—movie, TV, video, etc.—while the publication controls all worldwide publishing rights.

All Periodical or All Serial Rights. This leaves you both book and dramatic rights, while worldwide newspaper and magazine rights go to the publisher.

Reprint or Second Serial Rights. These are the rights you sell to a secondary market or markets after your piece has been published elsewhere.

Work Made for Hire. In this situation, you give away all rights to your material, including the copyright. You are essentially a temporary employee, without claims to authorship, including byline. The publisher even has the right to put another byline, such as that of an expert or a celebrity, above your writing.

As a writer, the best deal you can strike is to sell only Onetime or First NAS rights, probably the most common agreements freelance writers make. Most publications you submit to will not demand all rights, realizing it's unfair and unrealistic; some publishers, however, are firm about it, but are usually willing to pay handsomely to get so much. Others may be willing to negotiate for lesser rights.

Personally, if the money were good enough and the material had limited market appeal, I'd sell away all rights. But if the material was dramatic in nature, such as a true story, and exploitable in high-paying ancillary markets such as TV or films, I'd certainly think twice.

In some cases, publishers will insist on a split of proceeds earned in ancillary markets, figuring they deserve a share for giving the story its initial exposure.

A final area to consider is that of electronic rights. At this writing, definitions and agreements on rights regarding the electronic transmission and sale of material after publication in print are still evolving. With the proliferation of electronic databases, it's important that you fight for compensation when your work is resold in this way, just as music composers are given royalties whenever their work is recorded or broadcast, and as a freelance writer is paid when her material is sold to a wire service. These are issues and terms you may have to work out on an individual basis with each editor until they become more sharply defined and standardized.

THE COPYRIGHT QUESTION

Copyright law specifies that you hold the copyright to anything you write from the moment you write it—not the idea itself, or the general ideas therein, but how the work is executed, its form, the special way you put the words together.

Some writers, to signal awareness of their rights, affix a copyright symbol (©) under the date on their manuscripts (see sample first page, page 245); however, not all writers submit manuscripts bearing a copyright symbol (I never have). Copyright protects your work during your lifetime, plus fifty years (or, in the case of partners, the life of the last surviving partner, plus fifty years), unless, of course, you sell those rights.

The copyright symbol that appears on a newspaper or magazine does not apply to your work specifically; it's a "compilation copyright," which protects the publication as a whole.

CAN I USE A PSEUDONYM?

While the use of pseudonyms is common in fiction publishing, where name identification in connection with certain genres is considered important to marketing, it's not widely accepted in the nonfiction field.

Some nonfiction writers use phony names (or try to) for a variety of reasons, among them:

- They don't like the editing done to their article, and want their real name taken off.
- They are ashamed of the publication or the subject matter of the article.
- They are writing in a market that directly competes with another they contribute to regularly.
- If their real name were used, a conflict of interest would be apparent, such as a business or personal connection (or conflict) with their subject.
- They're in hiding — from the authorities, IRS, an ex-spouse, et al.

Many nonfiction editors frown on the use of a pseudonym, because it suggests the writer may have something to hide. It also deceives readers about who wrote an article, raising questions about honesty and accuracy.

Another reason not to use a pseudonym: It can confuse accounting and make getting paid more difficult.

If at all possible, use your real name.

With the exception of work-for-hire agreements, you own the copyright on your published work, which gives you the exclusive right to copy and distribute it in the future and to use it in other markets and forms, such as books.

For instance, throughout this book, I have been able to use sections of articles and columns written for *Writer's Digest* because I sold the magazine only First NAS rights the first time around. I do not need permission to reprint material *WD* has published under my byline; however, *WD* needs *my* permission if it wishes to reprint any of it.

Most freelance writers do not bother to register each article they write; however, if you have written a substantial piece or a more lengthy work such as a book, you may wish to go to the trouble and expense of having that extra protection; registration is also required to wage a copyright infringement lawsuit in federal court.

For more details on copyright regulations and procedures, or to get a registration form, write to the Copyright Office, Library of Congress, Washington DC 20559. A postcard should be sufficient.

MONEY MATTERS

Whether you make a comfortable living as a freelance writer or earn only nominal amounts (or expect to soon), you are self-employed; that means you face certain monetary concerns employees don't.

The first and most important part of these money matters is collecting a paycheck.

Getting Paid

After performing enough research, writing and revision to deliver a publishable product, you'd think being paid fairly and expeditiously would be a matter of routine. Unfortunately, collecting what's owed them becomes an increasing problem for self-employed writers.

Here are some steps to take that may help:

• Send an invoice with your manuscript. Some writers who submit on spec even include an invoice, although you may want to wait until you've gotten an acceptance. Include an itemization of out-of-pocket expenses, with receipts attached; most clients prefer that larger expenses, such as meals and accommodations, be paid by credit card, and they may require that you submit the original receipt. Keep photocopies for your own tax purposes. (For a sample invoice, see page 273.)

• If payment is weeks overdue, send a second billing. Be diplomatic, even friendly, when you write your reminder. Assume it's merely an oversight at this point. If you still haven't been paid after another two weeks, you know you're being given the runaround.

• Send a tougher letter that doesn't insult your editor, but doesn't mince words, either. Ask the editor to call you regarding the matter, and remind her that the money owed you is income you need right now.

• If you don't hear from her or receive payment within a week, call the editor directly. To make your point, call collect.

• If you still fail to get satisfaction, send a new invoice that includes interest calculated on payments owed you over thirty days, with a tough cover letter explaining that late payment means money taken from your pocket in the form of unearned interest. You may not get the interest, but it might shake loose what's owed.

STANDARD SAMPLE INVOICE
(Your Letterhead)

(Social Security or   (Date) _____
Employee I.D. No.)

To: (name of editor)
    (publication)
    (address)

For Services Rendered:

    Article title: _____

    Delivered: _____

    Amount due: $ _____

    Photos: _____

    Delivered: _____

    Amout due: $ _____

Expenses (taxes included; receipts attached):

    _____

    _____

    _____

    _____

    _____

Amount due: $ _____
Total due: $ _____
    Send check to:
    (your name and address)

If none of this works, you probably face a tough collection problem. There will be times when a publication, beset with financial troubles or just dishonest, will attempt to stiff you. Wringing money from a publication is difficult for writers, especially if much distance separates them, but there are a few steps you can take:

• If you belong to a national writers' organization, such as the American Society of Journalists and Authors or the National Writer's Union, or even a regional group, such as the Independent Writers of Southern California (my affiliation), it may be able to put pressure on the publication and even provide you with limited legal support. The bigger the organization and its clout, the more likely a publisher is to respond.

• Notify *Writer's Digest* and *Writer's Market*, which warn readers about errant publishers. Be succinct, sticking to specifics; keep the tone professional; avoid undue rhetoric and a complicated "pissing match." Include a copy of your contract, letter of acceptance, or other pertinent documentation. Send copies of your letter to the editor who owes you money to let her know you won't walk away without a fight.

• Alert other writers about the deadbeat publication any way you can, through writers' groups, newsletters, word-of-mouth, etc. Let the publication know you're spreading the word. Just be sure you can back up any of your claims.

• Ask a lawyer to write a letter to the publisher warning of possible legal action.

• Offer to negotiate for lower payment, if it's worth it to you to settle.

• Warn the publisher you will take them to small claims court; as a last resort, do it.

Whatever recourse you try, having a contract and copies of all submitted materials and correspondence is helpful.

TAXING CONCERNS

If you write as a professional—with the intent to make money—you are in business as far as the Internal Revenue Service is concerned, even if you show no profit. Paychecks from publishers, copies of query letters and manuscripts, membership in professional writers' groups, even rejection slips, are all evidence that you are a *working* writer, trying to make a profit.

Keep expense receipts for everything that is writing-related, including meals in which you discuss business, transportation costs, home office supplies, membership dues for writing groups, postage, etc.

Maintain a bookkeeping system, even if it's only in a single-entry ledger, available at any office-supply store. Simple, dated notations that keep your writing income and expenses orderly, shown in relationship to each other, will work fine.

To deduct an expense when you file your income-tax forms, that expense must be customary and reasonable in the course of conducting specific business activity, such as research or interviewing, or necessary in developing and maintaining your writing business, such as computer purchase or repair.

If you write about something and you must spend money *to be able to write about it*, those expenses should be deductible. If you travel to Borneo for pleasure, it's not deductible; if you travel to Borneo and sell an article or photos about your trip, many of your expenses, including travel and accommodations, will probably be acceptable as write-offs.

If you specialize in writing about gardening, gardening magazines will probably be approved by IRS auditors as tax deductible. If you write about horses, some expenses involved with raising, keeping or riding horses may be used to offset writing income. And so on.

Anyone can claim to be a freelance writer, of course, and many people make false claims and abuse their tax-deductible status, which means the IRS may look harder at forms filed by those claiming business deductions.

The IRS also has the so-called "2-5 rule," which requires that you show a profit in two of five consecutive years to be considered a legitimate business for profit. You are considered to show a profit when your writing income exceeds your writing expenses within the year.

If your profit is $400 or more, you must fill out the self-employment section on your 1040 tax form.

You also must pay estimated quarterly taxes; you may want to start making these quarterly "prepayments" even before you get into the profit stage, to make yourself "penalty-proof," as my accountant puts it. The law requires that you pay 80 percent of your owed taxes *by the time you file your annual tax return*. You may not have earned much last year, but if you suddenly get hot, and your freelance income accounts for 20 percent or more of your income this year, you'll be fined a penalty for not prepaying. If you estimate more than you actually earn, the prepaid taxes will be returned to you, or you can apply them to next year's payment.

Home Office Deductions

One area that has come under more intense scrutiny is that of home office deductions. Because of changing rules, claiming such deductions becomes more difficult for the part-time writer who holds a regular job and works primarily outside the home, and for the writer who uses, say, a kitchen table or corner desk in a room that's also used for other purposes. A 1993 Supreme Court ruling makes claiming the home office as a legitimate business expense complicated and difficult. Under this ruling, the two key questions for writers are:

How important are the activities performed at home to your writing business?

How much of your work time is spent in your home office?

Here are some suggestions for the home-based writer, as outlined by Jan Norman, business columnist for *The Orange County Register*:

- Keep a careful log of the hours you use your home office—to be deductible under the new guidelines, it must be your most essential place to do your work.

- To claim your home office as a deduction, it should be in a room used exclusively for professional work; if it's the dining room, you'd better serve meals elsewhere.
- Housing expenses such as utilities, security system and homeowner's insurance can be written off if you can justify your home office as a deductible expense.
- To simplify record-keeping for home telephone expense deductions, install a separate telephone line just for business.
- In addition, keep receipts of business-related dining and entertainment expenses over twenty-five dollars, detailed notes of those under twenty-five dollars; and log all business mileage, including beginning and ending odometer readings.

Norman also suggests that home-based "entrepreneurs" file the EZ tax form if they gross less than $25,000 from their business and claim less than $2,000 in expenses.

Claiming a home office deduction is said to be a red flag for IRS auditors, and some freelance writers simply omit it at tax time to avoid calling attention to their income-tax statements.

I've claimed a home office deduction every year that I've used a room in my home exclusively for writing, as well as related writing expenses, and have never been audited.

I believe there are several reasons:

- I pay quarterly estimated taxes, even when I'm employed full time and doing relatively little freelancing.
- At tax time, I use an accountant who knows the current rules and advises me on such matters as depreciation of equipment and "spreading income" to offset tax-heavy years when my earnings jump (the accountant's fee is tax-deductible).
- I keep receipts like a pack rat, maintain careful records, and use common sense when taking deductions.
- I include *all* writing income on my statement, including potentially "hidden income" such as foreign earnings and other payments that may not be reported to the IRS.

IRS auditors look for red flags about potential areas of cheating, but I suspect they also look for clues that indicate a taxpayer plays by the rules.

For current and more detailed guidelines about taxes, contact your local

IRS office or call (800) 829-1040, or pick up IRS publications at public libraries and some post offices.

SELLING TO SECONDARY MARKETS

We covered reslanting ideas for multiple markets in earlier chapters, but several avenues are left open for exploiting your material, among them:

Reprint anthologies. Although not as proliferous as they once were, publications that specialize in reprinting articles are still around. They range from *Reader's Digest*, which pays extremely well for a wide range of mainstream material, to the *Utne Reader*, which reprints more offbeat or controversial pieces published by the alternative press, dealing primarily with culture and politics.

Self-syndication. With self-syndication, a writer handles her own resales of an article, querying a string of newspapers simultaneously or sending the article unsolicited with a cover letter offering each paper exclusive rights to reprint the piece in its circulation area. The benefit, of course, is that you keep 100 percent of the resale money.

Unfortunately, with hard economic times and shrinking budgets, self-syndication has become more difficult in the 1990s.

Throughout the 1980s, I routinely sold articles first printed in *The Los Angeles Times* to any number of the fifteen or so major newspapers across the country, particularly pieces with strong, national appeal that involved extensive research on a "hot" or high-impact topic or public figure. I offered each newspaper two versions: the longer one, published in the *Times*, and a shorter version of 1,700 to 2,000 words tailored to the length restrictions of smaller papers. I did the same with a number of Sunday supplements, contracting to write an article with a strong national peg that each magazine would then get exclusively in its circulation area. That ended when newspapers started to "localize" their Sunday magazines, using local freelancers and cutting back on costs.

These days, self-syndication is harder; editors buy more selectively, pushing staff to increase productivity and picking up material off the wires. That said, I have self-syndicated articles fairly recently, and other established nonfiction writers continue to do it as well, and quite profitably.

The key to self-syndication is to offer editors:

• A story that gives them something special, such as a timely peg and a subject with high reader impact and broad appeal, which they're unlikely to get from staff or the wires.

• Service support, such as photos, or a list of photo sources for the specific subject you've covered, telephone numbers of sources for fact-checking and so on. Try to give them a complete "ready-made" feature package.

- A reasonable reprint price (editors usually have standard reprint rates).

As a group, travel writers probably do the most self-syndicating, in part because newspapers can't afford to send reporters hither and yon covering exotic locales. One enterprising travel writer bought a special airline ticket that allowed him to hop from city to city at a low price; he personally met editors throughout the country, setting up a network of about twenty newspapers that purchases his travel column each week, earning him twenty times what he'd make if he sold his article to only one market. That's self-syndication at its most efficient.

Some freelance writers also advertise their wares in the classified section of the weekly *Editor & Publisher.*

As a rule, when you self-syndicate, you pick up your own expenses.

The Editor & Publisher Yearbook, available at most libraries, lists virtually every newspaper in the United States, complete with departments, editors, addresses, telephone numbers and other pertinent data, including circulation; in my experience, the larger the readership and the higher the quality of the newspaper, the more likely it is to purchase reprints. (*The New York Times* generally buys no reprints, however.) Generally, the smaller the publication, the less it pays.

I've also found that, as a rule, section editors are fairly good about replying to queries accompanied by an SASE; some prefer to call, so include your telephone number.

Syndicates. If you use a syndicate to handle resales, it generally splits proceeds 50/50 (some try to sneak in a 10 percent "editing fee," so look closely to verify the exact split beforehand). The benefit of working through syndicates is that they are plugged into hundreds of subscribing newspapers and magazines, both in the United States and foreign countries, and set up to promote and distribute your material and collect payments.

Syndicates are not particularly good at selling one-shot articles unless they have a particularly strong sales hook, such as an exclusive interview with a hard-to-get celebrity or headline-making revelations involving a controversial issue. Syndicates are most effective at peddling columns and book excerpts on subjects with broad appeal.

Note: Many syndicates have poor reputations about responding to queries or submissions of one-shots, because the market for them has gotten so dry, and because syndicate editors are notoriously underpaid and over-worked.

Both *Writer's Market* and the annual *Editor & Publisher Syndicate Directory* cover syndication services.

Foreign markets. Because of the distance involved, selling to foreign publications can be complicated, time-consuming and costly. It's more diffi-cult to study foreign markets firsthand, although some newsstands in major cities offer limited selections of foreign periodicals.

As mentioned earlier in this book, freelance writer James Joseph, a cre-dentialed science and aerospace writer, has made a specialty for many years of marketing his articles overseas. Selling to the higher-paying foreign-lan-guage weeklies, Joseph has made as much as $20,000 from multiple sales of essentially the same package on one subject, frequently after first selling to a U.S. magazine. Note that he offers publications a *complete* package that includes appropriate photos, captions, graphs and other illustrations, and optional sidebars, all executed and presented with the highest professional standards. He also studies international markets zealously, maintains files by country, and makes regular trips abroad to meet with editors and promote his packages.

Sources for studying the international marketplace include *Ulrich's International Periodicals Directory, Ulrich's Quarterly, The Writers' and Artists' Yearbook, International Literary Market Place* (ILMP), *World Press Encyclopedia, Europa Yearbook* and *World Press Review.*

Because postal rates differ from country to country, you'll need International Reply Coupons (IRCs) for return postage when corresponding with foreign publications, unless you instruct the receiving editor to dispose of your material if it's not needed; IRCs are available at some, but not all, post offices. (For more details on international postal procedures, check the "Business of Writing" section in *Writer's Market.*)

Given the logistics of selling their wares abroad, some writers opt to let one of the major syndicates, such as The New York Times Syndicate or The Los Angeles Times International Syndicate, handle foreign sales of articles whose commercial appeal crosses language barriers.

Books. I often suggest to beginning writers who want to write books that they start by researching and writing articles. "If you can't write an article, or a dozen articles," goes my line, "how do you expect to handle an entire book?"

Gaining experience and sharpening skills first through articles has other advantages:

HOW TO SELL YOUR NONFICTION BOOK

Unlike novels, most nonfiction books are sold before they're written.

It happens like this: You write a query letter to a publisher or agent pitching your book project. If she's interested in the idea and likes your presentation, she might call and discuss it, or ask you to submit a book proposal.

Book proposals are a written *sales presentation* of your project that must stand out from the hundreds and thousands of proposals that flood a publishing house or an agent's office.

Most run thirty-five to sixty typed pages and include a chapter-by-chapter outline; the writing should reflect the skill with which you'll write the book.

Most proposals have the following elements:

Overview. Give an agent or publisher a good overview of the subject matter and the particular approach you'll take that will make it stand out from books in the same general subject area.

Specifics. Cover all the main points you intend to explore chapter by chapter, what kind of research you intend to do, your specific sources and so on. It must be detailed enough to give an agent or publisher a clear idea of the scope and depth of your proposed project, including word length, format, illustrations and other graphics.

Analysis of the book's target audience. For whom are you writing the book? Is there a large enough audience to justify publishing this book? If you try to sell to a major publisher, you'll need a book that appeals to hundreds of thousands of readers. Can you make a case that your book will appeal to general readers or a large segment of the general reading public, with specific figures to back up your claims?

If your target audience is narrow, you may want to try one of the nonmainstream or smaller presses, which publish books aimed at specialized audiences.

Marketplace comparison. How your book differs from others published recently is a key consideration for the publisher, who's looking for a fresh, promotable hook. It's up to you to seriously study the market and convince the publisher that your book will be different and better, and tell them why it should be published *now* (why it's timely). (*Books in Print*, available at your local library, should be a useful resource.)

Your credentials. Why are you the one to write this particular book?

continued

What is your track record, either as a writer or an authority in a given field, to warrant an advance and be trusted to deliver a book of substance and value? What is your special take or feel for the material that will cause the publisher to select you over another writer with a project in the same subject area?

Promotion possibilites. In what special ways does your idea lend itself to promotion and marketing? Is your topic appropriate for talk-show exposure? Can you market it through specialized organizations or associations? Can you personally help sell the book through print and electronic interviews? Do you have such experience?

If your proposal impresses a publisher, she may offer you an advance to write the book; a year is a customary time frame for delivery, but just like payments, deadlines are negotiable, and depend on the scope and complexity of the project.

Never sign a book contract without the representation and advice of a legitimate literary agent or lawyer.

If an agent requires a fee for her services, find another one; reputable agents earn their income by taking 10 to 15 percent from the advances and royalties they negotiate for authors.

◆ ◆ ◆

The best way to find appropriate publishers for your particular book? Study *Publishers Weekly*, bookstores and libraries to see which books are being printed by which publishers, and who's doing the best job of promotion.

Some publishers will only look at manuscripts submitted through agents; others may accept unsolicited submissions, but frequently take many months to respond.

Literary Market Place has a fairly comprehensive listing of publishers and author's agents. *Writer's Market* also lists publishers, and features sections on writing book proposals and working with book packagers. *The International Directory of Little Magazines and Small Presses* covers more offbeat and nonmainstream publishers.

The Society of Authors' Representatives (10 Astor Place, New York NY 10003) and the Independent Literary Agents Association (432 Park Ave. South, New York NY 10016), will send free lists of their voluntary members if you enclose an SASE with your request. You'll

continued

also find agents listed in *Guide to Literary Agents & Art/Photo Reps.*

For a detailed discussion of book contract terms, refer to *Writing A to Z*, edited by Kirk Polking.

If you have an interest in ghostwriting — being paid to write a book for a client, who gets the byline — read Eva Shaw's *Ghostwriting*, considered the bible of the ghostwriting trade.

- Your clips, particularly in a certain field, are evidence of your expertise and may help you land a book deal.
- The research that goes into writing those articles can be used as essential material for the book itself.
- Many nonfiction books germinate from published articles that catch a book editor or publisher's eye.

Without evidence of your research and writing skills in the form of articles, however, it's unlikely a publisher will have enough faith in you to give you a contract and an advance to put a book together.

In my proposal for this book, for instance, I referred to several articles on the craft of nonfiction writing I'd filed with *Writer's Digest*; I included clips to indicate the tone, style and type of book I had in mind.

Writing books is a logical goal for any nonfiction writer, but books demand far more research, concentration, stamina and organization than most articles. Cutting your teeth on articles — the more challenging and the more numerous, the better — is an excellent way to prepare.

Anyone with serious book-writing aspirations can study the field in *Literary Market Place*, *Writer's Market*, *Writer's Digest* and particularly *Publishers Weekly*, which not only covers news and trends in the book industry, but reviews upcoming books by category.

These sources also provide information and advice on literary agents. (See sidebar, "How to Sell a Nonfiction Book," page 280.)

Vanity/subsidy book publishing. With a subsidy- or vanity-publishing arrangement, you pay money to a subsidy "publisher" to print copies of your book. But be forewarned: It's a business fraught with fraud and con artists who rip off thousands of dollars from gullible writers desperate to be published. There may be legitimate publishers in this field, but they are few and far between. Stories are legion of writers getting only a fraction of the vanity books they pay for (or none at all), volumes of shamefully poor quality, books that receive no promotion or distribution as promised, etc.

As a reporter, I've investigated a few of these cases myself, and they can be heartbreaking.

If you consider any such "deal," have a good *literary* attorney go over the contract at the very least; even then, many vanity/subsidy presses are fly-by-night outfits, and finding them later to press legal actions can be difficult to impossible.

Don't let your need to have your work in print cloud your better judgment, and don't necessarily trust outfits just because they advertise in writing magazines that you otherwise respect or see recommended in this book. A reputable and recognized publisher is one that pays *you* for the right to publish your book, or at least guarantees royalties — *not the other way around.*

Self-publishing. This is an entirely different area than subsidy/vanity publishing. With self-publishing, you are in total control — in effect, your own publisher and distributor. Desktop publishing and new marketing technology have made this a viable alternative to more traditional publishing venues; it's a complex, demanding way to go, with a lot of technical and business know-how involved, but if you're game, success stories abound.

The Self-Publishing Manual, by self-publishing giant Dan Poynter, is an excellent guide on how to write, print and sell your own book, available from Para Publishing (P.O. Box 4232, Santa Barbara CA 93140-4232).

Just know what you're doing going in, and be willing to see it through to the end.

Book packagers. They will help you develop a proposal for a publisher, in exchange for a percentage of the take. *Writer's Market* has more details and a listing of packagers.

◆ ◆ ◆

For examples of how to write a variety of writing-related business letters, including book queries, I highly recommend *How to Write Irresistible Query Letters,* by Lisa Collier Cool.

I also recommend that you move on to Step Sixteen, and a few final thoughts before we bid each other goodbye.

Step Sixteen

Keeping the Faith

If you had asked me why I write before I started this book, I would have told you, in this order:

1. I write to entertain myself.
2. I write to make a living.
3. I write to get down on paper some of the ideas that clutter up my head, so I'll have some peace of mind.
4. I write because I like the attention.
5. I write because it gives me a voice, allowing me to impress upon others my thoughts, feelings and views; I write to express myself to the world, and to myself.

In the course of writing this book, however, I discovered that the order is wrong.

I began writing for publication almost thirty years ago, and continue to write, because writing gives me a voice.

Please indulge me for a moment, as I explain.

BACK TO THE BEGINNING

No one talked much in my family, not about things that matter: joy, fear, sadness, pain, dreams, goals, injustice, ethics, spirituality, relationships, sexuality, the nature of love; simple, direct affection and honest feelings were rarely, if ever, expressed. We talked; seldom did we communicate.

By family, I mean the family after my parents divorced; my mother remarried, and a stepfather dominated the household in which I was primarily raised. Although there were good times, and love and support in odd, measured doses, it became a household of terrible silences. A household where abuse flourished, but no one spoke a word about it. A household where children lived with fear and pain, but rarely cried out. A household made sick by a virulent strain of racism and anti-Semitism, where the words *nigger* and *kike* were heard day and night, spit out with frightening, inexplicable anger and loathing—which I would only understand years later as *self*-loathing and the bottled rage that comes with it. A household where, if you tried to express your own anger, or speak your own mind, a leather belt would likely be laid across your backside hard enough, and enough times, for blood to come and welts to rise.

My sister and I bore much of it in silence because silence felt safer.

Like many kids in such situations, I found sanctuaries: my pals, who remain among my closest and most supportive friends to this day; the stories I read, and admired; and sports, in part because of a warm and generous coach named Jack Fernandez, who became, by proxy, a surrogate father to boys who needed one.

When I was getting ready to go away to college, Coach asked me what I was going to study.

"English, I guess," I replied, with characteristic lack of focus or resolve.

"Ah," he said. "You're going to be a writer."

"No," I corrected him, "an English major. Then probably a teacher."

"All English majors secretly want to be writers," he said, with a wise and knowing grin. "You'll be a writer."

It was the first time anyone had suggested such a thing to me. The idea filled me suddenly in a way that felt both wonderful and scary; I said goodbye to Coach with the notion spinning wildly in my head, and went off to college.

Two years later, I started writing for my local newspaper. A few years after that, I started publishing my own small paper, on the thinnest of shoestrings. And, despite some ups and downs, I've made a living as a nonfiction writer pretty much ever since.

Only now, all these years later, and after writing this book, do I understand why: I needed a voice; and in nonfiction, I found a place where it felt safe to use it.

STAYING THE COURSE

I don't know why *you* write.

Your reasons may not be so rooted in personal need as mine, or your need may be even deeper and more profound. But I do know that you must feel at least a burning desire if you're going to stay the course, keep the faith, in a profession that promises more than its share of frustration and rejection.

If you have the wherewithal to see it through, every day of your life will be an exercise in doubt and procrastination, and a valiant battle to over-

HANDLING REJECTION

If you haven't faced at least a few rejections of your written work, I'm worried about you. All hard-working writers get rejected, not just when they start out, but throughout their lives. If you aren't accumulating some rejection slips, it probably means you aren't sending out many queries or completing many manuscripts.

Don't get me wrong; no rational writer has a goal of collecting as many rejection slips as possible. Your goal should be to score *more sales* than rejections, learning to take rejections in stride, even to be proud of them as testaments to your productivity.

In recent months, I've had submissions rejected by both *Writer's Digest* and *The New York Times*. Yet I've sold articles to both publications many times, and I'll sell to them again.

Was I disappointed? Sure. Did it depress me or cause me to lose belief in myself? Maybe, for a bleak moment, if I was having a bad day.

But I don't have that many bleak moments or bad days, because I'm a professional writer, and there isn't time for that kind of self-doubt or self-pity. If you're a working writer, you get back to work.

The key to dealing with rejection: *Never take it personally and always learn something from it.*

The rejection of a manuscript is the rejection of a particular piece of work at a particular time in a particular market by a particular editor, for any number of reasons that may have little or nothing to do with *you*. Don't make it more than it is; accept it as part of the professional writing life. If Babe Ruth expected to hit a home run every time up at bat—or even to *hit the ball*—he would have quit baseball long before he got to the major leagues.

How we deal with rejection and make use of it makes all the difference. Grow from it; stop expecting the work to be easy, or success to "happen." Figure out what went wrong and what you can do differently next time. Get back to work, determined to do a better job.

After a while, if you really apply yourself, rejections become fewer and fewer, and successes commonplace.

And never forget: A rejection in one market may be an acceptance in another.

Years ago, on assignment for *Cosmopolitan*, I tried and tried to bring an article up to the expectations of the publisher, Helen Gurley Brown.

continued

> Finally, the editor sent me a kill fee and a consoling note that said, "I guess you're just not a *Cosmo* boy."
>
> I deposited the check in my bank account and sold the same piece, slightly retailored, to *TV Guide*, which paid me top money and made it a cover story.
>
> Know who you are as a writer, know the markets, develop your nonfiction writing skills, then watch your sales increase as your rejections dwindle.

come both. You may or may not become a "great" writer, but you will certainly become great at finding excuses not to write; we all do. That's because writing for publication is risky; it means you must put your words and your work out there for all the world to see. It means laboring harder and longer and with different pressures than people who write primarily to amuse themselves or find a creative outlet.

In the beginning, you may start the same way, perhaps writing in a daily journal that's private, just for you; it's how many professional writers first feel their way, establish discipline, find their voice. But eventually you must take your writing to another level, if you intend to share it with the general reading public and get paid decently for it.

If you want badly enough to reach and stay at that professional level, you must find the extra discipline and drive that eludes those who fall short. That's really what separates the successful from the unsuccessful, the professional from the amateur — simple discipline, the willpower to put your behind in the chair.

In the end, all the explanations, justifications and excuses simply don't matter. Because unless you write, and until you get your writing out there, nobody "out there" knows you're alive. And, frankly, nobody cares.

THE FOOLPROOF, MONEY-BACK, GUARANTEED FIVE-STEP STAIRWAY TO SUCCESS

In my introduction, I said I could only give you guidelines about craft and marketing, but could make no assurances about how successful you might become; that was up to you. I'm going to amend that and make an ironclad guarantee: If you follow these five steps resolutely and religiously for one year, I promise that you will be a more effective and successful nonfiction writer than you are at this moment:

1. Write every day; *every* day, no days off. Find your voice and rhythm; nurture and strengthen them through daily writing.
2. Write with a routine, an established time and place only for writing, nothing else. Two hours minimum, preferably more.
3. Read some nonfiction every day, studying both the market and the craft with the eye and mind of a professional writer. One hour minimum, preferably more.
4. Send out only that writing of which you are truly proud, from cover letter to completed manuscript.
5. Finish every piece of writing you start; send out every piece of writing you finish. Continue sending it out until you have exhausted every possible market.

If this sounds unrealistic and impossible, I will only add: Many writers have applied themselves with this kind of commitment and discipline, and far more, under the most adverse circumstances imaginable.

The question remains: How badly do you want to be a professional writer, and how successful according to the terms you set?

The answer will not be in what you say, but in what you *do*.

THE WRITING LIFE

Back in the early 1980s, an article appeared in the *Columbia Journalism Review* analyzing the sorry state of freelance writing. One conclusion: The payment rates of most markets were not only failing to keep up with inflation, they were actually sliding.

The deck beneath the headline summed up the findings: *The pay is lousy, the editors are worse, and making a living writing for magazines has never been so tough. It's a wonder anybody tries.*

If anything, it's tougher today.

Cable and interactive TV, video, the emergence of electronic or "talking" newspapers and magazines, and declining literacy continue to make serious inroads on print markets. Economic realities have caused many publications to further shrink. Simply put, more print writers vie for fewer opportunities, often for decreasing pay and benefits.

I no longer attempt to freelance as a nonfiction writer full time. I'm not sure I would make a decent living at it again if I tried. During the year or so that I wrote this book under contract, I also derived income from television writing, a magazine column, teaching, freelance editing, and the occasional magazine article. I've diversified to survive.

That said, the newspaper and magazine markets are still there—thousands upon thousands in the United States alone, buying millions of dollars' worth of freelance writing every year. Beyond that is the book market, which changes, but thrives in some areas; at this writing, several friends are hard at work on nonfiction books for advances higher than they've ever earned.

If you sincerely want to be part of the professional writing community and are willing to work hard enough to get there, you will. Networking—being in touch with other writers through classes, conferences, writers' groups or organizations and the like—can be a big help, not only to tip you to work opportunities, but to remind you that you are not alone. It's also a good idea to work at a job that requires writing, *any kind of writing*, so that you constantly practice and sharpen your basic skills. Luck may also be a factor, particularly connecting with the right editors or mentors, those special people who can be both tough and supportive, and give you opportunities others might not.

The hard truth is, though, that you're ultimately on your own, with only your personal desire and discipline to count on.

Talent? Forget it.

"It strikes me now and then that talent may be one of the least important variables in the writing business," novelist Lawrence Block once wrote in *Writer's Digest.* "People without a superabundance of talent succeed anyhow. People with tons of talent never get anywhere. It happens all the time."

Another writer once wrote in *Reader's Digest:* "The reality is that writing is a lonely, private and poor-paying affair. For every writer kissed by fortune there are thousands more whose longing is never requited. Even those who succeed often know long periods of neglect and poverty. I did."

The writer was Alex Haley. He wrote *The Autobiography of Malcolm X* and *Roots*, two of the most important titles in the history of publishing. His work had incredible impact on generations of readers, as well as worldwide film and television audiences. He won a Pulitzer Prize and made a ton of money.

Most of us won't be so fortunate. But we want to write, we love to write, and we will write. It makes getting up each morning more purposeful. It provides a crucial thread through our lives. It keeps us in touch with ourselves and connected to the world around us. It entertains us, even as it provides us with income. It gives us the sense that we've done a worthwhile day's work. It makes us feel good about ourselves. It gives us a voice.

Even at its most frustrating, we continue to do it.

As long as we're doing it, is there any reason not to do it well?

YOU ARE NOT ALONE

There are literally thousands of writers groups around the United States, from local groups with only a handful of members to the mighty Council of Writers Organizations (1501 Broadway, Suite 1907, New York NY 10036), a consortium of writers' groups with a membership approaching 25,000 individual writers. Those groups can be a valuable source of networking, professional services and moral support.

Some other prominent national organizations include:

American Society of Journalists and Authors, Inc. (1501 Broadway, Suite 1907, New York NY 10036). ASJA is a nationwide organization of freelance nonfiction writers, which requires a certain number of bylined sales before you are invited to join.

The National Writers Club (1450 S. Havana, Suite 620, Aurora CO 80012). Both aspiring and published freelance writers can join this group, which represents more than 6,000 freelance writers.

The National Writers Union (13 Astor Place, 7th Floor, New York NY 10003). Founded in 1981 to fight for the protection of free speech and writers' rights in the workplace, this organization has local chapters in seven major cities.

The Author's Guild (234 W. 44th St., New York NY 10036). Membership in this organization is open to both book and magazine writers, with certain criteria about how much, where and when they've been published.

PEN American Center (568 Broadway, New York NY 10012). This international association includes poets, playwrights, novelists, essayists and literary editors, with a mission to promote and protect freedom of expression.

Many local and national writers' organizations offer such benefits and services as newsletters, group medical insurance, writing contests and conferences.

For a more complete listing, see *Writer's Market* or the *Encyclopedia of Associations*, available in most libraries. Check the alphabetical title listing and *keyword* index in the back of the latter volume, such as The Society of *Environmental* Journalists, Society of American *Travel* Writers, Associated *Business* Writers of America, etc.

◆ ◆ ◆

With that, I finish this book. I've probably said more about the craft and business of nonfiction writing, and more about myself, than you needed or wanted to hear. Besides, I have so much other writing to do.

And so do you.

INDEX